LEARN ANCIENT GREEK

"Have you seen my husband, he'll be a bull, a swan or a shower of gold."

LEARN ANCIENT GREEK

Peter Jones

Duckworth

Eleventh impression 2003
First published in 1998 by
Gerald Duckworth & Co. Ltd.
61 Frith Street, London W1D 3JL
Tel: 020 7434 4242
Fax: 020 7434 4420
Email: info@duckworth-publishers.co.uk
www.ducknet.co.uk

A catalogue record for this book is available
from the British Library

ISBN 0 7156 2758 9

Typeset by Ray Davies
Printed and bound in Great Britain by
Bookcraft (Bath) Ltd, Midsomer Norton, Somerset

CONTENTS

v

CONTENTS

PREFACE

This volume is constructed on the same principles and in the same format as *Learn Latin* (Duckworth, 1997). It has been written in response to insistent demand for an ancient Greek equivalent, especially from those who used *Learn Latin* in its earlier incarnations in the *Sunday Telegraph* and the *Daily Telegraph*. Its purpose is to provide users with just enough Greek (and no more) to read selected 'target' extracts from the *New Testament,* the *Greek Anthology*, Thucydides, Plato, Sophocles, the satirist Lucian and the historian Cassius Dio.

Purists will shudder at my frivolous mixing of Classical, *koine* and late Greek usage, not to mention the simplification and skating over of countless linguistic problems.

An audio-cassette pronunciation tape is available. Please send cheques for £6 or $14 (made out to L.M.H. Jones) to the address below.

Peter Jones
28 Akenside Terrace
Jesmond
Newcastle upon Tyne NE2 1TN
UK
February 1998

INTRODUCTION

The ancient Greeks

Talk about learning ancient Greek and someone is bound to ask 'Ancient Greek? What *use* is that?' The answer, I suppose, depends on whether you think pleasure is useful. Being a *joie de vivre* man myself, I can think of few things more useful than pleasure, but I do not want to stop anyone being as miserable as sin if they so choose.

As for ancient Greek being 'dead', that is the sort of claim made only by those ignorant of the language. I waste no more space on them.

Ancient Greece was not a nation state: it was just an area inhabited by people who spoke Greek, and there were almost as many dialects of Greek as there were city-states. By 'ancient Greeks', we usually mean Athenians (and their dialect, Attic Greek), specifically Athenians of the 5th-4th centuries BC, the 'golden age' of Athens, and even more specifically, Athenian intellectuals, politicians, historians, dramatists, architects, doctors, sculptors, potters and so on. Arguably, no single city-state, of such a small population (perhaps 50,000 male citizens at its maximum), has had such a profound impact upon the intellectual, cultural and political life of western civilisation.

And yet one does not patronise Athenian men in the street, *hoi polloi*, by paying tribute to them too. Athens was an open society, and in an open society, the achievements of the few are always predicated on the collusion or acquiescence of the many. The Athenian man in the street underpinned the world's first and last real democracy (and, with a few exceptions, showed remarkable restraint and maturity of judgement in running it); he provided passionately involved audiences for dramatists of the richness and complexity of Aeschylus, Euripides and Sophocles; he offered thinkers an environment in which some of the most radical and threatening ideas about the nature of the world and man's position and function in it could be freely discussed;

1

and he showed a visual taste in sculpture and architecture, for example, that we can only gasp at.

The foundations of Athens' achievements, however, were laid by earlier Greeks inhabiting not the Greek mainland, from which they had emigrated, but the islands off, and coast of, western Turkey. It was here, from the late 8th century BC, in contact with great near eastern civilisations, that the Greek flower started to bloom.

And what a bloom – Homer (c. 720 BC)! If Greek civilisation had contributed nothing else, the poems of Homer alone would stand as one of the very greatest of human achievements. Alas, this brief introduction to the language cannot, for reasons of dialect, encompass the greatest of all Greek authors. But I have placed a passage of Homer, with translation, as an end-piece, to give you the sense of a star never outshone – except, perhaps, by Shakespeare.

The story of this extraordinary civilisation and the impact of its culture and language on ours will be pursued in the brief essays at the end of each chapter, **The Greek world** and **Wordplay**. But if one wanted to identify the single characteristic that makes ancient Greeks so different and so important, one would point, I think, to their passion for independence, especially their determination to explain the world as far as they could in humanly intelligible terms, through the sole medium of rational human thought processes, without reference even to the supernatural, let alone to any earthly 'authority'.

It is thrilling, for example, to read the fragments of the world's earliest philosophers as they decide that one entity, whatever it is, lies at the root of the physical world; as they grapple with explaining how that one entity changes into the different phenomena of the world we see about us (wood and water, rock and blood, thought and spirit); as Parmenides decides that, logically, change is impossible (if something is, it is; if something isn't, it isn't; you cannot change an is into an isn't; therefore change is impossible) – and draws the stunning conclusion that the world we see about us with all its changes (like, for example, movement) must therefore be an illusion; and how his successors began to grope their way towards an 'atomic' theory of matter – that the basic substance of the world is below the level of perception and does indeed remain unchanged itself,

2

but by combining and recombining in different ways creates everything we see about us. No one in the west, as far as we know, had ever even begun to think like this. In area after area of human intellectual, political and cultural endeavour Greeks laid down principles that have informed our thinking about the subject – for good or ill – ever since.

For any westerner, then, to come into even brief contact with the ancient Greek language is to open oneself to one of the richest linguistic and cultural experiences imaginable. And I have not even mentioned the *New Testament*.

Some suggestions

Anyone learning a language reaches a crunch point, where what has been up till then a smooth and easy path suddenly turns rocky and perilous. I know of no language course that successfully negotiates that crunch, and I make no claims for this one. The simple fact is that, at that crunch point, those with a gift for languages will move on, the rest will not.

The alphabet is the first problem with ancient Greek, and some will fall there. I would very much hope, however, that anyone who gets past that hurdle would be able to reach Chapter 3, and thus be able to read some very simple Greek from the *New Testament* about God being love. That in itself will be a heroic and thrilling achievement.

But it is better to warn you now that you will probably find learning by heart rather difficult. Learning is for many people a visual business, and the new alphabet inevitably makes it even less easy than usual. All one can do is practise writing and reading the language till its shapes and sounds become second nature, and diligently keeping lists of words and forms to be learnt.

I cannot stress too much the advantages of working in a group and of having help available when you need it. There is a useful address below where you can find a list of postal tutors.

As with *Learn Latin*, I have been rigorous in selecting for analysis only what needs to be known in order to read the 'target' extracts. You will, for example, learn no noun-types in this course – news that will shake Latinists rigid – but there it is: in Greek, one can get by without. Or rather, one can in this course.

And there will be no jokes either about the last line of the Homer extract in **End-piece** duplicating your feelings about learning ancient Greek, please.

Postal tuition

For a list of postal tutors, write to:

The Secretary
The Joint Association of Classical Teachers
Senate House
Malet Street
London WC1E 7HU

Classical organisations for the non-specialist

For the *Classical Association*, write to:
Dr Jenny March
PO Box 38
Alresford
Hants SO24 0ZQ

For *Friends of Classics*, write to:
Jeannie Cohen
51 Achilles Road
London NW6 1DZ

THE GREEK ALPHABET (1)

1. Straight in

The Greek alphabet is the ultimate source of the English alphabet (see **Wordplay**, Chapter 2).

It contains 24 letters. Of these, eleven are instantly recognisable, as long as you got plenty of gammas at school – g is a hard 'g', as in *g*amma – and remember the value of π 'p' to infinity.

Write these out in Greek, with their English equivalents, a trillion times, thus αaαaαaαa, and concentrate on the minuscule letters:

A α = a
B β = b
Γ γ = g
Δ δ = d
E ε = e
I ι = i
K κ = k
O o = o
Π π = p
Σ ς = s
T τ = t
Y υ = u

Already, therefore, you are master of *a b g d e i k o p s t* and *u*. You should now write out in Greek, say in Greek, and then change into English letters (transliterate) the following.

You will begin with a famous figure of myth, while most of the other words have derivations in English.

Notes
* Pronounce vowels short: h*a*t, p*e*t, p*i*t, p*o*t, p*u*t

Aα=a, Bβ=b, Γγ=g, Δδ=d, Eε=e, Iι=i, Kκ=k, Oo=o, Ππ=p, Σς=s, Tτ=t, Yυ=u

- Ignore for the moment the little hook thingy over vowels at the start of words (e.g. ἱ, ἰ, ἀ) – though you may be able to work out what it is doing

Οἰδιπους (pronounce οι as in 'boy', ου as 'too')
N.b. no dots on Greek ι.

πους, stem ποδ- , 'foot' – English chiropodist
γιγας, 'giant' – English gigantic
τοπος, 'place' – English topical
ποτος, 'drinking, carousal' – cf. English potable, via Latin potabilis
βιος, 'life' – English biology
δις, 'twice' – English diode
εἰδος, 'shape, form' (pronounce ει as 'fiancée') – English (wait and see)
ἰδεα, 'idea' – English idea
ποποι, 'ouch!' – English? Er, no (nothing to do with spinach-eating sailors)
οἰκος, 'house' – English economy (nomoi are 'laws')
παις (plural παιδες), 'boy' (pronounce αι as 'high') – English paediatrics
ἀκουε, 'listen!' – English acoustics
᾿Αττικα, the territory where Athens was located.

Notes
- We spell *Oidipous* Oedipus because we tend to use the Roman spellings of Greek names. Thus the ancient historian Θουκυδιδης *Thoukudides* becomes (via Latin) Thucydides. See **Wordplay**, Chapter 3.
- Greek υ (not in diphthongs) often transliterates into English 'y'.

2. An *L* of a time

Now add Λ λ, lambda, *l*, (λlλlλl etc) and you can write out, transliterate and say:

καλος, 'lovely, beautiful, handsome, fine' (so what does a *kal-eido*-scope look at?)

Αα=a, Ββ=b, Γγ=g, Δδ=d, Εε=e, Ιι=i, Κκ=k, Οο=o, Ππ=p, Σς=s, Ττ=t, Υυ=u, οι=boy, ου=too, ει=fiancée, αι=high, Λλ=l

6

πολλοι 'many' (the many = οἱ (*hoi*) πολλοι)
βιβλος, 'papyrus, book'
λεγε, 'speak!'
λογος, 'word' (in the beginning was the λογος)
βαλλε, 'throw!'
γλαυκος, 'blue, grey' (pronounce αυ as 'how')

And you can now write out, transliterate, say and translate your first Greek inscription:

καλος ὁ (*ho*, 'the') παις 'beautiful the boy', 'the boy [is] beautiful'.

This is found scratched on thousands of pots given by adult males to the handsome young boys they were in love with – only in capital letters, with no gaps between the words: ΚΑΛΟΣΟΠΑΙΣ or ΟΠΑΙΣΚΑΛΟΣ.

3. The S bend

So what's the Greek for 'is', then? Add another letter to your quiver – σ, sigma, *s*, (σσοσος etc) which is used everywhere except at the end of a word (at the end of the word our chum ς is used, as we have seen. σ and ς are pronounced identically).

'Is' is ἐστι – and we at once remember: Latin *est*, French *il est*, German *ist*, English *is*. So, in full our inscription now reads:

καλος ὁ (*ho*) παις ἐστι, 'beautiful the boy is'.

Write out, transliterate and say:

σκοπ-, meaning 'look at, examine' (as in kaleido-)
βασιλευς, 'king' (king Basil)
Ὀδυσσευς (who he?)
ἀλγος, 'pain' – neur*algi*a
στασις, 'revolt' – *stasis*
βασις, a 'walk' or 'pedestal' – *basis*
διαβολος, 'slanderous' – *diabol*ical.

Αα=a, Ββ=b, Γγ=g, Δδ=d, Εε=e, Ιι=i, Κκ=k, Οο=o, Ππ=p, Σς=s, Ττ=t, Υυ=u, οι=b*oy*, ου=t*oo*, ει=fianc*ée*, αι=h*igh*, Λλ=l, αυ=h*ow*, Σσ=s

And we haven't actually learned any Greek at all yet. And your pronunciation is also probably all over the place (unless you have got the tape). But who cares? We're just having fun.

4. Effing away

Now add Φ φ, phi, *f*, (φfφfφ etc) and you can write out (etc) the well-known animal the ἐλεφας and the well-known subject:

φιλοσοφια, where φιλο- means 'love, like' and σοφ- means 'wisdom'. And the chap who does it is a φιλοσοφος.

What do the following people do? Write out (etc):

φιλολογος
φιλοπαις (we reverse the two stems)
φιλοδεσποτος (guess from the English)
φιλοδικος (the δικ- stem means 'justice')
φιλιππος (ἱππ- 'horse').

ἀδελφος means 'brother', so what happens in Phil-adelphia?

5. Breathings

Now for the little hook thingy.

Words beginning with a vowel *always* indicate whether the word *starts* with an 'h' sound or not. Write out (etc) (it is getting boring saying this. Take it for granted):

' above a vowel (smooth breathing) indicates the absence of the sound 'h': ἰδεα = *idea*. Thus, as you have seen, ἀδελφος, Οἰδιπους, Ὀδυσσευς, Ἀττικα, οἰκος, ἀλγος, εἰδος.

' above a vowel (rough breathing – some prefer heavy breathing, pant gasp) indicates the *presence* of the sound 'h' at the *start* of a word: ὁσος = *hosos*, οἱ = *hoi*. Try ὁ, αἱ (both 'the'), ὁς, ἁ ('who', 'what'), ἱππος ('horse'), ἁγιος ('holy', cf. the famous Byzantine

---

Αα=a, Ββ=b, Γγ=g, Δδ=d, Εε=e, Ιι=i, Κκ=k, Οο=o, Ππ=p, Σς=s, Ττ=t, Υυ=u, οι=b*oy*, ου=t*oo*, ει=fianc*ée*, αι=h*igh*, Λλ=l, αυ=h*ow*, Σσ=s, Φφ=f, ῾=h

church Ἁγια Σοφια), ὁλος ('whole'), ὁπλα ('weapons'), ὑς ('pig'), ὑπο ('under'), υἱος ('son').

Notes

• Examine οἱος: when a word begins with a *diphthong*, the breathing goes over the second vowel

6. Three nasty ones: ν = *n*, ρ = *r* and η = *ê*

As you can see, the above Greek letters closely resemble different letters in English.

ν is *n* (νnνnνn etc), capital N (nu)

Write out and distinguish clearly between ν and υ: νανος 'dwarf'; ναυς 'ship'; νεος 'new'; νεανιας 'young man'; νεφελο-κοκκυγ-ια 'Cloud-cuckoo-land'; νους 'mind' (Greek now, not English, cf. ναυς above!); νυν 'now'; γενος 'race, descent', οἰνος 'wine', ὑπνος 'sleep', κανναβις (no idea, officer).

ρ is r (ρrρrρr etc), capital P (rho)

Write out ἰατρος 'doctor'; νεκρος 'corpse'; νευρον 'nerve'; ῥαββι 'Rabbi' (no, not Burns); ῥακος 'rag'; παντα ῥει 'everything flows/changes/is in a state of flux'; ῥοδον 'rose'; δενδρον 'tree' (put ῥοδο- in front and ...?); Ῥοδος 'Rhodes'; ῥυππαπαι 'yo heave ho!'; πυρα 'pyre'; Βοσπορος 'Bos [ox]-porus [ford]'; γερανιον 'geranium'; παραδεισος 'garden'; περι 'around'; οὐρανος 'heaven', ἐργον 'work', παραλυσις 'paralysis'.

Note

• ρ at the *start* of a word always carries a rough breathing, ῥ

η is long *ê* (h*ai*r) (ηêηêηê etc), capital H (eta)

Write out καταστροφη 'overturning'; γραφη 'writing, drawing, painting, writ'; γυνη 'woman'; γυναικες 'women'; ἀνηρ 'man';

Αα=a, Ββ=b, Γγ=g, Δδ=d, Εε=e, Ιι=i, Κκ=k, Οο=o, Ππ=p, Σς=s, Ττ=t, Υυ=u, οι=b*oy*, ου=t*oo*, ει=fianc*ée*, αι=h*igh*, Λλ=l, αυ=h*ow*, Σσ=s, Φφ=f, ʽ=h, Νν=n, Ρρ=r, Ηη=*ê* h*ai*r

9

ἀνδρες 'men'; νησος 'island'; νικη 'victory' (*now* you know why the trainers are so called); νοησις 'thought, intelligence'; νη τον (the) Δ(=δ)ια! 'yes [by] (the) Zeus!'; Δηλος 'Delos'; γηρας 'old age'; εὑρηκα 'I've got it!' (watch the breathing!); πατηρ 'father'; κρατηρ 'cup' (shaped like a crater); and the historian Ἡροδοτος. -η is also a favourite noun-ending: so e.g. δικη 'justice'; σπονδη 'libation'; βοη 'shout'; ὀργη 'anger', ἡδονη 'pleasure'.

-ης is a favourite person-ending (so ναυτης 'sailor'; δικαστης 'juror'; ποιητης 'poet') and name-ending (Εὐριπιδης, Π(=π)ερικλης, Σ(=σ)οφοκλης).

Αα=a, Ββ=b, Γγ=g, Δδ=d, Εε=e, Ιι=i, Κκ=k, Οο=o, Ππ=p, Σς=s, Ττ=t, Υυ=u, οι=b*oy*, ου=t*oo*, ει=fianc*ée*, αι=h*igh*, Λλ=l, αυ=h*ow*, Σσ=s, Φφ=f, ʽ=h, Νν=n, Ρρ=r, Ηη=ê h*air*

10

THE GREEK ALPHABET (2)

Maintain the reading and pronouncing, writing out and trans-literating routine. The more you do it, the better you become at it.

1. μ = m (mu) (μmμmμm) M and χ = kh (chi, as in 'lo*ch*')
(χchχchχch) X

You surely remember the curate from Kew, who learnt ancient Greek diddly do, he ompty pom pom and tiddle om tom, but his kitten could only say μ? Or however it went?

Well, here it is: μ for mu for *m*, just like English 'm'. So babies in Greek cry μαμμα and when they grow up call for their μητηρ and so on. Here is a squeaky little μυς (does it have πνευμονια?) here the pure white μαρμαρος, here a verb meaning 'I imitate' μιμεομαι, and the imitator himself, the μιμος – what a μιμικος – and here the dread plant μανδραγορας. A memorial is a μνημα: mnemonic, right? νυμφη is a 'young woman, nymph'; and someone seized by violent, unattainable desire is a νυμφοληπτος, cf. nympholepsy. No, there is no Greek word νυμφομανια. Get back to work. But μανια does mean 'madness'.

χ is not English 'x'. It is English 'ch', pronounced as in 'lo*ch*', a hard 'ch' – as in the following, all giving us English words, which you must match with the English given below them:

χαος χασμα Χριστος ἀρχαιος χρισμα Χριστιανος σχημα χαρακτηρ χορος χρονος χρυσος χρυσελεφαντινος τριηραρχος

Character, chryselephantine, Christian, chaos, chorus, trierarch, chasm, scheme, chronology, chrism, Christ, archaeology (one missing – which?).

Αα=a, Ββ=b, Γγ=g, Δδ=d, Εε=e, Ιι=i, Κκ=k, Οο=o, Ππ=p, Σς=s, Ττ=t, Υυ=u, οι=b*o*y, ου=t*oo*, ει=fianc*é*e, αι=h*igh*, Λλ=l, αυ=h*ow*, Σσ=s, Φφ=f, ʽ=h, Νν=n, Ρρ=r, Ηη=*ê* h*ai*r, Μμ=m, Χχ=kh

11

2. ω = ô (omega) (ωôωôωô) Ω and θ = th (theta) (θthθthθth) Θ

We have already met one 'o', ὁ μικρον 'little o' (cf. micro). Now we meet ὠ, omega, pronounced as in 'saw': ὠ μεγα 'big o' (cf. mega). It is the last letter of the Greek alphabet (I am ἀ and ὠ, the first and the last). You cannot worship God and Μαμμωνας, as the Greeks called this Syrian god of wealth. ὠμοι is a common Greek cry of despair and plain ὠ a common exclamation. One day you may write an odd ὠδη or pay a visit to the seaside and the ὠκεανος, and give a cry of ὡσαννα (Hebrew, 'save, we pray!'), a Greek saviour being σωτηρ. You could paint the sea in a pale shade of ὠχρος. The suffix ων is a very common ending for jobs like an ἀρχιτεκτων, names like the philosopher Πλατων, the gods Ἀπολλων and Ποσειδων and the place Μαραθων, and ω is the common ending for verbs, like φωνω, 'I speak'. φωνη is a good word: 'voice', 'language'. Add τηλε 'afar off'...and listen for the lovely ἠχω.

θ = th (theta) is pronounced as in 'thigh' – a soft 'th'. 'God' is θεος, and the goddess Ἀθηνη lived in Ἀθηναι. A place to watch plays is a θεατρον, where you will be a θεατης. An acolyte is Greek ἀκολουθος, one who accompanies. Do a PhD and you will write a θεσις. Treacle derives from theriac, a concoction made from a wild beast, θηριον. A king sits on a θρονος, and devotees of Bacchus carry a θυρσος with their delicious and highly alcoholic μεθη (which is connected with ἀμεθυστος, α- meaning 'not': you put amethyst in your drink if you wish to remain sober. You can now do the Christian acronym ἰχθυς ('fish') – Ἰησους Χριστος Θεου υἱος σωτηρ, 'Jesus Christ, God's son, saviour'.

In the next section you will look at the *diphthongos* – διφθογγος.

3. Diphthongs

αι   as in 'high': thus νικαι, δικαι, σπονδαι, αἱ, αἱμα
αυ   as in 'how': thus αὐτος, παραυτικα, ταυτα

Αα=a, Ββ=b, Γγ=g, Δδ=d, Εε=e, Ιι=i, Κκ=k, Οο=o, Ππ=p, Σς=s, Ττ=t, Υυ=u, οι=boy, ου=too, ει=fiancée, αι=high, Λλ=l, αυ=how, Σσ=s, Φφ=f, ῾=h, Νν=n, Ρρ=r, Ηη=ê hair, Μμ=m, Χχ=kh, Ωω=ô saw, Θθ=th

ει   as in 'fiancée': thus εἰδη, σκοπει, παυει, δειπνον, εἰεν, εἰη
ευ   pronounce both elements separately ('e-oo', cf. cockney
     'belt up'): thus Ζευς, εὐλογια
οι   as in 'boy': thus ἀνθρωποι, γενοιτο, οἱ, ποιοιη, τοις
ου   as in 'too': thus λουω, σου, τουτου, σοφου, τους, που, του
γγ   as in 'finger': thus ἀγγελοι, τεγγου, ἐγγυς, ἀγγειον,
     διφθογγος

4. ψ = ps (psi) (ψpsψpsψps) Ψ and
ζ = sd/z (zeta) (ζzζzζz)Z

The psalmist sings a ψαλμος on his harp, his ψαλτηρ. A shrink tends to a person's ψυχη. A psephologist studies voting-patterns, Greek ψηφος, a pebble (with which votes were registered in the courts). Let us hope we never find ourselves in *Private Eye*'s Corner dedicated to the ψευδης (verb ψευδω, 'I cheat, beguile'). A false messenger is a ψευδαγγελος and a false brother a ψευδαδελφος. And who is the one-eyed giant? Κυκλωψ – 'round-face' (not 'eye'). Write a συνοψις of his story.

Zeta, ζ, was pronounced 'sd' in classical times: he's not Zeus but Sdeus – Ζευς. The west wind that blows so agreeably is the ζεφυρος and we all know what lives in the zoo – yes, an animal, ζωον, many coming from a tropical ζωνη no doubt (it means 'belt, girdle') and, as far as we are concerned, a long way over the ὁριζων.

5. Punctuation

Greek uses:
. for a full stop (like English)
, for a comma (like English)
; for a question-mark
· for a colon.

Αα=a, Ββ=b, Γγ=g, Δδ=d, Εε=e, Ιι=i, Κκ=k, Οο=o, Ππ=p, Σς=s, Ττ=t, Υυ=u, οι=boy, ου=too, ει=fiancée, αι=high, Λλ=l, αυ=how, Σσ=s, Φφ=f, ̔=h, Νν=n, Ρρ=r, Ηη=ê hair, Μμ=m, Χχ=kh, Ωω=ô saw, Θθ=th, Ψψ=ps, Ζζ=sd/z

6. ξ = x (xi) (ξxξxξxξx – tricky, this) Ξ

How to write this odd-looking letter? Take heart. Ἀλεξανδρος could do it: so can you. Try a backwards 3, with a top and a tail. It is pronounced like English 'x' (so ξ and χ need very careful distinguishing). You had better be aware that γξ is pronounced 'ngx'. Thus the animal, the λυγξ. See one of those at the dead of νυξ (on the island of Ναξος?), and, struck with ἀποπληξια and ἀσφυξια as it tears at your σαρξ (good word σαρκασμος, lit. 'flesh-tearing'), you may be tempted to make a quick ἐξοδος, uttering sharp cries through the λαρυγξ. ξυλον is Greek for 'wood', but there is no Greek word ξυλοφωνη. There is, however, ἀνθραξ ('charcoal', cf. anthracite) and ὀνυξ 'finger-nail'. One of the most interesting Greek words is ξενος, a guest, host, stranger or foreigner. Greeks did not have a word ξενοφοβια, though they did have ξενοφωνια, 'uttering strange noises'. Better word than telephone.

The Greek alphabet

That's your lot, then. Here is the full, 24-letter monty.

The letters are diagnosed in the order – capital, minuscule, the name of the letter, English equivalent, English pronunciation. Now is the time to learn it. This is the big one:

A α	(alpha)	*a*:	as in 'c*u*p' or 'c*a*lm'
B β	(beta)	*b*:	as English
Γ γ	(gamma)	*g*:	hard, as in '*g*ot'
Δ δ	(delta)	*d*:	as English
E ε	(epsilon)	*e*:	short, as in 'p*e*t'
Z ζ	(zeta)	*z*:	'sd', as in 'wi*sd*om'
H η	(eta)	*ê*:	long, as in 'h*ai*r'
Θ θ	(theta)	*th*:	as in 't*h*igh' (or as in 'ho*t-h*ead')
I ι	(iota)	*i*:	as in 'h*i*t'
K κ	(kappa)	*k*:	as English
Λ λ	(lambda)	*l*:	as English

Αα=a, Ββ=b, Γγ=g, Δδ=d, Εε=e, Ιι=i, Κκ=k, Οο=o, Ππ=p, Σς=s, Ττ=t, Υυ=u, οι=b*oy*, ου=t*oo*, ει=fianc*é*e, αι=h*igh*, Λλ=l, αυ=h*ow*, Σσ=s, Φφ=f, ʽ=h, Νν=n, Ρρ=r, Ηη=*ê* h*ai*r, Μμ=m, Χχ=kh, Ωω=*ô* s*aw*, Θθ=th, Ψψ=ps, Ζζ=sd/z, Ξξ=x

Μ μ (mu)	m:	as English
Ν ν (nu)	n:	as English
Ξ ξ (xi)	x:	as English
Ο ο (omicron)	o:	short, as in 'hot'
Π π (pi)	p:	as English
Ρ ρ (rho)	r:	as English
Σ σς (sigma)	s:	soft, as in 'sing'
Τ τ (tau)	t:	as English
Υ υ (upsilon)	u:	as in French 'lune' or German 'Müller'
Φ φ (phi)	ph:	as English (or as in 'top-hole')
Χ χ (chi)	ch:	as in 'loch' or 'cool'
Ψ ψ (psi)	ps:	as in 'lapse'
Ω ω (omega)	ô:	as in 'saw'

Exercise

1. Write out, say and transliterate the following. All of them are the source of easily recognisable English words:

Plants, flowers, trees
κροκος πεταλον μηλον ιρις ευκαλυπτος ανεμωνη ορχις κυκλαμις δελφινιον σπογγος

Animals
καττα μυς λεων τιγρις πανθηρ ελεφας καμηλος ρινοκερως κροκοδειλος

Politics
πολις δημοκρατια μοναρχια τυραννος αριστος αναρχια

The Arts
ποιημα μυθος τραγωδια δραμα ιστορια κινημα παντομιμος σκηνη ορχηστρα θεατρον

Αα=a, Ββ=b, Γγ=g, Δδ=d, Εε=e, Ιι=i, Κκ=k, Οο=o, Ππ=p, Σς=s, Ττ=t, Υυ=u, οι=boy, ου=too, ει=fiancée, αι=high, Λλ=l, αυ=how, Σσ=s, Φφ=f, '=h, Νν=n, Ρρ=r, Ηη=ê hair, Μμ=m, Χχ=kh, Ωω=ô saw, Θθ=th, Ψψ=ps, Ζζ=sd/z, Ξξ=x

Medicine

φαρμακον πνευμων ἀσθμα δυσπεψια ναυσια ἐπιληψις ἐκστασις

The body

κρανιον σκελετος ὀφθαλμος γαστηρ καρδια σπλην

Education

σχολη μαθημα παραγραφη κομμα κωλον τεχνη διλημμα θεωρια

From the Bible

Πετρος Παυλος Ματθαιος Μαρκος Λουκας Ἰωανης Ἀβρααμ Ἰωσηφ Μαρια Μαρθα Γαλιλαια Ναζαρεθ Βηθλεεμ Ἱερουσαλημ Ποντιος Πειλατης Θωμας Ἰουδας Ἰσκαριωτης

2. Who are the following famous Greeks, real and mythical?:

Ἀριστοτελης Πλατων Σωκρατης Αἰσχυλος Ἀρχιμηδης Εὐκλειδης Ἀφροδιτη Ἀθηνη Ἀπολλων Ἀρτεμις Ποσειδων Ἀρης Ἡρα Κασσανδρα Ἀχιλλευς Ἡρακλης Ἀτλας Ἀντιγονη Ἀγαμεμνων

3. Here are some Greek exclamations and animal noises:

παπαι (ouch! ah!), οἰμοι (alas!), ὠμοι (alas!), ἰου ἰου (hoorah!), βαυ βαυ αὐ αὐ (dog), βη βη (sheep), κοκκυ (cuckoo), κοι κοι (pig), and most famous of all, the frogs from Aristophanes' comedy *Frogs*, who cry βρεκεκεκεξ κοαξ κοαξ.

The flatulent, by the way, go παππαξ or παππαππαππαξ or, well, just carry on... .

Αα=a, Ββ=b, Γγ=g, Δδ=d, Εε=e, Ιι=i, Κκ=k, Οο=o, Ππ=p, Σς=s, Ττ=t, Υυ=u, οι=*boy*, ου=*too*, ει=*fiancée*, αι=*high*, Λλ=l, αυ=h*ow*, Σσ=s, Φφ=f, ʽ=h, Νν=n, Ρρ=r, Ηη=ê h*air*, Μμ=m, Χχ=kh, Ωω=ô s*aw*, Θθ=th, Ψψ=ps, Ζζ=sd/z, Ξξ=x

16

"I must say, Apollo, that was divine."

CHAPTER 1

From chaos to cosmos

Congratulations! The worst is over. You are now fluent in the alphabet and pronunciation of ancient Greek. You can tell the difference between a φ, a ψ and mother's apple π and are ready to take on the κοσμος.

Interesting word, κοσμος. It means the ordered universe (or world), created out of its opposite, χαος, the gaping void, or chaos. Same root as 'cosmetics', which also create order out of chaos.

Ho ho, very satirical. Now pay attention.

1a The verb 'to be' always seems *not* to be (yes, Hamlet, a question?) regular. But it is so common one may as well learn it first and get the agony out of the way.

There is also an important gain in doing this. With a very few extra words, you can enjoy the most gripping exchanges with other Greeks at once, asking (for example) 'who are you?' and replying 'I am who I am' or 'alpha and omega' or whatever. This is known as the 'oral method' and is, apparently, fantastically up-to-date as an educational technique. Nice to know that one is at the cutting edge.

Present indicative εἰμι 'I am'

1s	εἰμι	'I am'
2s	εἰ	'you (*singular*) are'
3s	ἐστι(ν)	'he, she, it, there is'
1pl	ἐσμεν	'we are'
2pl	ἐστε	'you (*plural*) are'
3pl	εἰσι(ν)	'they are'

Notes
- Whereas English uses two words to express any form (the person, e.g. 'I', and then the verb, 'am'), Greek uses only one.

18

- ἐστι and εἰσι add a final ν when they end the sentence or the next word begins with a vowel, e.g. ἐστιν. ἐστιν ἄλλα, εἰσιν οὐ.
- **Record** and learn this verb. All such charts will be repeated in the **Grammatical Summary** at the back, but it is best to build up a grammatical notebook of your own.

Vocabulary

When we recommend that you **record** something, it means that the words involved will recur frequently from now on. You must therefore *learn* them. Such words will be repeated in the **Learning Vocabulary** at the back of the book, but it is much the best thing to set up your own alphabetical notebook, English-Greek and Greek-English.

Record

εἰπέ μοι 'tell (to) me' (addressed to one person)
τίς; 'who?' (*s*)
τίνες; 'who?' (*pl*)
καί 'and', 'too', 'as well', 'also'.

Note
- Please **record** the accents on εἰπέ μοι, τίς and τίνες. Their purpose will emerge later on (for accents, see **Wordplay**, Chapter 4).

Exercise 1

Notes
- in English we reverse person and verb in a question, e.g. 'who *are you?*' Greek cannot: it uses the same word for 'you-are' and 'are-you', i.e. εἰ.
- remember that Greek punctuates a question with ; thus 'who are-you?' = τίς εἰ;
- ἐστι can mean 'X is' or 'it is X'. Judge from context which is preferable.

Translate into English:
1. εἰπέ μοι, τίνες εἰσιν;
2. ἐσμεν

19

CHAPTER 1

3. εἰμι
4. εἰπέ μοι, τίς ἐστιν; Παυλος ἐστιν [see last note above]
5. τίνες ἐστε; Παυλος και Πετρος ἐσμεν
6. εἰ
7. τίς εἰμι; α και ω εἰμι· εἰμι ὁστις (who) εἰμι
Now translate into Greek: 1. We-are. 2. You (s)-are. 3. She-is. 4.
Tell me, who is-he? 5. Who [s or pl?] are-they? 6. I-am Petros
(=Peter). 7. You (pl)-are. 8. Tell me, who am-I? 9. He-is who
(ὁστις) he-is. 10. You-are [s or pl?] Peter and Paulos.

Pronouns

1b Now we break the one-word verb rule described above. Or
rather, we modify it. Or expand it. Shut up, Jones. Just do it.

If you want to *emphasise* the person, and especially *contrast*
him/her with someone else, Greek *does* use its words for 'I', 'you',
etc. Such words are called pronouns. We shall be using the
following pronouns (**record** them now):

ἐγω 'I', συ 'you' (s); ἡμεις 'we', ὑμεις 'you' (pl)

Example: *I* am Peter, *you* (are) Paul – ἐγω Πετρος εἰμι, συ
Παυλος (εἰ).

Learning hint: we all know ἐγω because it is an English word
and we usually have it all over our face. Note that the first
syllables of συ and ὑμεις rhyme (sort of) with 'you'. That leaves
poor old ἡμεις, 'we', out on its own – unless ἡ- recalls 'we'.

Vocabulary
Record
ἀλλα 'but' (ἀλλ' when next word starts with a vowel, e.g. ἀλλ'
 ἐστι)
Ἑλ̄ην (Ἑλλην-) (s) 'Greek'
Ἑλλην-ες (pl) 'Greeks'
βαρβαρ-ος (s) 'non-Greek speaker, barbarian' (because they say
 'bar bar')
βαρβαρ-οι (pl) 'non-Greek speakers'
οὐ, οὐκ (when a vowel comes next, e.g. οὐκ ἐστι), and οὐχ (when
 'h' comes next, e.g. οὐχ Ἑλλην) 'no, not'; οὐχι 'no'.

20

Notes
- The words for 'Greek' and 'barbarian' above have their *stem* marked in the vocabulary list: thus the stem of Ἕλλην is Ἑλλην-, the stem of βαρβαρος is βαρβαρ-. These stems are *very* important: they give you the root meaning of the word and *never* change. Make sure you **record** them.
- The *endings* tacked on to the stem *do* change. You will find e.g. Ἑλλην-ες, Ἑλλην-ας, βαρβαρ-οι, βαρβαρ-ους, and so on. For the moment, these endings need not concern you. Just know the meaning of the word, by *recognising its stem*.
- Greek word-order is frequently different from English. Translate into English word-by-word first, then make the changes necessary to produce good English.
- Remember: και means 'and' together with 'as well', 'too', 'also'.

Exercise 2

Translate:
1. συ εἰ Πετρος, ἐγω Παυλος
2. ὑμεις βαρβαροι ἐστε, ἡμεις Ἑλληνες ἐσμεν
3. εἰπέ μοι, τίνες εἰσιν; βαρβαροι εἰσιν
4. συ εἰπέ μοι, τίς εἰ; Ἑλλην εἰμι ἐγω· και συ; Ἑλλην και ἐγω
5. Πετρος Ἑλλην οὐκ ἐστιν ἀλλα βαρβαρος
6. τίς ἐστιν; οὐ βαρβαρος; οὐχι, ἀλλα Ἑλλην
7. Πετρος και Παυλος Ἑλληνες εἰσιν· ἐγω και συ οὐχ Ἑλληνες ἀλλα βαρβαροι ἐσμεν

1. *I* am Greek, *you* are non-Greek. 2. *You* are not Peter but Paul. 3. *We* are non-Greek, *you* (*pl*) are Greek. 4. *We* are Peter and Paul – who are *you* (*pl*)?

Vocabulary

Record
χαιρ-ε (addressing one person) 'hello'
χαιρ-ετε (addressing more than one person) 'hello'
ὦ 'O' (addressing someone).

Notes
- names ending in -ος e.g. Πετρ-ος end in -ε when the person is addressed. Thus χαιρε, ὦ Πετρ-ε 'Hello, (o) Peter'.

21

* names ending in -ης end in -ες or -εις when the person is addressed. Thus Σωκρατ-ης, but χαιρε, ὦ Σωκρατ-ες.
* Observe the stem χαιρ- (that is the bit that means 'hello'); the *endings* tell you whether one person or more than one person is being addressed.

Exercise 3

Translate the following scintillating dialogue, almost Platonic in its rich understanding of the infinite subtleties of human interaction:

Σωκρατης: εἰπέ μοι, τίς εἰ συ;
Σοφοκλης: ἐγω; Σοφοκλης εἰμι· ἀλλα τίς εἰ συ;
Σωκρατης: Σωκρατης ἐγω, ὦ Σοφοκλεις· χαιρε.
Σοφοκλης: ἀλλα χαιρε και συ, ὦ Σωκρατες.
(Enter another tremendous bore.)
Σοφοκλης: ἀλλ᾽ εἰπέ μοι, ὦ Σωκρατες, τίς ἐστιν;
Σωκρατης: Εὐριπιδης ἐστιν, ὦ Σοφοκλεις· χαιρε, ὦ Εὐριπιδες.
Εὐριπιδης: χαιρε και συ, ὦ Σωκρατες· ἀλλα τίς εἰ συ;
Σοφοκλης: Σοφοκλης εἰμι ἐγω.
(At this point enter two apostles, 500 years too soon, but never mind. The latest literary theory says you never need to pay any attention to anything as boring as dates.)
Εὐριπιδης: ἀλλ᾽ εἰπέ μοι, τίνες εἰσιν;
Σοφοκλης: Πετρος και Παυλος εἰσιν. χαιρετε, ὦ Πετρε και Παυλε.
Π και Π: χαιρετε και ὑμεις, ὦ Σοφοκλεις και Σωκρατες.
(A million other bores promptly storm the scene, so that the gripping conversation goes on forever. Enough, however, is enough.)

Particulars

1c Now we get classy. Ancient Greek groans with particles (lit. 'little parts' – no giggling at the back there). These are little words, like (in English) 'so', 'therefore', 'but', 'at any rate' which add nuances of meaning (see? 'Nuance.' That's class) to sentences.

μεν means (no cynical comments, *please*, ladies) 'on the one hand' (add cynical comment here). It jumps up and down waving a flag (yes, yes, ladies, contain yourselves) which says 'Keep the

22

eyes peeled, folks, for very soon I am going to announce a contrast which will be signalled by my very old chum δε, meaning "on the other hand".'

Slip, therefore, the lemon into overdrive and consider the following:

ἐγω μεν Παυλος εἰμι, συ δε Πετρος 'I (on the one hand) am Paul, you (by contrast, on the other) [are] Peter.'

ἡμεις μεν Ἑλληνες ἐσμεν, ὑμεις δε βαρβαροι 'We (on the one hand) are Greeks, you (on the other) are non-Greeks.'

As soon as you see μεν, therefore, jump up and down in feverish anticipation of a δε.

As another tactic, you could translate μεν as 'while' and not translate δε at all: e.g. 'While *we* are Greeks, *you* are barbarians.' This gets the contrast, but not in so sharp a form.

As another (on the other hand), you could refuse to translate μεν and translate δε as 'but'. Thus, '*we* are Greeks but *you* are barbarians'.

δε *on its own* means 'and' or 'but'. It is very common near the start of a sentence to show that that this sentence connects with the previous one in some way or other.

Vocabulary

Record

μεν...δε 'on the one hand...on the other hand'; δε 'and, but'
ἀγαθ-ος 'good, brave' (*s*, i.e. referring to one person)
ἀγαθ-οι 'good, brave' (*pl*, i.e. referring to many people)
κακ-ος 'bad, cowardly' (*s*)
κακ-οι 'bad, cowardly' (*pl*)
ὁ 'the' (*s*)
οἱ 'the' (*pl*)
ὁ θε-ος 'the god' (*s*)
οἱ θε-οι 'the gods' (*pl*)
ὀλιγ-οι few; οἱ ὀλιγ-οι 'the few'
πολλ-οι many; οἱ πολλ-οι 'the many' (and now you know who *hoi polloi* are – and they are not 'the *hoi polloi*', right?).

23

CHAPTER 1

Notes

• δε loses its last vowel if the next word begins with a vowel, e.g. ὁ δ᾽ Εὐριπιδης, etc.

• People's names are often prefaced by 'the' in Greek, e.g. ὁ Σωκρατης '[the] Socrates'.

Exercise 4

Translate:
1. ὁ μεν Σωκρατης ἀγαθος ἐστιν, ὁ δ᾽ Εὐριπιδης κακος
2. ὑμεις μεν ἀγαθοι ἐστε, ἡμεις δε κακοι
3. οἱ μεν Ἑλληνες εἰσιν ἀγαθοι, οἱ δε βαρβαροι κακοι
4. χαιρε, Εὐριπιδες· οἱ δε βαρβαροι οὐ κακοι εἰσιν ἀλλ᾽ ἀγαθοι
5. ὁ θεος δ᾽ οὐ κακος ἐστιν ἀλλ᾽ ἀγαθος
6. συ μεν ἀγαθος εἰ, ἐγω δε κακος
7. χαιρετε· τινες ἐστε; Ἑλληνες ἐσμεν
8. ὑμεις μεν Ἑλληνες ἐστε, ἡμεις δε βαρβαροι ἐσμεν
9. πολλοι μεν εἰσιν οἱ Ἑλληνες, ὀλιγοι δε οἱ θεοι
10. οἱ δε πολλοι οὐκ ἀγαθοι εἰσιν ἀλλα κακοι
11. χαιρε, ὦ Πετρε· εἰπέ μοι, τίς ἐστιν ἀγαθος, τίς κακος; ὁ μεν θεος ἐστιν ἀγαθος, οἱ δε Ἑλληνες κακοι
12. τινες εἰσιν οἱ πολλοι; οὐχ οἱ ὀλιγοι

The Greek world

From myth to Mycenae

As we have seen, Greeks called themselves Hellenes – people of the mythical Hellen. Hellen was son of Deucalion, a sort of Greek Noah, who re-peopled the earth after a flood by throwing stones behind him, from which humans sprang up. We call them Greeks because the Romans called them *Graeci*, 'men of Graea' – wherever that might have been (no one knows – Oropus is a recent guess).

We do not know when people speaking Greek entered what we now call Greece, but they were certainly there by the 2nd millennium BC. From about 1600-1200 BC (during the bronze age), Greece was controlled by great palaces like those at Mycenae, Pylos, Tiryns and Thebes (the age is called the 'Mycenaean age'), and their inhabitants spoke Greek. We know this because

24

"Don't worry about drowning. Unfortunately I only take a
moment."

the script they left behind, which we call Linear B, is a form of Greek (the earlier Linear A, used widely in Crete, looks very similar but has not yet been deciphered). Of the words you have met, δε and θεος occur in Linear B form – though looking nothing like the Greek we know. We have, however, found no literature or history recorded in this language, only economic records of staggering bureaucratic complexity and detail.

For reasons not yet fully understood, the Mycenaean palaces were destroyed, abandoned or reduced to villages from about 1200 BC onwards, and their script disappeared with them. When written texts next emerge in Greece in the 8th century BC (the iron age), they are in a quite different form of Greek (the basis of the Greek and English scripts that we know today). Fascinatingly, the first Greek literature to appear – Homer's great epics the *Iliad* and *Odyssey* (8th-7th century BC) – tells of bronze age heroes battling it out in what sometimes looks somewhat like a Mycenaean world...

Word play

Greek and the family of languages

Ancient Greek shares linguistic roots with Latin (the basis of Italian, French, and Spanish), German (the basis of English) and the Indian language Sanskrit. We know this because none of these languages derives from any of the others, yet they all share too many roots for it to be mere coincidence. Thus German *Mutter* (English 'mother'), Latin *mater*, Greek μητηρ, Sanskrit *matar*; German *Vater* (English 'father'), Latin *pater*, Greek πατηρ, Sanskrit *pitar* – and so on and endlessly on (cf. ist, est, ἐστι; ich, ego, ἐγω).

Conclusion? Once upon a time these languages were one language, spoken by one people (we call this language, for convenience, Indo-European). This people then split up, and over time, as they diverged geographically, so the language began to diverge too (as e.g. Italian, French and Spanish all diverged in their different ways from Latin, but all obviously come from a single common language).

Most of the pure Greek words in English, however, have been consciously taken over for some purpose or other (especially for educational purposes during the renaissance). Many have been lifted straight from Latin, which eagerly took over Greek words like φιλοσοφια and simply transliterated them (Latin *philosophia*). You have already met the Greek words that are used in '*the*ology', '*olig*archy', '*poly*technic' ('many skills'), *Agath*a, and *barbar*ian. We shall be exploring many more in the course of this book.

Answers
Notes
• as you will have seen, Greek word-order is very flexible. So when you translate English into Greek, your word order may be different from that of the 'answer'. Do not worry. Just make sure you have the correct form of the word (especially singulars and plurals). 'He/she/it' are often interchangeable too.
• likewise, a word such as και has many possible translations. If the answer shows 'too' and you have used 'as well' or 'also', that is fine.

Exercise 1
1. Tell me, who are they? 2. We are. 3. I am. 4. Tell me, who is it/he/she? It is Paul. 5. Who are you? We are Paul and Peter. 6. You are. 7. Who am I?, I am alpha and omega, I am who I am.
1. ἐσμεν. 2. εἰ. 3. ἐστι. 4. εἰπέ μοι,τίς ἐστιν; 5. τίνες εἰσιν; 6. εἰμι Πετρος. 7. ἐστε. 8. εἰπέ μοι, τίς εἰμι; 9. ἐστιν ὁστις ἐστιν. 10. ἐστε Πετρος και Παυλος.

Exercise 2
1. You are Peter, I Paul. 2. You are non-Greeks, we are Greeks. 3. Tell me, who are they? They are non-Greeks. 4. You tell me, who are you? I am Greek. And you? I [am] Greek as well. 5. Peter is not a Greek but a non-Greek. 6. Who is he? [Is he] not non-Greek? No, but Greek. 7. Peter and Paul are Greeks, I and you [=we] are not Greeks but non-Greeks.
1. ἐγω Ἑλλην εἰμι, συ βαρβαρος (εἰ). 2. συ Πετρος οὐκ εἰ ἀλλα Παυλος. 3. ἡμεις βαρβαροι ἐσμεν, ὑμεις Ἑλληνες (ἐστε). 4. ἡμεις Πετρος και Παυλος ἐσμεν· τίνες ὑμεις ἐστε;

Exercise 3
Socrates: Tell me, who are you? *Sophocles*: I? I am Sophocles. But who are you? *Socrates*: I [am] Socrates, o Sophocles. Hello. *Sophocles*: Hello [to] you too, o Socrates. *Sophocles*: But tell me, Socrates, who is he? *Socrates*: It is Euripides, o Sophocles. Hello,

o Euripides. *Euripides*: Hello [to] you too, o Socrates. But who are you? *Sophocles*: I am Sophocles. *Euripides*: But tell me, who are they? *Sophocles*: They are Peter and Paul. Hello, o Peter and Paul. *P and P*: Hello [to] you too, o Sophocles and Socrates.

Exercise 4

1. Socrates on the one hand is good, Euripides on the other hand bad. 2. You otonh are good, we ototh bad. 3. The Greeks otonh are good, the non-Greeks ototh bad. 4. Hello, Euripides. But/and the non-Greeks are not bad but good. 5. But/and the god is not bad but good. 6. You otonh are good, I ototh bad. 7. Hello, who are you? We are Greeks. 8. You otonh are Greeks, we ototh are non-Greeks. 9. The Greeks otonh are many, the gods ototh few. 10. But/and the many are not good but evil. 11. Hello, Peter: tell me, who is good, who evil? The god otonh is good, the Greeks ototh evil. 12. Who are the many? Not the few.

Afore ye go

Make certain you know by heart:

- εἰμι (**1a**)
- the pronouns ἐγω συ ἡμεις ὑμεις (**1b**)
- the contents of the four vocabulary lists (30 words in all, but really only 17, given that many are the same word in different forms). These words will not be given again, but will be found in the **Learning Vocabulary** at the back.

CHAPTER 2

Keeping regular

2a With a sigh of relief we leave the irregularities of εἰμι 'I am' and set our sights on the regular verb forms. Basically there are only two sorts of verb in Greek. In this chapter we deal with the first sort 'active'.

Present indicative active παυ-ω 'I stop'

1s	παυ-ω	'I stop' 'I do stop' 'I am stopping'
2s	παυ-εις	'you (s) stop', 'you do stop', 'you are stopping'
3s	παυ-ει	'he, she, it stops', 'he, she, it does stop/is stopping'
1pl	παυ-ομεν	'we stop', 'we do stop', 'we are stopping'
2pl	παυ-ετε	'you (pl) stop', 'you do stop', 'you are stopping'
3pl	παυ-ουσι(ν)	'they stop', 'they do stop', 'they are stopping'

Present imperative active

2s	παυ-ε	'stop!' (addressed to one person)
2pl	παυ-ετε	'stop!' (addressed to more than one person)

Terminology
- 'Present' (a tense) refers to the time the action is happening – now. There are different tenses (e.g. past).
- 'Indicative' (a mood) means that the action really is regarded as happening – it *indicates* what is the case. There are different moods – see 'imperative' below.
- 'Active' (a voice) means the subject of the sentence is doing the action: '*he stops* the car' means 'he' is actively doing something. Cf. the passive voice (which we shall come to but not yet) '*he is being stopped* by the car' – a quite different picture.

29

- 'Imperative' (like indicative, a mood) does not tell what is the case, but what ought to be the case – do it!

Notes

- Observe that, as with εἰμι, Greek requires one word to express two or three in English. English, in fact, has three ways to express the present tense – Greek only one. A useful saving of effort.
- The present stem, παυ-, remains fixed. It means 'stop'. On to it are added the present indicative active endings -ω -εις -ει -ομεν -ετε -ουσι and the imperative endings -ε -ετε. These help to indicate tense, mood and person (who is doing the action). So in English we hear the person first, then the verb, 'I stop', in Greek the reverse, 'stop I'.
- Like ἐστι and εἰσι, παυουσι becomes παυουσιν at the end of a sentence or if the next word begins with a vowel, e.g. οὐ παυουσιν ἀλλα...
- Er, that's it.
- Er, no it isn't. Observe that the imperative (order) forms in -ε -ετε are already old chums: cf. εἰπ-έ 'tell!'; and χαιρ-ε *s*, χαιρ-ετε *pl* 'hello!', 'welcome!'
- Observe, however, that παυ-ετε can mean either 'you stop' or 'stop!'

Vocabulary

Record the following verbs (with παυ-ω):
μεν-ω 'I remain, wait, stay'
γι(γ)νωσκ-ω 'I recognise, get to know, learn'
ἐχ-ω 'I have'.

Exercise 1

Translate:
1. παυομεν
2. μενουσι
3. γινωσκει
4. ἐχεις
5. παυετε (two meanings)
6. μενε

30

7. γιγνωσκομεν
8. ἐχουσιν
9. παυω
10. μενετε (two)
11. γιγνωσκουσιν
12. ἐχομεν
13. παυουσι
14. μενεις
15. γινωσκετε (two)
16. ἐχω
17. ἐχε
18. εἰπέ μοι

1. They stop. 2. She gets to know. 3. We do have. 4. You (s) are staying. 5. She is. 6. They have. 7. We are stopping. 8. She has. 9. They do not learn. 10. They are. 11. Stay! (s). 12. You are (pl). 13. You have (s). 14. We are. 15. Know! (pl). 16. Hello! (pl).

Vocabulary

Record

ἡ ἀγαπ-η '(the) love'
αὐτ-ος 'he'
ἐν 'in'
ἐκ 'from'
ἡ 'the' (s)
ὁτι 'that'

Notes

- We have now met three words for 'the': ὁ and ἡ (s); οἱ (pl).
- Greek sometimes uses these in places where we leave them out. Thus Greek will write ἡ ἀγαπη 'the love', where we would say, simply, 'love'; Greek writes ὁ Θεος, 'the god', where we would write 'God'; Greek writes ὁ Σωκρατης where we write 'Socrates'.
- Note that after ἐν 'in', ὁ Θε-ος becomes τῳ Θε-ῳ, αὐτ-ος becomes αὐτ-ῳ, and ἡμ-εις becomes ἡμ-ιν. Thus ἐν τῳ Θεῳ, 'in [the] God'; ἐν ἡμιν, 'in us', ἐν αὐτῳ 'in him' etc.
- What is this funny ῳ with that embarrassing little dropping extruding from it? Answer: it is ωι, with the ι written 'sub-script', i.e. *underneath* the ω instead of after it. It happens

31

also with η and ᾳ, originally ηι and αι. Why, you ask? If αι, ηι and ωι were good enough for ancient Greeks, why are they not good enough for us? Just one of those things, I fear – a convention. But it does have a small use, as we shall find later on.

• Note that after ἐκ 'from', ὁ Θεος becomes του Θε-ου. Thus ἐκ του Θεου 'from (the) God'.

Exercise 2

Polish up your lapels, Philhellenes. Here you are in only your second Greek lesson and you are about to read extracts from the real thing, i.e. the first epistle of John, chapter 4. Who said there are no such things as miracles?

Translate:

4.4 ὑμεις ἐκ του Θεου ἐστε

4.6 ἡμεις ἐκ του Θεου ἐσμεν

4.7 ἡ ἀγαπη ἐκ του Θεου ἐστιν

4.8 ὁ Θεος ἀγαπη ἐστιν

4.12 If we love one another, ὁ Θεος ἐν ἡμιν μενει, και ἡ ἀγαπη αὐτου [of him] ἐν ἡμιν ἐστιν. By this γινωσκομεν ὁτι ἐν αὐτῳ μενομεν και αὐτος ἐν ἡμιν...

4.15 Whoever agrees that Jesus is the son of God, ὁ Θεος ἐν αὐτῳ μενει και αὐτος ἐν τῳ Θεῳ

4.16 And we know and have believed in the love which ὁ Θεος ἐχει ἐν ἡμιν. ὁ Θεος ἀγαπη ἐστιν, και he who remains ἐν τῃ ἀγαπῃ, ἐν τῳ Θεῳ μενει και ὁ Θεος ἐν αὐτῳ μενει

Def Art (1)

2b As we have seen, 'the' is the definite article, and we have now met three different forms of it – ὁ, ἡ (s), οἱ (pl).

There are more forms of this innocuous word to come, but do not despair. Lay off the gin just a bit longer. For this little word is quite the most useful word in the whole Greek language. Hug it to your bosom, love it to bits and it will amply repay your devotion. Because if you know Def Art (you'll have to speak up, you know), you will have mastered a huge amount of grammar all at one go.

To see why, we must open our cases.

Cases

2c Greek, like Latin, has a case structure. Latinists know all about cases so can skip this bit. Non-latinists, eyes down.

'Peter recognises Paul'. 'Peter' is doing the action. He is the 'subject' of the sentence. Subjects in Greek take the form that we call the nominative case (nom.). The nom. of Πετρος is, er, Πετρος.

'Paul' is on the receiving end of the recognition. He is the 'object' of the sentence. Objects in Greek go into the accusative case (acc.). The acc. of Παυλος is Παυλον.

In Greek, therefore: Πετρος γιγνωσκει Παυλον.

But now see what the implications of this case system are. Since Πετρος announces by its form (nom.) that it is the subject of the sentence, he can appear anywhere in the sentence he likes. He will still be the subject. So too for Παυλον: his form (acc.) announces that he is the object and object he will remain, wherever he appears in the sentence.

So Παυλον Πετρος γιγνωσκει, Πετρος Παυλον γιγνωσκει, γιγνωσκει Πετρος Παυλον – indeed, any order of those three words you like – will yield exactly the same meaning. Πετρ-ος screams 'Ooo sir look sir me sir I'm the *subject* sir' while Παυλ-ον moans 'Ooo sir help sir no sir gosh sir I am the *object* sir'. Change Πετρος to Πετρον and Παυλον to Παυλος and the situation is, of course, reversed. Paul will be doing the action, and Peter will be on the receiving end.

Thus word order in a Greek sentence can be, indeed usually is, different from English. Word order, in a sense, 'does not matter' in Greek: it's the forms of the words that tell you what job they are doing (subject, object, whatever), not their position in the sentence.

In English, however, position is all. 'Peter recognises Paul' means one thing. Rewrite it 'Paul recognises Peter' and the meaning is quite different. Rewrite it 'Recognises Peter Paul' and we are already ringing for the men in white coats.

Enter, to tumultuous applause (not that he can hear it, bless him), Def Art, 'the'.

Def Art (2)

2d Here are the full forms of Def Art. Pay attention only to those <u>underlined</u>:

	M	F	N
Announcing subject, singular:	<u>ὁ</u>	<u>ἡ</u>	το
Announcing subject, plural:	<u>οἱ</u>	αἱ	τα
Announcing object, singular:	<u>τον</u>	<u>την</u>	το
Announcing object, plural:	<u>τους</u>	<u>τας</u>	τα

And what, you ask, are M F N? A cheap furniture warehouse? No. They stand for masculine, feminine and neuter. All nouns, whether people or things, are given a gender in Greek (small boys, for example are neuter. Hmmm). Def Art will use m. forms when going with m. nouns, f. forms when going with f. nouns, etc.

Now the really vital point about Def Art – and this is where Greek is so much easier than Latin which has no Def Art – is that Def Art alerts you to what is to come next. It screams at you 'Ee-oop, subject singular coming, or object plural' before you have even come to it.

So: see ὁ and you can say: whatever this is, there is one of them, it is m., and it is subject of the sentence. So ὁ Θεος – ah. 'God', subject, doing the action.

See τους and you can say 'Ho ho, Watson, there are a number of these blighters and they are m. and the object of the sentence, on the receiving end of the action'. So: τους βαρβαρους – 'the non-Greeks', object.

See την, however, and, your thoughts will go: 'Hmm: one of these, f. too, and the object of the sentence.'

You are allowed, of course, to be moderately interested in the fact that, for example, 'Greeks' (subject, plural) are οἱ Ἑλληv-ες while in the object plural they are τους Ἑλληv-ας but as long as you know what the stem Ἑλληv- means you can translate away perfectly happy because οἱ has told you 'these chappies are subject plural' while τους tells you 'these chappies are object plural'.

In other words, you do not need to pay attention to the *ending* of the nouns as long as you have:

(i) a firm grip on the *meaning* of the noun-stem, and
(ii) an even firmer grip on what Def Art is telling you about it –
that it is subject/object, whatever.

And in fact, in this course we will say almost nothing about the ending of nouns at all. Let Def Art take the strain! The curious, however, can peek at **Grammatical Summary 30-33.**

Remember: the Greek words can come in any order. To translate them into English:
(i)   put Greek subject first (if there is a Greek subject)
(ii)   then verb (start with the verb if there is no subject)
(iii)   then Greek object (if there is an object).

For example: τον Εὐριπιδη γιγνωσκει ὁ Σωκρατης.
(i)   Euripides? Hmm. τον – therefore object. Hold.
(ii)   γιγνωσκει – he/she/it recognises . So 'he/she/it recognises Euripides'.
(iii)   Socrates? Ah. ὁ. Therefore subject.
(iv)   Therefore 'Socrates recognises Euripides'.
(v)   βιγγω (if there were such a word).

Or: τον Σωκρατη γινωσκουσιν. Humph.
(i)   τον object – it's Socrates – hold.
(ii)   γινωσκουσι um 'they recognise'. OK.
(iii)   Any οἱ knocking around, subject plural to replace 'they'? Or any (say) ὁ X και ὁ Y, to make a plural subject? No.
(iv)   Therefore 'they recognise Socrates'.

Exercise 3

Define the following as subject or object, singular or plural:
ἡ
τον
τους
ὁ
την
οἱ
Translate and say what the case is (nom. if subject, acc. if object), e.g. τον Θεον '(the) God, acc.':
την ἀγαπην
ὁ Ἑλλην
τους ὀλιγους
οἱ πολλοι

35

τον βαρβαρον
οἱ ἀγαθοι [pl, i.e. good people]
τον κακον [s, i.e. bad person]
τους Ἑλληνας
ὁ Θεος
τον Σωκρατη
ἡ ἀγαπη
Translate:

1. ὁ Ἑλλην τον βαρβαρον γιγνωσκει
2. οἱ δε πολλοι τους ὀλιγους γινωσκουσιν
3. οἱ βαρβαροι τους Ἑλληνας γιγνωσκουσιν
4. συ μεν τον Σωκρατη γινωσκεις, ἐγω δ᾽ οὐ
5. γινωσκεις δ᾽ ὁτι οἱ ἀγαθοι τους κακους παυουσιν
6. ἡμεις μεν την ἀγαπην ἐχομεν, ὑμεις δ᾽ οὐ
7. γιγνωσκει ὁ Παυλος ὁτι την ἀγαπην ἐχει ὁ Θεος
8. τον Εὐριπιδη γινωσκετε (two meanings)
9. τους δε κακους οἱ πολλοι οὐ παυουσιν
10. γιγνωσκει ὁ Εὐριπιδης ὁτι οἱ μεν πολλοι κακοι εἰσιν, οἱ δε ὀλιγοι ἀγαθοι
11. την ἀγαπην ἐχετε, ὦ Ἑλληνες (two meanings)

The Greek world

Greeks and the near east

When we think of the 'the glory that was Greece', we tend to think of the Parthenon, Pericles, all those statues (many originally had little umbrella hats to keep bird-droppings off), democracy, Greek tragedies and 5th-century Athens. Fair enough: but it is important to understand that the foundations of this 'glory' were laid elsewhere, and that many of the most important cultural and intellectual breakthroughs were made much earlier, by Greeks who did not even live on mainland Greece, let alone in Athens.

Homer, for example, whose epics the *Iliad* and *Odyssey* were composed in the late 8th-7th century BC and are the western world's first literature, lived somewhere on or off the west coast of modern Turkey (we can tell this from the dialect in which the epics were composed). Greeks had been populating this coastline and its adjacent islands since the end of the Mycenaean era (*c.* 1200 BC), and it is not surprising that so much of the Greek

"How do I *know* you're Zeus?"

achievement had its origins here, close as Greeks now would be to the stimulating influences of great near Eastern cultures – Hittite (central Turkey), Phoenician (Lebanon), Syrian, Babylonian (Iraqi).

The Greek creation myth, for example, of the castration of Uranos by his son Cronos is clearly lifted from earlier Hittite myth, where Kumarbi is the castrator. Pythagoras' theorem was known to Babylonians a thousand years earlier. The Homeric epics have many similarities with the epic of Gilgamesh and other Babylonian masterpieces.

So the distinctive Greek achievement comes about as a result of these early interactions. But the edifice that Greeks were to build on these foundations bears witness to a whole new way of looking at and thinking about the world.

Word play

The Greek alphabet

The single most influential example of interaction between Greeks and near eastern cultures was surely the development of the Greek alphabet, the basis of ours. The Greeks invented their alphabet in the 8th century BC on the model of the Phoenician alphabet. Very broadly, Greeks took Phoenician symbols and where necessary changed both their look and their value to suit Greek needs. Major changes included:

- Phoenician script runs right-to-left. In time Greeks settled on left-to-right, and thus reversed all Phoenician non-symmetrical signs. So e.g. Phoenician gimel (ꓶ) became Greek gamma Γ.
- Greeks created separate signs to represent vowels. They took Phoenician consonants aleph (alpha), he (epsilon), yod (iota) and ain (omicron) and turned them into the vowels A E I O, and then invented Y to complete the hand. This was the first time that proper vowel signs became an established part of an alphabet, and was a very important development.
- They created H (long E) and Ω (long O).
- Since Phoenician did not have aspirates, Φ X (and Ψ) were added too.

None of this happened at once. Different Greek states used different versions of the alphabet for some time, both in appearance and number of letters (as we know from inscriptions). But by about 370 BC the Greek alpha-bet (α β, Phoenician aleph beth) had stabilised into the one we use today.

Or rather, into the one we do not use today. Our script bears no relation to that of the ancient Greeks. Ancient Greeks wrote in capital letters, with no punctuation and no gaps between the words. They would have written 1 John 4.4 as

ΥΜΕΙΣΕΚΤΟΥΘΕΟΥΕΣΤΕ

Punctuation and minuscule writing as we know it are essentially an invention of the middle ages. Hey ho.

At all events, this alphabet is the basis of the western alphabet, taken as it was by Greeks to Italy, and thus to Rome, and thus to the whole of the west. And the order of letters in our alphabet is still strikingly similar to that of the Phoenician alphabet too... .

Answers
Exercise 1
1. We stop. 2. They stay. 3. He gets to know. 4. You have. 5. You stop/stop! 6. Wait! 7. We get to know. 8. They have. 9. I stop. 10. You wait/wait! 11. They learn. 12. We have. 13. They stop. 14. You stay. 15. You recognise/recognise! 16. I have. 17. Have! 18. Tell me!

1. παυουσιν. 2. γιγνωσκει. 3. ἐχομεν. 4. μενεις. 5. ἐστιν. 6. ἐχουσιν. 7. παυομεν. 8. ἐχει. 9. οὐ γιγνωσκουσιν. 10. εἰσιν. 11. μενε. 12. ἐστε. 13. ἐχεις. 14. ἐσμεν. 15. γιγνωσκετε. 16. χαιρετε.

Exercise 2
4.4 You are from God. 4.6 We are from God. 4.7 Love is from God. 4.8 God is love. 4.12 God remains in us and his love is in us...we know that we remain in him and he in us. 4.15 ...God remains in him and he in God. 4.16 ...God has in us. God is love and...in love, remains in God and God remains in him.

Exercise 3
Subject singular; object singular; object plural; subject singular; object singular; subject plural.
Love (acc.); the Greek (nom.); the few (acc.); the many (nom.); the non-Greek (acc.); the good [people] (nom.); the evil [person] (acc.); the Greeks (acc.); God (nom.); Socrates (acc.), love (nom.).
1. The Greek recognises the non-Greek. 2. And/but the many recognise the few. 3. Non-Greeks recognise Greeks. 4. You rec-

ognise Socrates, I don't. 5. And/but you learn that the good [people] stop the bad [people]. 6. We have love, you don't. 7. Paul gets to know that God has love. 8. You recognise/Recognise! Euripides. 9. And/but the many do not stop the wicked [people]. 10. Euripides gets to know that the majority are evil, the few good. 11. You have/Have! love, o Greeks.

Afore Ye Go

Make certain you know by heart:
- The indicative and imperative of παυω (**2a**)
- The ten new words in the two vocabulary sections
- The underlined forms of Def Art at **2d**

Make certain you understand:
- The vital principle of cases and the function of Def Art (**2b-d**)

CHAPTER 3

Congratulations! Your first contract

3a The stems of some Greek verbs end in a vowel, α in the following cases (all of which **record**): ἀγαπα-ω, 'I love', ὁρα-ω, 'I see', and νικα-ω 'I conquer, win, am victorious'. See now what happens when α blends, or contracts with, the regular verb-endings, and work out what the rules are:

Present indicative active of νικαω 'I conquer'

1s	νικα-ω	becomes	νικ-ω 'I conquer'
2s	νικα-εις	becomes	νικ-ᾳς 'you conquer'
3s	νικα-ει	becomes	νικ-ᾳ 'he, she, it conquers'
1pl	νικα-ομεν	becomes	νικ-ωμεν 'we conquer'
2pl	νικα-ετε	becomes	νικ-ατε 'you conquer'
3pl	νικα-ουσι	becomes	νικ-ωσι 'they conquer'

Present imperative active

2s	νικα-ε	becomes	νικ-α 'conquer!'
2pl	νικα-ετε	becomes	νικ-ατε 'conquer!'

3b The rules of α contract Greek?

$$α + ε = α \ (2s \text{ and } 2pl, \text{ imperatives})$$
$$α + ει = ᾳ \ (2s, 3s)$$
$$α + \text{any } o/ω = ω \ (1s, 1pl, 3pl)$$

Exercise 1

Translate:
1. νικωμεν
2. ὁρατε (two)
3. ἀγαπᾳς

41

4. νικωσι
5. ὁρα
6. ἀγαπωμεν
7. νικας
8. ὁρωσιν
9. ἀγαπω
10. νικατε (two)
11. ὁρας
12. ἀγαπωσι
13. νικα
14. νικα
15. ὁρωμεν
16. ἀγαπατε (two)
17. ὁρα
18. νικωμεν

Translate: 1. You (pl) love. 2. She sees. 3. He conquers. 4. They love. 5. We see. 6. You (s) conquer. 7. She loves. 8. See! (pl). 9. They see. 10. I conquer.

Inscription

Vocabulary: δια or δι' + acc., 'because of, through'; τον Δια '(the) Zeus' (acc.). You are not expected to record these (keenies can, if they wish): they just refer to this passage.

Here in a 5th-century BC inscription Greeks living in Selinus (οἱ Σελινοντιοι) in Sicily record a victory, listing the gods responsible. You can guess most of the gods:

δια τους θεους τουσδε ('these', with 'gods') νικωσι οἱ Σελινοντιοι. δια τον Δια νικωμεν και δια τον Φοβον (Phobos, god of fear) και δια Ἡρακλεα και δι' Ἀπολλωνα και δια Ποτειδανα (=Poseidon) και δια Τυνδαριδας (Tyndaridae, Castor and Pollux) και δι' Ἀθηναιαν και δια Μαλοφορον (sheep-bringer= Demeter) και δια Πασικρατειαν (all-conquering: being next to Demeter, perhaps the Selinuntine Persephone?) και δια τους ἀλλους (other) θεους, δια δε Δια μαλιστα (most of all).

Participles

3c A participle is a verb ending in '-ing', e.g. 'having', 'conquering', 'seeing'. The Greek participle ends in -ων, e.g.

ἐχ-ων	'having'
γιγνωσκ-ων	'getting to know'
νικ-ων	'conquering'

It is a very common Greek idiom to preface this with ὁ (subject), to mean 'the person -ing', 'the one who -s', 'the -er', e.g.

ὁ νικων 'the one conquering, the person who conquers, the conqueror'
ὁ ἐχων 'the person having', 'the one who has'
ὁ μενων 'the person who remains', 'the one remaining'

Notes
- Observe that (for the moment anyway) verbs ending in -ω and -αω both have participle forms ending in -ων, e.g. ἐχ-ων 'having', ὁρ-ων 'seeing'.
- Watch out for participle + object, e.g. ὁ ἐχων την ἀγαπην, 'the [one] having (the) love' – την ἀγαπην being object of ὁ ἐχων; ὁ γιγνωσκων τον Θεον 'the [one] recognising (the) God', and so on.

Exercise 2

Translate the following clauses:
1. ὁ ἀγαπων τον Θεον
2. ὁ νικων τους βαρβαρους
3. ὁ ὁρων τον Παυλον
4. ὁ παυων τον Πετρον
5. ὁ μενων ἐν ἀγαπῃ
6. ὁ γιγνωσκων τους Ἑλληνας
7. ὁ ὁρων τους πολλους
8. ὁ νικων τους ὀλιγους

Vocabulary

Record

ἡ ζω-η '[the] life'
ἡ ἀληθει-α '[the] truth'
ἡ μαρτυρι-α '[the] witness, evidence'
πιστευ-ω 'I trust, have faith (in), believe'
ὁ Πατηρ (Πατ(ε)ρ-) '[the] Father'
ἀκου-ω 'I hear, listen to'
ὁ Υἱ-ος '[the] Son'
ὁ Ἰησ-ους '[the] Jesus'
ὁ Χριστ-ος '[the] Christ'

Remember ἐν 'in'.
Note the phrase ὁ Υἱος τ̲ο̲υ̲ Θ̲ε̲ο̲υ̲ 'the Son o̲f̲ (̲t̲h̲e̲)̲ God'.

Exercise 3

Translate:

1. εἰπέ μοι, τίς ἐστιν ὁ Υἱος του Θεου; Ἰησους Χριστος ἐστιν ὁ Υἱος του Θεου
2. χαιρετε· ἡμεις μεν τον Θεον ἀγαπωμεν, ὑμεις δε οὐ
3. ὁ Υἱος του Θεου ἀγαπα ἡμας ['us']
4. ὁ γιγνωσκων τον Θεον ἀκουει αὐτου ['him']
5. ἡ μαρτυρια ἐστιν ὁτι Ἰησους ἐστιν ὁ Υἱος του Θεου
6. ἐγω εἰμι ἡ ὁδος [guess!] και ἡ ἀληθεια και ἡ ζωη (John 14.6)
7. οὐ πιστευεις ὁτι ἐγω ἐν τω Πατρι και ὁ Πατηρ ἐν ἐμοι ['me'] ἐστιν; (John 14.10)
8. ἐγω ἐν τω Πατρι εἰμι και ὑμεις ἐν ἐμοι ['me'] και ἐγω ἐν ὑμιν ['you']
9. ἡ μαρτυρια ἐστιν ὁτι ἡ ζωη ἐν τω Υἱω του Θεου ἐστιν
10. εἰπέ μοι, τίς ἐστιν ὁ ἀγαπων τον Θεον; ὁ ἀγαπων τον Υἱον τον Θεον ἀγαπα
11. πιστευετε και ἀγαπατε τον Υἱον!
12. τίς οὐ πιστευει ὁτι ὁ ἀγαπων την ζωην ἀγαπα και την ἀληθειαν;

Exercise 4: more from 1 John

Note

An underlining represents a change of wording from the original epistle. Remember του Θεου 'of [the] God' – distinguish from τον Θεον (acc.)!

Translate:

1. ὁ γιγνωσκων τον Θεον ἀκουει ἡμων ['us'], ὁς ['he who'] οὐκ ἐστιν ἐκ ['from'] του Θεου οὐκ ἀκουει ἡμων (1 John 4.6)
2. ὁ ἀγαπων ἐκ του Θεου <u>ἐστι</u> και γινωσκει τον Θεον (1 John 4.7)
3. Whoever agrees ὁτι Ἰησους ἐστιν ὁ Υἱος του Θεου, ὁ Θεος ἐν αὐτῳ ['him'] μενει και αὐτος ['he'] ἐν τῳ Θεῳ (1 John 4.15)
4. ὁ Θεος ἀγαπη ἐστιν, και ὁ μενων ἐν τῃ ἀγαπῃ, ἐν τῳ Θεῳ μενει και ὁ Θεος ἐν αὐτῳ μενει (1 John 4.16)
5. ὁ ἀγαπων τον Θεον ἀγαπᾳ και τον ἀδελφον ('brother') (1 John 4.21)
6. ὁ πιστευων ὁτι Ἰησους ἐστιν ὁ Χριστος ἐκ ('from') του Θεου <u>ἐστιν</u> (1 John 5.1)
7. τίς ἐστιν ὁ νικων τον κοσμον ('the world') εἰ ('if') μη ('not') ὁ πιστευων ὁτι Ἰησους ἐστιν ὁ Υἱος του Θεου ('of God'); (1 John 5.5)
8. ὁ πιστευων εἰς ('in') τον Υἱον του Θεου ἐχει την μαρτυριαν ἐν αὐτῳ ('him') (1 John 5.10)
9. ὁ ἐχων τον Υἱον ἐχει την ζωην. ὁ μη ('not') ἐχων τον Υἱον του Θεου την ζωην οὐκ ἐχει (1 John 5.12).

More questions

3d So far we have asked questions with τίς and τίνες, 'who?' *s* and *pl*.

If you want to convert a plain statement into a plain question in English you just switch the verb round, e.g. 'you are staying' becomes 'are you staying?'. In Greek the verb stays the same but you flag the question with ἀρα, e.g.

μενεις 'you are staying' – ἀρα μενεις 'are you staying?'

Compare: ἀρα παυομεν 'are we stopping?'; ἀρα ἐχει 'does he have?' etc.

The Greek for 'why?' or 'what?' is τί; You will have to work out which is more appropriate from context, e.g. τί ἐχεις probably means 'what do you have?' while τί μενομεν probably means 'why are we waiting?'

Record ἀρα and τί.

Exercise 5

Translate:
1. εἰπέ μοι, τί ἐστιν;
2. τί οὐκ ἀγαπας την ἀληθειαν;
3. ἀρα γιγνωσκετε τους ἀγαθους;
4. ἀρα ἐχετε την μαρτυριαν ὁτι ὑμεις μεν τον Θεον ἀγαπατε, ἡμεις δ' οὐ;
5. τί παυετε τους Ἑλληνας;
6. ἀρα γιγνωσκει τον Εὐριπιδη ὁ Σωκρατης;
7. εἰπέ μοι, ἀρα πιστευουσιν οἱ βαρβαροι ὁτι τους Ἑλληνας ἀει (always) νικωσιν;
8. ἀρα οἱ πολλοι την ἀληθειαν ἀγαπωσιν; οὐχι, ἀλλα οἱ ὀλιγοι
9. τί ὁρᾳς; ἀρα ὁρᾳς τον Σωκρατη; οὐχι, ἀλλα τον Εὐριπιδη
10. τί την ζωην ἀγαπᾳς;

The Greek world

The world of epic

Homer's *Iliad* (Ἰλιας) and *Odyssey* (Ὀδυσσεια) are well known as the first works of western literature (8th century BC). The *Iliad*, named after the town of Ilium (Ἰλιον) – Troy (Τροια) is the region – tells of an incident during the Trojan War when Achilles withdraws from the fighting against Ilium because he is insulted by the Greek leader Agamemnon. This leads directly to the death of his best friend Patroclus (Πατροκλος), the death of the Trojan hero Hector and Achilles' own death (foretold, not witnessed in the epic itself). The *Odyssey* tells how Odysseus spent ten years returning from Troy, with many an adventure on the high seas before reaching his home island of Ithaca, where he finds his wife Penelope (Πηνελοπεια) besieged by 108 suitors.

A less well-known epic poet is Hesiod (Ἡσιοδος), c. 700 BC, traditionally the second poet of western literature, and rated very highly indeed in the ancient world. His *Works and Days* describes work down on the farm, his advice about how to live an honest life and his battle for justice against his brother Perses, who seems to have grabbed too large a portion of an inheritance. The tone is agreeable grumpy. It contains the story of Pandora's box, when the woman Pandora lets all the evils of the world fly out, leaving only Hope inside, and of the decline of the world from a golden age to the present ghastly iron age. Life is tough.

His *Theogony* is a cracking read, describing how the world began and how the Olympian gods with Zeus at their head fought their way to become top of the heap. This is very important for our understanding of Greek gods. They were not external to the world, but made by it. The earliest gods are not, for example, Zeus and Poseidon, but Chaos (Χαος), Earth (Γαια) and Eros (Ἐρως) – Eros being logically needed so that Earth can mate with Sky (Οὐρανος) and produce the subsequent family of gods. Cronus (Κρονος) comes to power after Sky by castrating him as he descends to make love to Earth. Cronus in his turn is eventually overthrown by Zeus.

Zeus came to power by force and struggle – a reflection of Greeks' own values. They adored competition, and especially winning. The Greek for competition, game, battle, struggle, trial, is ἀγων – whence our 'agony', 'antagonist'. Hesiod knew what struggle was like, both among the gods and down on his farm – in his ceaseless battle against the elements and his wretched, cheating brother Perses.

Word play

Speaking and writing Greek

Issues of spelling and pronunciation always loom large with ancient languages. Spelling is an especially thorny one with Greek. The reason is that, historically, Latin ruled the roost when Greek words were being adopted in their multitudes into the English language (especially during the renaissance). The result was that if there was a Latin form of the word that English wanted to adopt, however far it 'misspelt' the Greek, it

47

was that form that was adopted, and Latin rules in general have been used to 'translate' Greek words into English. So, for example, Greek names ending in -ος conventionally end in Latinate '-us' in English (e.g. Ἡροδοτος becomes Herodotus); Greek κ becomes 'c' (Σοφοκλης – Sophocles); Greek υ becomes 'y' (πολυ – poly) and so on. Greeks, naturally, played the same tricks on Romans. When they had to transliterate Caesar, they made him Καισαρ...(there is no Greek for 'Bill').

Pronunciation too presents many thorny problems, though not as thorny as some people might think. We know roughly how ancient Greek sounded. Ancient grammarians talked extensively about how it sounded; misspelt inscriptions are very useful; Greek is transliterated into other languages whose pronunciation we do know; and comparative linguistics plays its part.

For example, a grammarian talks of ρ being pronounced 'by the tongue rising to the palate near the teeth' and 'fanning' or 'beating' the air. Obviously a rolled 'r' is being described here. Latin transliterates Φιλιππος as Pilippus and Philippus, but never Filippus – suggesting Greek φ was pronounced not as our 'f' but as aspirated 'p' (top-hat). Simple spelling suggests that ζ was pronounced 'sd' – e.g. the Greek for 'to Athens', Ἀθηνασ-δε, was spelt Ἀθηναζε.

Answers
Exercise 1

1. We conquer. 2. You see/See! 3. You love. 4. They conquer. 5. He sees. 6. We love. 7. You conquer. 8. They see. 9. I love. 10. You conquer/Conquer! 11. You see. 12. They love. 13. He conquers. 14. Conquer! 15. We see. 16. You love/Love! 17. See! 18. We conquer.

1. ἀγαπατε. 2. ὁρα. 3. νικα. 4. ἀγαπωσι. 5. ὁρωμεν. 6. νικας. 7. ἀγαπα. 8. ὁρατε. 9. ὁρωσιν. 10. νικω.

Inscription

Because of these gods the Selinuntines are victorious. Because of Zeus we are victorious and because of Fear and because of Heracles and because of Apollo and because of Poseidon and because of the Tyndaridae and because of Athene and because of Demeter and because of Persephone and because of the other gods, but most of all because of Zeus.

Exercise 2

1. The one/person loving God/ he who loves God. 2. The one (etc.) conquering the barbarians. 3. The one seeing Paul. 4. The one stopping Peter. 5. The one remaining in love. 6. The one recognising the Greeks. 7. The person seeing the many. 8. The person conquering the few.

Exercise 3

1. Tell me, who is the Son of God? Jesus Christ is the Son of God. 2. Hello! We on the one hand love God, you don't. 3. The Son of God loves us. 4. He who knows God hears him. 5. The evidence is that Jesus is the Son of God. 6. I am the way, and the truth and the life. 7. Do you not believe that I [am] in the Father and the Father is in me? 8. I am in the Father and you in me and I in you. 9. The evidence is that life is in the Son of God. 10. Tell me, who is the one who loves God? The one who loves the Son loves God. 11. Have faith and love the Son! 12. Who does not believe that he who loves life loves also the truth?

Exercise 4

1. He who knows God hears us, he who is not from God does not hear us. 2. He who loves is from God and knows God. 3. Whoever agrees that Jesus is the Son of God, God remains in him and he in God. 4. God is love and he who remains in love remains in God and God remains in him. 5. He who loves God loves the [=his] brother too. 6. He who believes that Jesus is the Christ is from God. 7. Who is the one conquering the world if not the one who believes that Jesus is the Son of God? 8. He who believes in the Son of God has the evidence in him. 9. He who has the Son has life. He who does not have the Son of God does not have life.

Exercise 5

1. Tell me, what is it? 2. Why do you not love the truth? 3. Do you recognise the good (people)? 4. Do you have the evidence that you love God, but we do not? 5. Why do you stop the Greeks? 6. Does Socrates recognise Euripides? 7. Tell me, do the non-Greeks believe that they always conquer the Greeks? 8. Do the many love the truth? No, but the few (do). 9. What do you see? Do you see Socrates? No, but (I see) Euripides. 10. Why do you love life?

CHAPTER 3

Afore ye go

- Learn the α- contract verb at **3a-b**
- Make sure you know the fourteen new words
- Do you understand how participles work (**3c**)?
- Check questions involving τί and ἆρα again at **3d**

"She's a nymph, they named a mania after her."

CHAPTER 4

Here come the contractions again

In the last chapter, we inspected verbs whose stem ended in -α and noted what happened when they 'contracted' that a with the person endings. Now we shall do the same with verbs that end in -ε.

-ε contract verbs

4a Here is the very common verb φιλε-ω, 'I love' (non-Christian sense):

Present indicative active

1s	φιλε-ω	becomes	φιλ-ω	'I love'
2s	φιλε-εις	becomes	φιλ-εις	'you love'
3s	φιλε-ει	becomes	φιλ-ει	'he, she, it loves'
1pl	φιλε-ομεν	becomes	φιλ-ουμεν	'we love'
2pl	φιλε-ετε	becomes	φιλ-ειτε	'you love'
3pl	φιλε-ουσι	becomes	φιλ-ουσι	'they love'

Present imperative active

2s	φιλε-ε	becomes	φίλ-ει
2pl	φιλε-ετε	becomes	φιλ-ειτε

Note
- Observe the accent on φίλ-ει 'love!'. This distinguishes it from φιλει 'he, she, it loves'.

4b Your conclusions, however, about the ε- contract, Watson? Correct:
- ε + ω = ω
- ε + ε or ει = ει

- ε + ο or ου = ου

Vocabulary

Record

ἀδικε-ω 'I harm, do wrong'
μισε-ω 'I hate' (misogyny)
ὁμολογε-ω 'I confess, admit'
ποιε-ω 'I make, do' (poet)
φιλε-ω 'I love' (philo-, -phile)
γραφ-ω 'I write' (graph)
λεγ-ω 'I say, speak'

Exercise 1

Translate:
1. μισουμεν
2. ὁμολόγει (n.b. accent)
3. ἀδικειτε (two)
4. γραφετε (two)
5. ποιεις
6. γραφουσι
7. λεγει
8. φιλουσι
9. ἀρα ὁμολογουμεν;
10. ποίει
11. ἀδικουσι
12. λεγετε (two)
13. μίσει
14. ποιει
15. ὁμολογει
16. ἀρα λεγουσιν;
17. φιλεις
18. ἀδικουμεν
19. ποιουσιν
20. μισει

Translate: 1. I write. 2. She loves. 3. He makes. 4. You (*pl*) hate. 5. Does he harm? 6. I say. 7. They write. 8. She does. 9. Do wrong (*s*)! 10. He says. 11. Love (*s*)! 12. Do we make?

More accusatives: pronouns singular

4c ἐγω 'I' takes the forms ἐμε or με when it is the object of the sentence (accusative case), 'me'

e.g. φιλεις με 'you love **me**'.

συ 'you' (*s*) takes the form σε when it is the object of the sentence (accusative case), 'you'

e.g. φιλω σε 'I love **you**'.

Exercise 2

Translate:
1. τίς σε φιλει, ὦ Σωκρατες;
2. συ μεν ἐμε φιλεις, ἐγω δε σε μισω
3. ὁ θεος σε ἀγαπα
4. συ μεν τον θεον ἀγαπας, ἐγω δε σε οὐκ ἀγαπω, ἀλλα μισω
5. συ μεν ἐμε ὁρᾳς, ἐγω δε σε οὐ γιγνωσκω
6. ἀρα πιστευουσιν ὁτι ὁ ἀγαπων ἐμε τον Θεον ἀγαπα;
7. τίς εἰ συ; συ μεν ἐμε γιγνωσκεις, ἐγω δ' οὐ σε γιγνωσκω
8. τίς ἀδικει σε, ὦ Ευριπιδες; γιγνωσκω ὁτι ὁ Σωκρατης με ἀδικει
9. γιγνωσκω ὁτι ἐμε μεν οἱ Ἑλληνες φιλουσιν, σε δε μισουσιν
10. ὁ ἀδικων ἐμε, ἐμε μισει
11. φίλει με, Σωκρατες
12. τί ποιειτε; τί ἐστιν; τί ἀδικειτε με; τί μισειτε;

1. I love (non-Christian) you. 2. He hates me. 3. They harm me 4. We recognise you. 5. You (pl) stop me. 6. Love (*pl*) (non-Christian) me. 7. You (s) on-the-one-hand love (Christian) me, I on-the-other-hand wrong you. 8. Does he conquer me? 9. We conquer you. 10. I love (Christian) you.

Pile on the accs: pronouns plural

4d ἡμεις 'we' has the object/accusative form ἡμας 'us'

e.g. φιλει ἡμας 'he loves us'.

ὑμεις 'you' (*pl*) has the object/accusative form ὑμας 'you' (*pl*)

e.g. φιλουμεν ὑμας 'we love you'.

Exercise 3

Translate:

1. ἐγω μεν ὑμας φιλω, ὑμεις δε οὐ φιλειτε με
2. ὑμεις μεν ἡμας μισειτε, ἡμεις δε ὑμας ἀγαπωμεν
3. οἱ μεν βαρβαροι ἡμας νικωσιν, ὑμεις δε τους Ἑλληνας παυετε
4. συ μεν ἡμας ἀδικεις, ὑμεις δε ἐμε νικατε
5. ἐγω ὑμας και τους βαρβαρους ὁρω, συ δε με οὐ γιγνωσκεις
6. ὦ Σωκρατες και Σοφοκλεις, ἀρα φιλειτε με;
7. ἡμεις μεν σε οὐκ ἀδικουμεν, συ δε ἡμας [ἀδικεις]
8. ὑμεις μεν ἐμε ὁρατε, ἐγω δε ὑμας οὐ [ὁρω]
9. συ μεν ἡμας ἀγαπας, ἡμεις δε σε
10. ἡμας μεν οἱ βαρβαροι φιλουσιν, ὑμας δε μισουσιν

Def Art again

4e We return to the chart at **2c**:

	M	F	N
Announcing subject, singular:	ὁ	ἡ	το
Announcing subject, plural:	οἱ	αἱ	τα
Announcing object, singular:	τον	την	το
Announcing object, plural:	τους	τας	τα

So far we have wrestled the underlined forms, panting, onto the mat, observing that they variously indicate subject or object, singular or plural. Now we do the same with the *italic* forms, *αἱ* (nom., f., indicating subject, *pl*) and *τας* (acc., f., indicating object, *pl*).

Vocabulary

Record

ἡ γ-η 'the land' (geo-graphy)
ἡ θαλαττ-α 'the sea'
ἡ ἀρχ-η 'beginning; rule; principle' (archbishop, -archy)
ἡ δημοκρατι-α 'people (δημος)-power (κρατος), democracy'
ὁ δημ-ος 'people'
ὁ λογ-ος 'word, reason, argument' (logic, -logy cf. λεγω)

γαρ 'because, for' (second or third word in Greek, first in English)
που; where?

Particles again

4f We now meet another particle, γαρ, 'because, for' to add to μεν...δε 'on the one hand...on the other hand'. Note γαρ usually comes second or third word in the sentence, but should be translated first. Thus: κακος ειμι. αδικω γαρ σε 'I am evil. For/because I wrong you'.

Exercise 4

Translate:
1. τας δημοκρατιας μισω· τους γαρ δημους ου φιλω
2. που εισιν αι γαι; τας γαρ γας ουχ ορωμεν
3. οι Ελληνες την γην νικωσιν· πολλοι γαρ εισιν
4. εν τη αρχη υμεις ημας νικατε· ολιγοι μεν γαρ ημεις εσμεν, πολλοι δε υμεις
5. πιστευετε οτι την ζωην εχομεν εν Θεω· ο γαρ Θεος ημας αγαπα
6. εχουσιν οι βαρβαροι την γην· πολλοι γαρ εισιν
7. αδικει την δημοκρατιαν ο δημος
8. τας μεν θαλαττας νικωμεν, τας δε γας ουχι
9. εν αρχη αι δημοκρατιαι ολιγαι εισιν
10. τας μαρτυριας και τους λογους ουκ ακουει· την γαρ αληθειαν φιλει

John 1.1 (distinguish John [the gospel] from 1 John [the epistle]):
εν αρχη ην (was) ο λογος, και ο λογος ην (was) προς (with) τον θεον, και θεος ην ο λογος.

Euripides *Trojan Women* 1051:
ουκ εστ᾽ εραστης [lover] οστις [who] ουκ αει [always] φιλει.

The Greek world

Free thought

One of the most striking and important features of Greek thought is its independence. This is probably associated with the Greeks' almost unique lack of any form of ruling religious authority (contrast, for example, Egypt). It comes through strongly in Homer, where men respect but do not live in terror of the gods and priests have ritual functions but no other.

So when 7th century BC Greeks in Greek cities on and off the coast of Ionia (modern western Turkey) started arguing about how the world was made and what it was made of, we can understand how it came about that they did so without reference to the gods. The thinkers involved – people like Thales and Anaximander – doubtless acknowledged the existence of divinities, but the explanations they came up with intentionally kept the supernatural at a distance. Their aim was to produce humanly intelligible explanations for what had probably always been felt to be divine phenomena. The crucial intellectual assumption they made was that the world was a rational place, and could therefore be apprehended by reason (λογος). Apply the human thought processes, in other words, and the world was comprehensible without the need to appeal to any heavenly machinery.

This was a striking enough moment in the history of human thought. Even more important were the consequences. If there are no officials sanctioning this or that explanation, there is no official line. All conclusions therefore are open to debate. If thinker A argues that the world is basically made of water, thinker B is quite entitled to call him a charlatan and argue that it is made of air. This is essentially why the Greeks are so important in western history: they established the ideal of open, public debate controlled by reason. Such an intellectual leap was not likely to be greeted with applause by any society where religious or other authorities had their own agendas to impose on the people.

Wordplay

Accents

As you have seen, the Greek in this text only occasionally carries an accent. The reason for accenting the words we do is that the accent will help you distinguish them from other words. Hence, φίλ-ει 'love!' as against φιλει 'he, she, it loves'.

We have been highly selective about this. This is a beginners' text, and accents, frankly, can wait. When you read a full ancient Greek text, however, you will see that virtually all the words carry accents, and very pretty they look too. But what were they for?

There are three Greek accents – acute (ὀξεια, 'high, sharp' e.g. έ), grave (βαρεια, 'heavy, low' e.g. è) and circumflex (περισπωμενη, e.g. ῶ). They begin to appear on manuscripts from round about 200 BC, and seem to have been used to resolve ambiguities in pronunciation and word division (remember that there were no gaps between words at this time). The details are disputed, but very broadly they seem to have represented the *pitch* of a syllable – the acute representing a high pitch, the grave perhaps a low pitch or no change in normal pitch, and circumflex, which is found only on long vowels or diphthongs, a rise and fall in pitch (it is sometimes called ὀξυβαρεια).

Ancient Greeks, in other words, did not stress syllables (in the way that we do) but pitched them. A Greek sentence would thus have sounded rather melodic or musical to our ears – and very difficult indeed for us to imitate precisely, even if we were certain about the principles. These days, we tend to compromise and stress the accented syllables rather than try to pitch them. This, indeed, is what happened to the language itself. The pitch accent gradually gave way to a stress accent, the change probably being complete by about the 4th century AD. Modern Greek is entirely stressed.

Answers
Exercise 1
1. We hate. 2. Confess! 3. You harm/Harm! 4. You write/Write! 5. You make/do. 6. They write. 7. He says. 8. They love. 9. Do we admit? 10. Make/do! 11. They harm/do wrong. 12. You say/Say! 13. Hate! 14. He makes/does. 15. He admits. 16. Do they say? 17.

You love. 18. We harm/do wrong. 19. They make/do. 20. He hates.

1: γραφω. 2. φιλει/ἀγαπᾳ. 3. ποιει. 4. μισειτε. 5. ἀρα ἀδικει; 6. λεγω. 7. γραφουσι. 8. ποιει. 9. ἀδίκει. 10. λεγει. 11. φίλει/ἀγαπα. 12. ἀρα ποιουμεν;

Exercise 2

1. Who loves you, Socrates? 2. You love me while I hate you. 3. God loves you. 4. You love God but I do not love you, but (I) hate (you). 5. You see me but I do not recognise you. 6. Do they believe that the one loving me/he who loves me loves God? 7. Who are you? You recognise me but I don't recognise you. 8. Who wrongs you, Euripides? I know that Socrates wrongs me. 9. I know that the Greeks love me, but they hate you. 10. The one harming me/The one who harms me hates me. 11. Love me, Socrates! 12. What are you doing? What is it? Why do you harm me? Why do you hate (me)?

1. φιλω σε. 2. μισει με. 3. ἀδικουσι με. 4. γιγνωσκομεν σε. 5. παυετε με 6. φιλειτε με. 7. συ μεν ἐμε ἀγαπας, ἐγω δε σε ἀδικω. 8. ἀρα νικα με; 9. νικωμεν σε. 10. ἀγαπω σε.

Exercise 3

1. I love you, but you do not love me. 2. You hate us but we love you. 3. The barbarians conquer us but you stop the Greeks. 4. You harm us, but you conquer me. 5. I see you and the barbarians, but you do not recognise me. 6. O Socrates and Sophocles, do you like me? 7. We do not harm you but you [harm] us. 8. You see me but I [do] not [see] you. 9. You love us, we [love] you. 10. The barbarians love us, but hate you.

Exercise 4

1. I hate democracies. For I do not love the peoples. 2. Where are the lands? For we do not see the lands. 3. The Greeks conquer the land. For they are many. 4. In the beginning you conquer us. For we are few, but you many. 5. You believe that we have life in God. For God loves us. 6. The barbarians have the land. For they are many. 7. The people wrongs the democracy. 8. We conquer the seas, but not the lands. 9. In the beginning democracies are few. 10. He does not hear the evidence(s) and words. For he loves the truth.

In the beginning was the Word, and the Word was with God, and the Word was God.

There is no lover who does not always love.

Afore ye go

- Learn φιλεω **4a-b**
- Know the accusatives (ἐ)με, σε, ἡμας, ὑμας **4c-d**
- Learn the fifteen new words and especially the particle γαρ at **4f**
- Ensure you understand the function of the two new forms of Def Art αἱ and τας at **4e**.

"He's going into Politics."

CHAPTER 5

Oh my! Getting it in the middle

5a We have met and mastered a whole range of verbs whose first person singular ends in -ω, like λεγω, μενω, γιγνωσκω, ἐχω, ὁρω, φιλω and so on (all called 'active').

But there is another sort of Greek verb, called 'middle' for reasons too boring to go into at the moment, which conjugates in a different way. These verbs all end in -ομαι (cue 'Oh my! -ομαι) in the first person singular, and conjugate as follows:

Present indicative middle ἐρχ-ομαι 'I go'

1s	ἐρχ-ομαι	'I go', 'I do go', 'I am going'
2s	ἐρχ-η	'you (s) go', 'you do go', 'you are going'
3s	ἐρχ-εται	'he, she, it goes', 'he, she, it does go/is going'
1pl	ἐρχ-ομεθα	'we go', 'we do go', 'we are going'
2pl	ἐρχ-εσθε	'you (pl) go', 'you do go', 'you are going'
3pl	ἐρχ-ονται	'they go', 'they do go', 'they are going'

Present imperative middle

2s	ἐρχ-ου	'go!'
2pl	ἐρχ-εσθε	'go!'

Note
• As usual, the 2pl imperative is the same as the 2pl indicative.

Another negative

5b So far the only negative 'no(t)' in Greek we have met is οὐ and its various different forms (see Vocabulary at **1b**). Greek has a second negative, meaning precisely the same, used in various jolly contexts – μη (the only form of the word). For our purposes the importance of μη is that it is used with impera-

62

tives, e.g. μη ἐρχου 'not go!' – or 'don't go!', as those of us aged over two tend to say.

If you want to think of μη as meaning 'don't', please do. Or don't. It's up to you.

Vocabulary

Record

ἀποκριν-ομαι 'I reply'
γιγν-ομαι 'I become, happen, am made/born, am' (genetics, genesis)
ἐρχ-ομαι 'I come, go'
μαχ-ομαι 'I fight'
πορευ-ομαι 'I walk, journey, travel'
μη 'no(t)'; 'don't' (with imperatives).

Note
• Distinguish carefully between γιγν-ομαι 'I become' and γιγνωσκ-ω 'I know'.

Exercise 1

Translate: 1. ἐρχεσθε (two). 2. μαχεται. 3. γιγνονται. 4. πορευου. 5. ἀποκρινῃ. 6. μαχομαι 7. γιγνεται. 8. ἐρχονται. 9. ἀποκρινομεθα. 10. πορευεται. 11. ἐρχεται. 12. ἀποκρινονται. 13. μη μαχεσθε. 14. πορευῃ. 15. γιγνομεθα. 16. μη ἀποκρινου.
1. We become. 2. They fight. 3. You (s) walk. 4. He replies. 5. You (*pl*) come. 6. They journey. 7. He fights. 8. Don't reply (*pl*). 9. We come. 10. He is born. 11. Fight! (*s*). 12. She journeys. 13. You (*s*) go. 14. They go. 15. They become. 16. It happens.

Prepositions

5c What with all this coming and going we had better find out how we come and go to and from places. **Record** therefore the prepositions 'to' (and 'into') and 'from' (and 'out of'):

προς 'to', 'towards', e.g. προς την γην 'to, towards the land'
εἰς 'into', e.g. εἰς την θαλατταν 'into the sea'

Note: προς and εἰς are followed by nouns in the *accusative* case.

ἀπο, ἀπ᾽ ἀφ᾽ '(away) from', e.g. ἀπο της γης '(away) from the land', ἀπ᾽ αὐτου 'from him', ἀφ᾽ Ἱεροσαλημ 'from Jerusalem'
ἐκ, ἐξ 'out of', e.g. ἐκ της θαλαττης 'out of the sea', ἐξ αὐτης 'out of her'

Note: ἀπο and ἐκ are followed by nouns in some other case we have not met yet. Ssh, don't tell anyone, but it's called the genitive case. On the other hand, what does it matter? These prepositions could be followed by the suit case, book case or pyjama case for all you care. You know what the prepositions mean. That is all that counts for the moment.

Just to prove it, you have already met ἐν 'in'. This, in fact, is followed by the, er, um, nut case, but you have not blenched, turned pale and fled to take up Integrated Sociopathological Studies when you have met it. ἐν τῳ Θεῳ means 'in [the] God'. τῳ Θεῳ is the (cough) nut case. Big deal.

Hint: it is the dative case, actually. This has nothing to do with dates.

At some stage, of course, we shall have to learn about these various sorry cases properly, but not at the moment. The great advantage of meeting them in this way is that you can get used to the forms early on without it mattering much. You can say to yourself 'Well, strike me pink, ἐν is followed by the dative, so the dative of ὁ is τῳ and the dative of Θεος is Θεῳ, whatever that may actually *mean*, but is it not simply fascinating, who would have thought it' (etc. etc.). So when you have to grapple with the cases properly, you will be able to fall weeping on their shoulders and greet them like lost friends.

This also is a fantastically advanced educational technique rediscovered, year after year, by brilliant educational theorists.

Vocabulary

Record
ὁ ἀγγελ-ος 'the angel' (evangelist) 'messenger'
αὐτ-η 'she' ('her')
αὐτ-ος 'he' ('him') (autistic)
ὁ μαθητ-ης 'student, disciple' (maths)

ὁ οἰκ-ος 'house, home' (eco-logy, -nomy)
ἡ πολ-ις 'city, city-state' (politics).

Exercise 2

Note: there are many names of biblical towns and people here. Work them out.

Translate: 1. τί λεγει προς τους μαθητας; 2. μη ἐρχου ἐκ της πολεως προς τον οἰκον. 3. που εἰσιν οἱ ἀγγελοι; 4. οἱ ἀγγελοι γιγνωσκουσιν ὁτι ὁ Ἰησους γιγνεται ἐν Βηθλεεμ. 5. εἰπέ μοι, ἀρα πορευονται οἱ μαθηται ἀπο της Γαλιλαιας προς την πολιν; 6. ὁ δ' Ἰησους ἀποκρινεται προς τους μαθητας. 7. αὐτος λεγει προς αὐτην. 8. μη ἐρχεσθε ἀπο του οἰκου εἰς την Γαλιλαιαν. 9. πορευεσθε ἀπο της θαλαττης προς την πολιν και ἐκ της πολεως εἰς τον οἰκον! 10. λεγει δε προς τους μαθητας ὁ Ἰησους και ἀποκρινεται.

Translate (mostly from the bible): 1. [ὁ] Ἰωσηφ πορευεται ἀπο της Γαλιλαιας, ἐκ [της] πολεως Ναζαρηθ, εἰς την Ἰουδαιαν εἰς [την] πολιν [of] Δαυειδ...Βηθλεεμ. 2. ὁ ἀγγελος Γαβριηλ ἐρχεται ἀπο του Θεου εἰς πολιν... Ναζαρηθ. 3. ἡ Μαριαμ πορευεται εἰς πολιν [of] Ἰουδα και ἐρχεται εἰς τον οἰκον [of Zacharias]. 4. γιγνωσκομεν ὁτι ὁ Χριστος ἐστιν ἐν [τῃ] πολει [of] Δαυειδ. 5. ὁ Ἰησους μενει ἐν Ἰεροσαλημ. 6. ἐρχονται ἀπο του Ἡρῳδου εἰς τον οἰκον και ὁρωσι τον Ἰησουν. 7. ὁ Ἰωσηφ και Μαριαμ πορευονται ἀπο Αἰγυπτου εἰς γην Ἰσραηλ. 8. πορευεται ὁ Ἰησους ἀπο της Γαλιλαιας εἰς τον Ἰορδανην προς τον Ἰωανην. 9. που εἰ συ; εἰμι ἐν Ἀθηναις ἐγω. πορευομαι γαρ ἐκ Κορινθου προς Εὐβοιαν. 10. ὁ γαρ Παυλος πορευεται ἀπο Καισαριας προς την Ἰταλιαν, και ἐρχεται εἰς Μυρρα (Myra) και προς Κνιδον και Κρητην και εἰς Μελιτην.

The Greek world

The Greek polis

Man, said Aristotle, is a πολιτικον ζῳον – not 'political animal' but 'an animal living in a πολις'. The *polis* (*pl. poleis*) is the 'city-state', the most characteristic form of ancient Greek urban community.

Ancient Greece, it must be stressed, was not a nation-state:

indeed, it was hardly a political entity at all. Ancient Greece was simply a place where ancient Greek speakers lived. It was the small, individual, independent, self-contained, homogeneous, autonomous *polis* – Athens, Sparta, Thebes, Corinth, etc. – with its own institutions, laws, rituals, customs and coinages, and often at war with its neighbouring *poleis*, that was the focus of a Greek's loyalty. *Polis* would ally with *polis* for a variety of reasons, of course, but at no time did all Greek *poleis* sink their differences and engage in communal action as 'the Greek nation' (the closest they came to that was during the wars against the invading Persians in 490-479 BC).

The development of the *polis* system can be traced to the 8th century BC. Homer gives indications of knowing what it was, and at that time both small sites and archaeological sites in the countryside become few and far between. Greeks are moving to live in or near the city – a secure, walled city too.

A *polis* typically controlled a chunk of surrounding agricultural land (Athens and Sparta had very large chunks), but it was the city that was the political and economic focus. If it was located by the sea – and many were – it developed trade interests, and many sent out colonies, small replicas of themselves, to nourish useful connections elsewhere in the Mediterranean, east to the coast of modern Turkey and the Black Sea, south to Africa and Egypt, and west to southern Italy, Sicily, France and Spain – like frogs around a pond, as Plato says. By the 6th century BC, Greeks were everywhere – as we can see from Greeks ruins which pop up in the most unlikely places.

It was in this context that democracy was invented.

Wordplay

The language of politics

Greeks may not have been political animals, but theirs was certainly a political language, and English derives a vast range of political vocabulary from it. Greek κρατεω 'I rule, hold sway over' gives us all the '-cracy/-crat' words – rule of the δημος ('people'), of the ὀχλος ('mob'), of the ἀριστοι ('best'), of those with πλουτος ('wealth'), of Θεος ('God'), of αὐτ-ος ('oneself').

Likewise Greek ἀρχω 'I rule, hold office' gives the very common '-archy/arch' stem, e.g. rule of the μονος ('alone, single'), of the ὀλίγοι ('few'), of the ἱερος ('holy'), of the μητηρ ('mother') and of no one. The Greek prefix ἀ(ν) has a negating force – so ἀναρχια, 'anarchy', means no rule at all. Then there are all the arch-people: bishops, priests and so on.

πολις 'city-state' gives us 'politics' and its cognates, and e.g. metropolitan, the 'mother city' (μητροπολις). τυραννος did not necessarily mean anything worse than 'Prime Minister' (depending on which Prime Minister you meant, of course) – it was used of a sole leader who came to power with others' backing – but gradually developed more sinister overtones. νομος means 'law' – the rule of law so vital to any democracy – and all our '-nomy' words derive from it: the laws controlling the οἰκος ('household'), the γαστηρ ('stomach'), the ἀστρα ('stars'), etc.

Answers
Exercise 1
1. You go/Go! 2. He fights. 3. They become. 4. Journey! 5. You reply. 6. I fight. 7. He becomes. 8. They go. 9. We reply. 10. He journeys. 11. He goes. 12. They reply. 13. Don't fight! 14. You walk. 15 We are made. 16. Don't reply!

1. γιγνομεθα. 2. μαχονται. 3. πορευῃ. 4. ἀποκρινεται. 5. ἐρχεσθε. 6. πορευονται. 7. μαχεται. 8. μη ἀποκρινεσθε. 9. ἐρχομεθα. 10. γιγνεται. 11. μαχου. 12. πορευεται. 13. ἐρχῃ. 14. ἐρχονται. 15. γιγνονται. 16. γιγνεται.

Exercise 2
1. What does he say to the disciples? 2. Don't go out of the city towards the house. 3. Where are the angels? 4. The angels know that Jesus is being born in Bethlehem. 5. Tell me, are the disciples walking from Galilee towards the city? 6. And/but Jesus answers [to] the disciples. 7. He speaks to her. 8. Don't go from the house into Galilee. 9. Journey from the sea towards the city and out of the city into the house! 10. And/but Jesus speaks to the disciples and answers.

1. Joseph journeys from Galilee out of the city Nazareth, into Judaea into the city of David...Bethlehem. 2. The angel Gabriel comes from God into the city Nazareth. 3. Mary travels to the city [of] Judah and comes into the house of Zacharias. 4. We know that the Christ is in the city of David. 5. Jesus waits in Jerusalem. 6. They come from Herod into the house and see Jesus. 7. Joseph and Mary travel from Egypt into the land

Israel. 8. Jesus travels from Galilee into Jordan towards John. 9. Where are you? I am in Athens. For I am travelling from Corinth to Euboea. 10. For Paul journeys from Caesarea towards Italy and goes into Myra and towards Cnidus and Crete and into Malta.

Afore ye go

Make certain you know by heart:
- The indicative and imperative forms of ἔρχομαι (**5a-b**)
- The four prepositions προς, εἰς, ἀπο and ἐκ
- The twelve new words in the vocabulary sections

"*Of course* you're suffering from single vision."

CHAPTER 6

Middling participles

6a In **3c** we met the participle forms of -ω verbs. They ended in -ων, e.g. ἀγαπων 'loving'. Stick ὁ in front, and you got 'the one -ing, the one who -s', e.g. ὁ ἀγαπων 'the one loving', 'the one who loves'.

Now we can experience the unspeakable thrill of meeting the participle forms of -ομαι verbs. Hold tight and peer closely at the following:

ἐρχ-ομενος	'coming/going'
πορευ-ομενος	'travelling'
μαχ-ομενος	'fighting'

Your conclusion? Right! With -ομαι verbs, the participle is formed by slyly changing -ομαι to -ομενος. Tricky, or what?

And as we would expect, add ὁ and you get 'the one -ing', 'the one who -s', e.g. ὁ ἐρχομενος 'the one who comes/goes', ὁ πορευομενος 'the one who travels', 'the traveller'.

Exercise 1

Translate: 1. ἐγω μεν πορευομενος εἰς την πολιν μαχομαι, συ δε ἐρχομενος ἀπο της θαλαττης μενεις. 2. ἀποκρινομενος ὁ Ἰησους λεγει προς τους μαθητας. 3. ὁ μαχομενος κακος οὐκ ἐστιν ἀλλ' ἀγαθος. 4. εἰπέ μοι, τίς ἐστιν ὁ ἐρχομενος ἐκ της θαλαττης; 5. τί λεγει ὁ μαθητης; ὁ μαθητης λεγει ὁτι ὁ Ἰησους ἐστιν ὁ ἐρχομενος. 6. ἀρα ὁ μαχομενος νικα τους βαρβαρους; 7. ἐρχομενος προς την γην μη μαχου! 8. ἀγαθος γιγνομενος μη γιγνου κακος!

Gender-bending

6b Observe now something of extreme usefulness, which adds a whole sheaf of new arrows to our quiver with almost no effort whatsoever.

Recall our old friend Def Art, the word meaning 'the' and declining:

	M	F	N
Announcing subject, singular:	ὁ	ἡ	το
Announcing subject, plural:	οἱ	αἱ	τα
Announcing object, singular:	τον	την	το
Announcing object, plural:	τους	τας	τα

We have seen that ὁ + participle means 'the one -ing', 'the one who -s' (**3c**). Now it can be told: ὁ and his cronies οἱ τον τους are all masculine in gender – they are blokes. So ὁ ἐρχομενος means in fact 'the [bloke] coming/going'.

This is obviously an outrage. Blokes don't come or go. They sit at home cradling a lager asleep in front of the telly. Only women have the intelligence and wit to come and go. Thus: ἡ ἐρχομενη 'the [female] coming/going', 'the female who comes/goes'.

But ὁ and ἡ mark subject singular: what if there are lots of them going? Or what if they are not subjects, but objects? Good old Def Art will tell you, bless his little cotton socks, e.g.

ὁρω τας ἐρχομενας 'I see the ones (feminine, *pl*) coming', 'I see the women who come'

ὁρω τους ἐρχομενους 'I see the ones (masculine, *pl*) coming', 'I see the men who come'

νικω την μαχομενην 'I conquer the one (feminine, *s*) fighting', 'I conquer the woman who fights/fighting woman'

νικω τον μαχομενον 'I conquer the fighting man'

οἱ μαχομενοι νικωσι με 'the fighting men conquer me'

αἱ μαχομεναι ὁρωσιν ἡμας 'the fighting women see us'

You will appreciate the fiendish cunning of it all. Def Art + participle means 'the one -ing', 'the -er' and Def Art will tell you

71

whether you are talking of chaps or gels, singular or plural, subject or object.

What you have to do is keep an eye open for the word after Def Art and look for the give-away verb-stem + some form of -ομενος.

Exercise 2

Translate: 1. οὐ γιγνωσκομεν τας πορευομενας· οὐ γαρ ἐγγυς (near) εἰσιν. 2. αἱ ἀποκρινομεναι λεγουσιν προς τους μαθητας. 3. ὁρα τους πορευομενους εἰς τον οἰκον· οἱ γαρ εἰς τον οἰκον πορευομενοι ἐγγυς εἰσιν. 4. ἀρα αἱ μαχομεναι μισουσι τους πορευομενους προς την πολιν; 5. ἡ ἐρχομενη ἀπο της πολεως οὐχ ὁρα τον ἐρχομενον εἰς την πολιν. 6. εἰπέ μοι, που ἐστιν ὁ μαθητης ὁ πορευομενος εἰς την πολιν; οὐ γαρ ὁρωμεν τον πορευομενον. 7. μη λεγε προς τους γιγνομενους κακους. 8. μη πιστευετε εἰς τους προς ('against') τον Θεον μαχομενους.

Active participles

6c You will be even more stunned to learn that this trick also applies to active verbs like ἀγαπαω, μενω, παυω, φιλεω and so on. We have already met e.g. ὁ ἀγαπων 'the one loving/who loves' but now that we know such a lover is masculine, singular, subject, we are immediately banging the table demanding to know what we must do if we want to talk about (say) 'those-who-love', feminine, plural, object.

Cast therefore a beady eye over the following:

ὁ μεν-ων ὁρα με	'the one (male) waiting sees me'
ὁρω τον μεν-οντ-α	'I see the one (male) waiting'
ὁρω τους μεν-οντ-ας	'I see the ones (males) waiting'
ἡ μεν-ουσ-α ὁρα με	'The one (female) waiting sees me'
ὁρω την μεν-ουσ-αν	'I see the one (female) waiting'
ὁρω τας μεν-ουσ-ας	'I see the ones (females) waiting'

See? The male participle stem changes from -ων to -οντ-; the female participle stem ends in -ουσ-. The following chart orders all this:

72

	M		F	
Nom. *s*	ὁ	παυ-ων	ἡ	παυ-ουσα
Nom. *pl*	οἱ	παυ-οντες	αἱ	παυ-ουσαι
Acc. *s*	τον	παυ-οντα	την	παυ-ουσαν
Acc. *pl*	τους	παυ-οντας	τας	παυ-ουσας

The rule is still to hang on to Def Art and let him tell you what you are dealing with (subject/object, *s/pl*, m/f). But it is also useful to see how active verbs form their participles (very different from middle verbs). Let me re-emphasise:

Active participle masculine: stem παυ- + -οντ-
Active participle feminine: stem παυ- + -ουσ-

Participles with contractions

6d Contract verbs will, naturally, play their contract tricks. But they follow rules already established at **3b** and **4b**. Thus:

Active participle masculine: stem ἀγαπα- + -οντ- = ἀγαπ-ωντ-
Active participle feminine: stem ἀγαπα- + -ουσ- = ἀγαπ-ωσ-

Active participle masculine: stem φιλε- + -οντ- = φιλ-ουντ-
Active participle feminine: stem φιλε- + -ουσ- = φιλ-ουσ-

6e In summary:

(i)   Watch our for Def Art + verb-stem
(ii) Check the verb stem is followed by either some form of -μενος (middle verbs) or -οντ -ωντ -ουντ or -ουσ -ωσ (active verbs)
(iii) Then you know you are dealing with a participle, 'the one -ing, the one who -s, the -er'.

Exercise 3

Translate the following and say whether they are subject/object, *s/pl*, m/f.

Observe: Def Art has cruelly been omitted! So you must get your answer by using the charts above and paying attention to the verb forms (see also **Grammatical Summary 21-23**). Remember that, with Def Art omitted, these participles will mean simply '-ing', not 'the one -ing'.

E.g. παυοντας 'stopping, object, *pl*, m':

μενουσας, φιλουντες, πιστευοντα, ποιουσαν, ἀδικουντα, ἀκουουσας, γραφοντες, ἐχουσαν, νικωσαι, μισουντας.

Mind bender, what? See how one misses dear old Def Art. Good for the brain, though. Now treat yourself to a well-deserved piece of fish, get the synapses throbbing, and do this next exercise, being very specific about men and women:

Exercise 4

Translate: 1. τίς γιγνωσκει τους ἐν τη πολει μενοντας; 2. ὑμεις μεν φιλειτε τας ἀδικουσας, ἡμεις δε μισουμεν. 3. ἀρα οἱ ἐχοντες την ζωην ἀγαπωσι τον Θεον; 4. αἱ ὁμολογουσαι ὁτι ὁ Θεος ἀγαπη ἐστι την ζωην ἐχουσιν. 5. πολλοι εἰσιν οἱ μαθηται οἱ πιστευοντες ὁτι ὁ Ἰησους κυριος (Lord) ἐστιν. 6. μισω τους ἀδικουντας την δημοκρατιαν. 7. οἱ Ἑλληνες νικωσι τους ὁμολογουντας ὁτι βαρβαροι εἰσιν. 8. οὐ φιλουμεν τας μισουσας την πολιν. 9. εἰπέ μοι, ἀρα μισεις τους την ἀληθειαν μισουντας; 10. τί ποιεις; τί λεγεις; μη λεγε ὁτι οἱ τους λογους ἀκουοντες οὐ πιστευουσιν.

The Greek world

From monarchy to democracy

Greek democracy is an extraordinary concept. One is tempted to say that only ancient Greeks, living in proudly autonomous and fairly small city-states, with their strong sense of independence and love of open debate, could have invented it and made it work.

One can broadly trace the development of Greek political life from Homeric times to 508 BC when the Athenian Cleisthenes made the democratic breakthrough. Homer's world seems to be one of monarchs, either hereditary or appointed, supported by councils of nobles and some sort of assembly of citizens summoned when necessary. But wealthy, land-owning aristocratic families, using their financial and military muscle (only they

74

could afford armour and horses), then seem to have absorbed the offices of state (ἄρχοντες, archons or rulers, was the title of these office-bearers), producing aristocracies; and tyrannies arose when enough of the wealthy (usually those not at the centre of power) saw fit to support an individual and impose him upon the fledgling πολις. Hesiod's world is one of aristocratic rule.

But the world was changing, and the development in the 7th century BC of hoplite-fighting seems to have been at the root of a major social change. Hoplite tactics required co-operation between large numbers of warriors attacking *en masse*, keeping the line straight and firm and working as a military unit. Consequently the security of the πολις was no longer in the hands of the wealthy few, but those who could afford hoplite-armour – the middle classes, if you like. Aristocratic rule became less and less tenable as commoners demanded their say (though aristocrats were not about to give up without a fight). At the heart of the solution to the resulting political, social and economic tensions was the development of the concept of a people's assembly and court. Though probably restricted to the middle classes in the first instance, this development is of the highest importance (it was associated in Athens with the reformer Solon in 594 BC). The idea that the people should stand in judgement is at the very heart of Greek democracy.

Wordplay

Beginnings and endings

Prefixes and suffixes are the unsung heroes of language. Take the prefix ἀ(ν)- that we saw in ἀν-αρχια, indicating negation – 'no-rule'. It occurs all over the place in English – in atom (ἄτομος 'not to be cut'), anaesthetic (cf. αἴσθησις 'feeling, perception'), asphalt (ἀσφαλης 'non-slip/fail'), agnostic (ἀγνοεω 'I do not know'), and so on. Consider the Greek word for 'truth', ἀληθεια. The ληθη root is connected with forgetfulness, cf. the river Lethe in the underworld, where souls of the dead (according to Plato) drank before returning to life in order to forget what they had seen. The truth is something you do not forget.

Look at the effect of two Greek suffixes -της and -μα on a word like ποιεω 'I make, do'. The suffix -της = the English suffix '-er', so a ποιητης is a 'mak-er/do-er' (or poet). The suffix -μα indicates

'something -ed', so a ποιημα is 'something made/done' (or poem).
γραφω means 'I write, draw'; γραμμα means 'something written
or drawn, a letter, painting' (so 'grammar' is to do with what is
written). κρινω means 'I decide': a κριτης is an arbitrator, judge
(hence 'critic'). πραττω also means 'I do, fare': a πραγμα is a
deed, fact, matter, business, concern (cf. pragmatic).

Answers
Exercise 1
1. I, travelling into the city, fight, but you, coming from the sea,
wait. 2. Replying, Jesus speaks to the disciples. 3. The fighter is
not cowardly but brave. 4. Tell me, who is the person coming
from the sea? 5. What does the disciple say? The disciple says
that Jesus is one who is coming. 6. Does the fighter conquer the
non-Greeks? 7. Coming to the land do not fight! 8. Becoming
brave, do not become a coward!
Exercise 2
1. We do not recognise the travelling women: for they are not
near. 2. The replying women speak to the disciples. 3. See the
men travelling into the house: for those travelling into the house
are near. 4. Do the fighting women hate the men travelling to
the city? 5. The woman coming from the city does not see the
man going into the city. 6. Tell me, where is the disciple who is
travelling into the city? For we do not see the traveller. 7. Do not
speak to those who are becoming evil. 8. Do not trust in those
who fight against God.
Exercise 3
Waiting, object, *pl*, f; loving, subject, *pl*, m; trusting, object, *s*, m;
making/doing, object, *s*, f; wronging, object, *s*, m; hearing, object,
pl, f; writing, subject, *pl*, m; having, object, *s*, f; conquering,
subject, *pl*, f; hating, object, *pl*, m.
Exercise 4
1. Who recognises the men staying in the city? 2. You love the
women who do wrong, but we hate [them]. 3. Do the men who
have life love God? 4. The women agreeing that God is love have
life. 5. Many are the disciples who trust that Jesus is lord. 6. I
hate the men who harm democracy. 7. The Greeks conquer those
men admitting that they are non-Greeks. 8. We do not like the
women who hate the city. 9. Tell me, do you hate the men who

hate the truth? 10. What are you doing? What are you saying? Do not say that the men who hear the words do not have faith.

Afore ye go

Since participles are very common indeed in Greek, it is important that you feel confident about the formation and meaning of:
- The full range of middle participles (-ομεν-ος), at **6a-b**
- The full range of active participles, on the masculine pattern παυ-ων παυ-οντ-, the feminine pattern παυ-ουσ-α, at **6c-d**

CHAPTER 7

From here to infinitive

7a What a wonderful thing it is when you're having fun. Now take a swift peep at the following fantastically difficult new fixed forms (they never change), known as 'infinitives':

Active infinitive: παυ-ειν 'to stop'
Middle infinitive: ἐρχ-εσθαι 'to go'

Killer, or what? Yes, I know you're keen to know what the contract forms are, so here they are:

νικα-ω becomes νικ-αν 'to conquer'
φιλε-ω becomes, er, φιλ-ειν 'to love'.

Note also the irregular infin. of εἰμι 'I am': εἰναι 'to be'

Exercise 1

Translate the following infinitives: γιγνεσθαι, γιγνωσκειν, ἀδικειν, ἐχειν, εἰναι, μαχεσθαι, ὁραν, πορευεσθαι, μισειν, ὁμολογειν, ἀκουειν.
Construct and translate the infinitives of: γραφω, μενω, λεγω, ἀποκρινομαι, ποιεω, εἰμι.

Verbs with the infinitive

7b **Record** the following: δει and χρη 'it is necessary for X (acc.) to, X (acc.) must', δοκεω 'I seem' (carrying the idea of having a reputation), βουλομαι 'I wish, want' (carrying the idea of planning), ἐθελω or θελω 'I wish, want', φαινομαι 'I seem, appear', οὐν 'therefore' (second word in a sentence, like γαρ).

Notes

- all these verbs are followed by an infinitive, as in English: 'it is necessary *to...*', 'I seem *to...*', 'I wish *to...*', 'I appear *to..*'.
- δει and χρη put the person who 'must' in the accusative case, e.g. δει με μαχεσθαι 'it is necessary for me (acc.) to fight', or 'I must (to) fight'.

Exercise 2

Translate: 1. τί οὖν δει με ποιειν; οὐ γαρ γιγνωσκω. 2. ἀρα βουλομαι μαθητης γιγνεσθαι; 3. τί οὖν θελεις γραφειν και λεγειν; εἰπέ μοι. 4. ὑμεις μεν λεγετε, δει δε ἡμας ἀποκρινεσθαι. 5. οἱ θεοι κακοι εἰναι φαινονται· οὐ γαρ δοκουσι θελειν ἡμας φιλειν. 6. τί οὖν γιγνεσθαι ἐθελεις; ἐθελω μαθητης γιγνεσθαι και ἐχειν την ζωην. 7. χρη τους πορευομενους εἰς την πολιν ἐρχεσθαι. 8. τους ἐν τη πολει μενοντας μαχεσθαι δει. 9. χαιρετε, ὠ Ἑλληνες· ὑμας μεν χρη λεγειν, ἡμας δε ἀκουειν την μαρτυριαν. 10. τους προς την γην ἐρχομενους δει μενειν ἐν τη πολει. 11. βουλονται οἱ βαρβαροι μαχεσθαι και νικαν τους Ἑλληνας· κακοι γαρ εἰσιν. 12. τί οὖν βουλη ποιειν; βουλομαι πορευεσθαι προς την θαλατταν και ὁραν. 13. δει με τον λογον λεγειν και ἀποκρινεσθαι προς τους Ἑλληνας. 14. μη οὖν βουλου κακος γιγνεσθαι ἀλλ᾽ ἀγαθος. 15. Aeschylus' *Seven against Thebes* (said of the Theban hero Amphiaraus): οὐ γαρ δοκειν ἀριστος (best) ἀλλ᾽ εἰναι θελει.

7c We have already met one irregular verb – the verb 'to be'. Here is another one, also tremendously common:

Present indicative οἰδα **'I know'**

1s	οἰδα	'I know'
2s	οἰσθα or οἰδας	'you know'
3s	οἰδε(ν)	'he, she, it knows'
1pl	ἰσμεν or οἰδαμεν	'we know'
2pl	ἰστε or οἰδατε	'you know'
3pl	ἰσασι(ν) or οἰδασι(ν)	'they know'

Infinitive: εἰδεναι 'to know'
Participle (m) εἰδως (εἰδοτ-), (f) εἰδυι-α 'knowing'

Vocabulary

Record: ὁ ἀνηρ (ἀνδρ-) 'the man' (android); ἡ γυνη (γυναικ-) 'the woman' (gynaecology); οὐδεν 'nothing'.

Exercise 3

Translate: εἰδεναι, ἰσμεν, οἰδας, οἰσθα, οἰδατε, ἰσασιν, οἰδε, οἰδαμεν, οἰδα, ἰστε; (give two answers where possible for the following) I know, we know, they know, you (s) know, he knows, to know.
Translate: 1. οὐκ οἰδα τίς ἐστιν ὁ ἀνηρ· φαινεται γαρ ὁ ἀνηρ βαρβαρος εἰναι και οὐχ Ἑλλην. 2. αἱ γυναικες, πορευομεναι προς την πολιν, οὐκ ἰσασι που εἰσιν. 3. ὁ οὐν Σωκρατης, εἰδως ὁτι οὐδεν οἰδεν, λεγει ὁτι οὐδεν οἰδεν. 4. οἱ ἀνδρες ἀρ' οἰδασι τί χρη ποιειν; 5. ὠ γυναικες, ἀρ' ἰστε τί βουλεσθε λεγειν; 6. ὁ ἀνηρ οὐκ οἰδε τί λεγει· οὐδεν γαρ λεγει. 7. τους ἀνδρας δει φαινεσθαι εἰδεναι τί ποιουσιν, ἀλλ' αἱ γυναικες ἰσασιν ὁτι οὐδεν οἰδασιν. 8. ὠ ἀνδρες, ἰσμεν ὁτι ἡμας χρη νικαν τους Ἑλληνας· οὐκ οὐν δει ἡμας μενειν, ἀλλα πορευσθαι ἀπο της θαλασσης προς την πολιν. 9. μη λεγε ὁτι οὐδεν εἰδεναι δοκεις, ὠ Σωκρατες. 10. δει οὐν την γυναικα λεγειν τί δει ποιειν και λεγειν· οὐ γαρ δοκει ὁ ἀνηρ εἰδεναι.

Sophocles' *Philoctetes* and Aristophanes' *Frogs*
Vocabulary

δειν-ος 'terrible, awful, awesome'; ἐξοπισθε 'behind'; ἰθι 'come along'; 'go! run!'; νυν 'well then'; ὁ παις (παιδ-) 'child, boy, slave' ('Ο child' = ὠ παι); παπα(ι) 'ouch!'; προσθεν 'in front'; πως; 'how?'; το τεκν-ον 'son, boy'.

Philoctetes wants to be rescued from the island where he has been stranded but has a painful foot. Here he bursts out screaming in agony and fears this will prevent young Neoptolemos from saving him:

ΦΙΛΟΚΤΗΤΗΣ: ἀ ἀ ἀ ἀ.
ΝΕΟΠΤΟΛΕΜΟΣ: τί ἐστιν;

ΦΙΛ: οὐδεν δεινον. ἀλλ᾽ ἰθ᾽, ὦ τεκνον.
(Neoptolemos enquires about the problem but Philoctetes does not really want to talk about it. Then:)
ΦΙΛ: παπαι
ἀπαππαπαι παπα παπα παπα παπαι
('Why this screaming?' enquires Neoptomelos)
ΦΙΛ: οἰσθ᾽, ὦ τεκνον;
NEO: τί ἐστιν;
ΦΙΛ: οἰσθ᾽, ὦ παι;
NEO: τί σοι (= [is] up with you?);
οὐκ οἰδα. ΦΙΛ: πως οὐκ οἰσθα; παππαπαππαπαι.

Here from the comic poet Aristophanes' *Frogs*, the god Dionysus has gone down to the underworld with his (human) slave Xanthias, and is absolutely terrified at the prospect of all the monsters down there. Xanthias suddenly hears a noise and the cowardly Dionysus asks:

ΔΙΟΝΥΣΟΣ: που που 'στιν; ΞΑΝΘΙΑΣ; ἐξοπισθεν. ΔΙΟ: ἐξοπισθ᾽ ἰθι.
ΞΑΝ: ἀλλ᾽ ἐστιν ἐν τῳ προσθε. ΔΙΟ: προσθε νυν ἰθι.

The Greek world

Greek democracy

The Athenian Cleisthenes, who invented democracy in 508 BC, was an aristocrat, a member of the Alcmaeonid family (of which Pericles, later, was a member too). Whatever the fledgling democracy looked like in 508 BC (and it is difficult to be sure), it is unlikely that Cleisthenes could have envisaged what it would become under Pericles in the 5th century BC and how it would further develop in the 4th century BC. But the final result was that, for the first and last time in the West, power to control the direction of their own world resided in the hands of all male citizens over the age of eighteen, irrespective of wealth or birth.

In the fully developed democracy, citizens met regularly about every nine days in the ἐκκλησια (Assembly, cf. ecclesiastical) to take all the decisions that our 'democratic' parliament takes today without any reference to us whatsoever. The ἐκκλησια was absolutely sovereign. That is one aspect of δημο-κρατια, 'people-power'.

Another is the βουλη, or Council. Clearly, the ἐκκλησια could not function if it did not have an agenda. The βουλη was a steering committee, consisting of five hundred citizens over thirty, who prepared the business of the ἐκκλησια and then made sure its decisions were put into effect. At any time, if the ἐκκλησια did not like what the βουλη had done, it could refer the matter back to it. Citizens were appointed to the βουλη for one year at a time, and could not be appointed more than twice.

But the final aspect is the most amazing of all. Nearly all executive officers (whose duty it was to carry out Assembly orders), including members of the βουλη, were appointed for one year *by lot* from among any citizens who put themselves forward. That is real citizen *power*. As Aristotle said, elections are aristocratic (or meritocratic, as we would say) because their aim is to choose the best. Real democracy appoints people at random, by lot.

Wordplay

Dramatic language

The vitality and inventiveness of the Greeks, especially the Athenians, are remarkable. They established ways of looking at, understanding and expressing the world that have had immense influence down the ages. This shows up most clearly in our vocabulary which (especially from the renaissance onwards) has consciously drawn on the Greek language (often through Latin and French) to provide us with the concepts we have needed.

Take drama (Greek δραμα, literally 'something enacted'). Tragedy is a Greek word: τραγῳδια, or 'song (ᾠδη) to do with a goat (τραγος)'. This has proved a baffling little word. Since we know that tragedy developed out of ritual songs praising the god Dionysus, it is possible that goat-sacrifices perhaps accompanied such rituals. Comedy, meanwhile, is κωμῳδια, or 'song to do with a revel' (κωμος).

The χορος, or chorus, was tragedy's all-singing, all-dancing 'collective' of 12-15 members, who took on a role in tragedy without being individually characterised. They danced and sang in the ὀρχηστρα, the large circular dancing area in front of the σκηνη – no, not 'scene' but literally 'tent', coming to mean 'stage'. The actors were all hypocrites (ὑποκριται), something to do with ὑποκρινομαι meaning 'I answer' or 'I interpret'. At the heart of tragedy is the hero (ἡρως) and the world of Greek myth (μυθος), to which tragedy usually looks back for subject matter, but which it then challengingly reinterprets to present the audience in the θεατρον (watching-place) with issues and debates relevant to its time.

Answers
Exercise 1
To become, to recognise, to wrong, to have, to be, to fight, to see, to travel, to hate, to agree, to hear.

γραφειν to write, μενειν to wait, λεγειν to say, ἀποκρινεσθαι to reply, ποιειν to do, εἰναι to be.

Exercise 2
1. What therefore must I do? For I do not know. 2. Do I wish to become a disciple?
3. What therefore you do wish to write and say? Tell me. 4. You speak, but we must reply. 5. The gods appear to be wicked. For they do not seem to wish to love us. 6. What therefore do you wish to become? I wish to become a disciple and have life. 7. Those travelling must go into the city. 8. Those waiting in the city must fight. 9. Welcome, Greeks. You must speak, but we must hear the evidence. 10. Those going to the land must wait in the city. 11. The non-Greeks wish to fight and conquer the Greeks. For they are evil. 12. What therefore do you wish to do? I wish to travel to the sea and see [it]. 13. I must speak the word and reply to the Greeks. 14. Do not therefore wish to become evil, but good. 15. For he wishes not to seem the best but to be [it].

Exercise 3
To know, we know, you know, you know, you know, they know, he knows, we know, I know, you know; οἰδα, οἰδαμεν/ ἰσμεν, οἰδασι/ ἰσασι, οἰδας/ οἰσθα, οἰδε, εἰδεναι.

1. I do not know who the man is: for the man seems to be non-Greek and not Greek. 2. The women, travelling towards the city, do not know where they are. 3. Therefore Socrates, knowing that he knows nothing, says that he knows nothing. 4. Do the

men know what it is necessary to do? 5. Women, do you know what you wish to say? 6. The man does not know what he is saying: for he is saying nothing. 7. The men must seem to know what they are doing, but the women know that they know nothing. 8. Men, we know that we must conquer the Greeks. We must not therefore wait, but march from the sea to the city. 9. Do not say that you seem to know nothing, Socrates. 10. The woman must therefore say what it is necessary to do and say: for the man does not seem to know.

Sophocles

Ph: Ah ah ah ah. N: What is it? Ph: Nothing terrible. But come, son.... Ph: Ooooouch.... Ph: You know, son? N: What is it? Ph: You know, child? N: What's up with you? I don't know. Ph: How do you not know? Oooooooouch.

Aristophanes

D: Where, where is it? X: Behind. D: Get behind [me]. X: But it's in front. D: Then get in front.

Afore ye go

Ensure that you know:

- the forms and meaning of the infinitives (especially εἶναι 'to be'), and how they are used (**7a-b**)
- the forms and meanings of οἶδα 'I know' (**7c**)
- the eleven new words given for recording

84

"What d'you mean, it's past closing time? This is Paradise!"

CHAPTER 8

Getting in the moods

8a We could, if you like, go into long discussions of Verbs In The Subjunctive Mood. We could say that the indicative mood says something is the case; the imperative mood that something must be the case; and the subjunctive mood that something might be the case, but we are not terribly certain.

But hey, life is short. All that needs to be said for our purposes is that, in Greek, verbs hop keenly into the subjunctive mood in some situations, often when English is using 'may' or 'might'.

Direct, therefore, the beams of ratiocination emanating from the brain via the oracular orbs at the following clauses:

ἐαν τις λεγη   'if (ἐαν) someone may say/says'
ἱνα τις λεγη   'in order that (ἱνα) someone may say'
ὁς ἀν λεγη   'whoever (ὁς ἀν) may say/says'

8b You will at once observe that indicative λεγει 'he says' has become subjunctive λεγη 'he may say/says'. So far, so boring.

Much more interesting are the introductory little formulas: ἐαν τις 'if someone', ἱνα τις 'in order that someone' and ὁς ἀν 'whoever'. These are important. ἐαν, ἱνα, and ἀν are markers, waving tiny flags that proclaim 'Oi, look out, subjunctives about'.

Record these formulas, especially as τις here means not 'who?' but 'someone'. Note the lack of accent. As we know, τίς meaning 'who?' appears with an accent (*pl* τίνες). Reckon now with τις meaning 'someone'.

Of course, ἐαν or ἱνα could be followed not by τις but by e.g. Σωκρατης. In that case, translate 'if Socrates' or 'in order that Socrates'. Or it might be followed by a subject in the verb, e.g. ἱνα γραφης 'in order that you may write'. It is just that ἐαν τις 'if someone' is very common.

8c For the record, here are the subjunctive forms of active and middle verbs. As you stare glassy-eyed at them, you will notice one very cheering feature: they are identical to the indicative forms in every way, except that the main vowel is lengthened. Thus:

Present subjunctive active παυ-ω 'I stop'

1s	παυ-ω	'I (may) stop'
2s	παυ-ῃς	'you (s) (may) stop'
3s	παυ-ῃ	'he, she, it may stop/stops'
1pl	παυ-ωμεν	'we (may) stop'
2pl	παυ-ητε	'you (pl) (may) stop'
3pl	παυ-ωσι(ν)	'they (may) stop'

Present subjunctive middle ἐρχ-ομαι 'I go'

1s	ἐρχ-ωμαι	'I (may) go'
2s	ἐρχ-ῃ	'you (s) (may) go'
3s	ἐρχ-ηται	'he, she, it may go/goes'
1pl	ἐρχ-ωμεθα	'we (may) go'
2pl	ἐρχ-ησθε	'you (pl) (may) go'
3pl	ἐρχ-ωνται	'they (may) go'

Present subjunctive εἰμι 'I may be/am'

1s	ὠ	'I may be, I am'
2s	ᾖς	'you (s) may be, are'
3s	ᾖ	'he, she, it may be, is'
1pl	ὠμεν	'we may be, are'
2pl	ἠτε	'you (pl) may be, are'
3pl	ὠσι(ν)	'they may be, are'

Notes

- The subjunctive of εἰμι is identical to the endings of the active subjunctive!
- For the record, the subjunctive of οἰδα 'I know' is εἰδ-ω, εἰδ-ῃς, εἰδ-ῃ etc.
- There are no infinitives or participles (phew).
- We have met the Greek for 'no(t)' many times – οὐ, οὐκ, οὐχι.

But μη is used when the verb is subjunctive, e.g. ἐαν μη ἐρχησθε 'if you do not come'.

But the important thing is to remember the meanings of the very common introductory formulas ἐαν, ἱνα, and ὁς ἀν. See one of those, say 'Bingo, here comes a verb in the jolly old subjunc., easy peasy', identify the person, and gallop on chortling merrily.

Exercise 1

Translate: 1. ἐαν τις ἐρχηται. 2. ἱνα μη μενωμεν. 3. ὁς ἀν γραφῃ. 4. ἐαν μη πορευωμεθα. 5. ἐαν τις γραφῃ. 6. ὁς ἀν πιστευῃ. 7. ἱνα μη εἰδῃς. 8. ἐαν γιγνησθε. 9. ἐαν γιγνωσκητε. 10. ἱνα ἠς. 11. ὁς ἀν μη μαχηται. 12. τίς ἐστι; 13. ἱνα τις ἠ. 14. ἐαν τις μη πιστευῃ. 15. ἱνα φαινωνται. 16. ἐαν μη δοκωμεν.

The genitive case

8d What joy! A shiny new case! And just in time for the AwayDay Weekend Break Offer Horror!

We have already met the nominative case (in which you pack your subjects) and the accusative case (in which you pack your objects). In the genitive case, you pack your belongings and possessions. This is a pathetic pun. I explain.

If you see a word in the genitive case, you should preface it with the word 'of'. Peer lugubriously at the following examples:

ὁ υἱος του Θε-ου 'the son OF [the] God'
ὁ υἱος του Πατρ-ος 'the son OF the Father'
οἱ λογοι της γυναικ-ος 'the words OF the woman'
ὁ λογος της ζω-ης 'the word OF [the] life'
οἱ λογοι των γυναικ-ων 'the words OF the women'
οἱ υἱοι των πατερ-ων 'the sons OF the fathers'

8e Er, that's it. You will now have observed that in the genitive case Def Art appears as:

του (m) and της (f) in the singular
των in the plural

See, therefore, του, της or των, write 'of the whatever-it-is' and away you go cackling hideously.

Incidentally, you can now see why you take down your genitive case when you are dealing with belongings and possessions. 'The basket of the cat', or 'the cat's basket' means 'the basket belonging to/in the possession of the cat'. The genitive has other functions too, e.g. 'the words of the women' means 'the words which emanate from the women', so we talk of the genitive as expressing 'source', and so on.

But whatever the technical functions of the genitive, 'of' covers most examples for the purpose of translation.

Now revise **5c**, where you will remember you met the genitive first of all – after the prepositions ἀπο 'away from' and ἐκ 'out of'.

Personal possessions

8f Here are the genitives of our friends the personal pronouns:

ἐγω	'I'	gen. ἐμου, μου	'of me, my, mine'
συ	'you'	gen. σου	'of you, your, yours'
ἡμεις	'we'	gen. ἡμων	'of us, our, ours'
ὑμεις	'you'	gen. ὑμων	'of you, your, yours'

Vocabulary

Record: ὁ ἀνθρωπ-ος 'the human, man, fellow' (anthropology); ὁ ἀποστολ-ος 'the apostle'; διδασκ-ω 'I teach' (didactic); ἡ ἐντολ-η 'the command'; ἡ ἐπιστολ-η 'the letter' (epistle); ὁ κυρι-ος 'the lord' (κυριε, ἐλεισον 'Lord, have mercy'); τηρε-ω 'I guard, keep'.

Exercise 2

Translate: του κυριου, των ἐντολων, του ἀνθρωπου, ὑμων, ἐκ της ἐπιστολης, σου, των ἀποστολων, του μαθητου, ἐμου, του Θεου, ἀπο των ἀνδρων, της γυναικος, των ὀλιγων, των πολλων, ἡμων, της ἀρχης, της γης, ἀπο της θαλαττης, ἐκ της πολεως, της ζωης.

Translate: 1. βουλομαι οὐν τους ἀνθρωπους τηρειν τας ἐντολας μου. 2. δει ἡμας ἀκουειν την ἐντολην του κυριου. 3. ὁς ἀν ἐχῃ τας εντολας μου, ἀγαπα με. 4. ἐαν τις ὑμων λεγη ὁτι ἀγαπα τον υἱον του Θεου, οὑτος (this man/he) ἀγαπα και τον Θεον. 5. οἱ ἀποστολοι του κυριου διδασκουσιν τους ἀνθρωπους ἱνα τηρωσιν τας ἐντολας του Θεου. 6. χρη γαρ σε λεγειν και διδασκειν τας ἐπιστολας ἡμων. 7. ὁς ἀν την ἐπιστολην σου ἀκουη, δει τηρειν τας ἐντολας μου. 8. ἐαν οὐν τις μη τηρη τας ἐντολας του Πατρος, μισει με. 9. εἰπέ μοι, ἐαν τις ὑμων και των ἀποστολων με διδασκειν βουληται, ἀρα δει με ἀκουειν; 10. ἐαν τις, πορευομενος ἐκ της πολεως, μη εἰδη ποι (where) ἐρχεται, χρη λεγειν. 11. τί οὐν δει με ποιειν ἱνα ἀγαθος ὠ; δει σε ἀκουειν τας ἐντολας του πατρος.

The Greek world

The lottery of democracy

The idea that people picked by lot should run a country may sound mad to us. But that is what happened in 5th century Athens, the world's first and last genuine democracy. Some executive posts were, it is true, elective, in particular the top posts of military commander (ten of them a year) and state treasurer, and these office-holders could be re-appointed year after year as well. But everyone else who, as official executive, wanted to carry out the Assembly's orders, was appointed by lot to serve for one year, and never again.

There was, however, something of a disincentive to serving. The people in Assembly were absolutely sovereign. Regular checks were kept on executive performance. At the end of your term, the Assembly reviewed your whole year of office, and if you were felt to have failed them in any way, penalties were imposed – anything from fines, loss of rights, and exile, through to execution. It was no good claiming that the Assembly had told you to do X, Y and Z and it was not your fault if it had turned out to be a disaster. The people in Assembly could do no wrong. Consequently no one was about to put themselves forward without some clear notion of what the job entailed and of their capacity to do it.

But if the Assembly was sovereign, where do great leaders like Pericles fit in? What role could an individual have in running the state when the Assembly called all the shots? The answer is that the Assembly had to decide first which shots to call, and for that it depended on advice. This is the source of Pericles' control. The people trusted him. Indeed, they appointed him to one of the top ten military posts for fifteen years running. But Pericles' power did not ultimately depend on this top executive decision. It depended ultimately on one thing alone – his capacity to persuade the Assembly to do his will. In other words rhetoric, the ability to persuade, was the key to power in the Greek democracy.

The Greek historian Thucydides summed up Athens under Pericles in the famous words: λογω μεν δημοκρατια, ἐργω δε ὑπο του πρωτου ἀνδρος ἀρχη 'In word on the one hand democracy, but in fact rule by (ὑπο) the first man'.

Wordplay

Long ologies

The ancient Greeks have given us a rich vocabulary of analysis (ἀναλυσις) and description. The '-logy' ending to so many words derives from λογος, 'reason, reasoned account' and is attached to e.g. βιος 'life', ψυχη 'soul', γυναικ- (stem of γυνη) 'woman', ἀρχαιος 'old', γη 'land', θεος 'god', ὀρνιθ- (stem of ὀρνις) 'bird', κοσμος 'universe', ἐτυμος 'true', οἰνος 'wine', χρονος 'time', and hundreds of others. The '-scope' ending is equally fruitful (σκοπεω, 'I examine') – στηθος 'chest', περι 'around', τηλε 'afar off', ἐνδον 'inside', ὡρα 'season', γυρος 'ring', and so on. Again, what of '-graphy' from γραφω, 'I write, describe'? Try it with εἰκων 'statue', πορνη 'prostitute', ἐθνος 'race', αὐτος 'oneself', παλαιος 'old', λιθος 'stone', ἁγιος 'holy'. Equally useful are '-archy' (ἀρχω, rule), '-sophy' (σοφια, wisdom), and '-phony' (φωνη, voice).

Not that one has to attach Greek words to them, of course. We all tut-tut at hybrid formations, but they are very useful and very common. Consider e.g. sociology (Latin *socius*, ally), cartology (Latin *carta*, map), criminology (Latin *crimen*, charge, crime), and so on.

Answers
Exercise 1
1. If someone comes. 2. In order that we may not wait. 3.

Whoever writes. 4. If we do not travel. 5. If someone writes. 6. Whoever has faith. 7. In order that you may not know. 8. If you become. 9. If you recognise. 10. In order that you may be. 11. Whoever does not fight. 12. Who is it/he/she? 13. In order that someone may be. 14. If someone does not have faith. 15. In order that they may appear. 16. If we do not seem.

Exercise 2

Of the lord, of the commands, of the man, of you, out of the letter, of you, of the apostles, of the disciple, of me, of God, from the men, of the woman, of the few, of the many, of us, of the beginning, of the land, from the sea, out of the city, of life.

1. I wish therefore the men to keep my commandments. 2. We must hear the command of the lord. 3. Whoever has my commandments loves me. 4. If someone of you says that he loves the son of God, he also loves God. 5. The apostles of the lord teach the men in order that they may keep God's commandments. 6. You must speak and teach our letters. 7. Whoever hears your letter, he must keep my commandments. 8. If therefore someone does not keep the father's commandments, he hates me. 9. Tell me, if someone of you and of the apostles wishes to teach me, must I listen? 10. If someone, travelling out of the city, does not know where he is going, he must speak. 11. What therefore must I do in order that I may be good? You must hear the commandments of your father.

Afore ye go

- Make sure you can recognise the subjunctives at **8c** and know ἐαν, ἱνα, and ὁς ἀν at **8b**
- Are you comfortable with the form and functions of genitives at **8d-e** (especially Def Art του της and των) and the personal pronouns at **8f**?
- Learn the seven new words in the vocabulary list

CHAPTER 9

Neutered!

9a We have found that Def Art, like the ancient prophet Teiresias, has masculine (ὁ, etc.) and feminine (ἡ, etc.) forms. But Def Art goes one better. He can be neuter too. Honestly, some lexical items have all the fun. Scrutinise warily:

	M	F	N
Announcing subject, singular (nom.):	ὁ	ἡ	το
Announcing subject, plural:	οἱ	αἱ	τα
Announcing object, singular (acc.):	τον	την	το
Announcing object, plural:	τους	τας	τα
Announcing 'of', singular (gen.):	του	της	του
Announcing 'of', plural:	των	των	των

9b Your razor-keen brain will have spotted an immediate problem. το serves as both subject and object singular; and τα as subject and object plural. What, sirrah, is going on? How can we translate a sentence if we cannot tell our subjects from our objects?

Good question. But I am afraid you will have to live with it. For example, in the sentence το X το Y φιλει, you cannot tell whether the X loves the Y or the Y loves the X.

But take heart. Greeks were not daft. They did not set out to sow confusion in the minds of their readers/listeners. We teachers of grammar, of course, must alert you to the problem and to illustrate it must set you teasing little sentences in which ambiguity abounds. This, like fish, is very good for the brain, increasing all-round awareness and alertness and giving you a Solid Preparation For Life. But Greek literature (for all that French literary theorists may try to persuade you otherwise) does not make a habit of it. Precision: clarity: pith – that is what Greek authors strive for.

CHAPTER 9

Vocabulary

Record: το βιβλι-ον 'the book' (bible); ὁ βι-ος 'the life' (biology); το δαιμονι-ον 'the divine sign; the devil, demon'; το ἐργ-ον 'the work, deed' (ergonomics, energy); κελευ-ω 'I order'; το παιδι-ον 'the small child, small slave' (paediatrics); το πληθ-ος 'the mob' (plethora); το τεκν-ον 'child, son, young man'; το τελ-ος 'the end, aim, purpose' (teleology).

Note
• Blench at this very strange feature of Greek:

τα τεκνα ἐστιν ἀγαθα 'the children are good.'

Spot the deliberate mistake? Right: why do we read ἐστιν 'is' and not the plural εἰσιν 'are'? V.g. question indeed. Wish I knew a convincing answer. But there it is. Neuter plural subjects take singular verbs. Natch.

This is certainly a feature to be stuffed, mounted and battle for pride of place in the World Museum of Top Linguistic Monsters.

Exercise 1

Translate two ways: 1. το τεκνον το παιδιον μισει. 2. φιλει το πληθος το δαιμονιον. 3. κελευει τα τεκνα το πληθος. 4. τα παιδια το δαιμονιον οὐκ ἀγαπα. 5. παυει τα πληθη τα τεκνα.
Translate: 1. τί οὖν ἐστι το τελος του βιου; ὁ Ἰησους ἡμας κελευει ἀγαπαν τον Θεον. 2. τί ἐστι το ἐργον του κυριου; 3. το ἐργον των μαθητων ἐστι πιστευειν. 4. δει οὖν ἡμας λεγειν τα βιβλια των ἀποστολων. 5. ἐαν τις γραφῃ τα βιβλια, το πληθος οὐ λεγει αὐτα [them]. 6. ὁ γαρ ἀποστολος γραφει το βιβλιον ἱνα πιστευῃς. 7. οἱ οὖν πιστευοντες εἰσι [τα] τεκνα του Θεου· τουτο [This] γαρ ἐστι το τελος του βιου. 8. ἐαν γαρ τις ποιῃ τα ἐργα του δαιμονιου, οὐκ ἀγαπα τον κυριον. 9. αὑτη [This] ἐστιν ἡ ἐντολη του Θεου, ἱνα ἀγαπωμεν ἀλληλους [each other]· οἱ γαρ ἀγαπωντες ἀλληλους ἀγαπωσι τον Θεον· ὁ γαρ Θεος ἀγαπη ἐστιν. 10. ἡ ἀρχη του βιβλιου ἐστιν ἀρχη του ἐργου· ἀλλα τί ἐστι το τελος;

Into the past

9c It had to come. For the last nine chapters we have been swimming in the murk of the present. But it is time to don the goggles and oxygen mask and plunge into the pure serene of the past: clear, limpid, crystal, bracing. What a relief. Attend therefore to the following Big Ones and **record** all:

9d ἦ(ν) 'I was'

1s	ἦ(ν)	'I was'
2s	ἦσθα	'you were'
3s	ἦν	'he, she, it was, there was'
1pl	ἦμεν	'we were'
2pl	ἦτε	'you were'
3pl	ἦσαν	'they were, there were'

9e Aorist indicative active ἦλθ-ον 'I came/went'

1s	ἦλθ-ον	'I went'
2s	ἦλθ-ες	'you went'
3s	ἦλθ-ε(ν)	'he, she, it went'
1pl	ἦλθ-ομεν	'we went'
2pl	ἦλθ-ετε	'you went'
3pl	ἦλθ-ον	'they went'

On the same pattern, **record**: εἶπ-ον 'I said, spoke'; εἶδ-ον 'I saw', ηὗρ-ον 'I found' (getting close to our friend ηὕρηκα, no?)

Notes
- This past tense in Greek is called the aorist. It means simply 'I -ed'.
- The 1s and 3pl forms both end in -ον. Keep a sharp eye on context (e.g. look for plural or single subjects) to decide which is which.
- Remember εἰπέ? You must now distinguish between εἰπέ and εἶπε(ν).

Exercise 2

Translate into English: ἦσθα, εἶπε, εἰπέ, ἦλθον (two possibilities), ηὗρε, εἶδες, ἦμεν, εἴπομεν, ἦλθες, εἶδε, ἤ, εἴπετε, ηὗρες, ἦν (two), εἶδον (two), ἦσαν, εἶπες, ἦλθεν, ηὗρομεν, ἦτε, εἶπον (two), ἤλθομεν, ηὗρετε.

Translate into Greek: I came, we saw, they said, he was, he came, they were, he saw, they came, you (s) were, he said.

Translate: 1. κελευω σε λεγειν· τίς ἦν ὁ Σωκρατης; οὐκ οἶδα τίς ἦν. 2. ἦσαν οἱ μαθηται του κυριου ὁ Μαθθαιος και ὁ Μαρκος και ὁ Λουκας και ὁ Ἰωανης. 3. ὁ Ἰησους ἀποκρινομενος εἶπεν προς τους μαθητας. 4. οἱ Ἑλληνες μαχομενοι ἦλθον ἀπο της θαλαττης εἰς την πολιν και ηὗρον τους βαρβαρους. 5. τεκνον, οὐχ ηὗρον σε. που οὖν ἦσθα; οὐ γαρ εἶδον σε. 6. τί βουλη με ποιειν; ἦλθον γαρ ἐκ της πολεως ἱνα γιγνωσκω. εἰπέ μοι οὖν και κελευε με. 7. ἡμεις μεν προς τους ἀνδρας εἴπομεν, οἱ δ' ἀνδρες οὐκ ἀποκρινονται· οὐ γαρ ἀκουουσιν. 8. τί εἶδον αἱ γυναικες ὑμων; ἦλθον γαρ ἱνα ὁρωσιν ἡμας. 9. ἐγω μεν προς σε εἶπον, συ δ' ἦλθες εἰς τον οἰκον. 10. οὐκ ἰσμεν που ἦσαν οἱ βαρβαροι· ἦλθον μεν γαρ οἱ βαρβαροι προς την πολιν ἡμων, ἡμεις δ' οὐκ εἰδομεν αὐτους [them] οὐδε [nor] ηὗρομεν. 11. ὦ τεκνα, τί δει ὑμας ποιειν; ἐαν κελευω ὑμας ἀκουειν τους λογους του πατρος, ἀκουετε. 12. μη κελευετε τους μαθητας ἐρχεσθαι εἰς την πολιν των βαρβαρων.

The Greek world

Defending Greek democracy

In modern eyes, three things spoil the astonishing achievement of Greek democracy. First, power was in the hands of citizens over the age of eighteen, and that meant males. Females remained outside the political process. Second, for all their democracy, the Greeks still owned slaves. Finally, democracy does not seem to sit particularly comfortably with empire, and at times a fairly ruthless one at that.

Of the first charge, it can be replied that the invention of male-run democracy – the enfranchisement of all citizen males to make every decision about the running of their political and legal life – was amazing enough anyway. It has never been tried since. But most of all, look at our own record. With the example of the Greeks before us for 2,500 years, it was only in the 19th century that franchise was extended in the UK to all males, and the 20th century to females – and we are still no nearer real democracy. Politicians – oligarchs to a man – really do hate the idea that the people can take decisions for themselves. This makes the Greek achievement even more remarkable.

Again, slavery was endemic all over the world till the 19th century. To demand that the Greeks (alone) should have outlawed it is about as reasonable as to demand that Greeks should have cured smallpox. Some argue that democracy 'depended' on slavery. But all societies once 'depended' on slavery. If that is one's sticking point, all past achievements are fatally flawed.

As for the Athenian empire, it was both a product of the democracy – it was what Athenians wanted – and also the means of democracy's radical development (**The Greek world** Chapter 12). The point is that the Athenian empire was a maritime empire. When Athens depended on its army, only the wealthier citizens could afford to arm themselves. So it was with the wealthier that political power lay. But with the development of a maritime empire in the 5th century BC, power shifted to those who rowed the triremes (the Athenian warships) – and these were not the wealthy, but the poor. It was at this time, when Pericles was such a persuasive force, that the ancient political structures fell away and democracy became more and more radicalised.

Wordplay

Greek names

Proper names are a rich source of words. The Bunsen burner was invented by Mr Bunsen, and Birdseye foods by Mr Birdseye. Jeans were first made in Genoa. Greek gods and heroes have likewise worked their way into English in most interesting ways.

Ἀτλας supported the world on his shoulders. Since early maps showed him doing this, the maps assumed his name too.

Κασσανδρα was a prophetess who resisted the advances of Apollo. He doomed her always to tell the truth and never to be believed – though a Cassandra nowadays tends rather to mean nothing but a pessimist.

The *Titanic* got its name from the Titans, Τιταν, *pl* Τιτανες, the race of giants who helped Cronos rule the earth before Zeus overthrew him and instituted the rule of gods on Mt Ὀλυμπος. Whence 'olympian', meaning calm, distanced, and masterful.

The only Greek human to be made a god was Ἡρακλης, Heracles, who turns up in Latin as Hercules. He carried out twelve labours – herculean tasks all. (Another Greek who undergoes astonishing transformation from Greek into Latin is Γανυμηδης, Ganymede, Zeus' beautiful cup-bearer. He emerges in Latin as *catamitus*.)

Ἡλυσιον, or Elysium, or the Elysian fields, are the dwelling-places of the blessed after death. The word may be connected with ἐνηλυσιος, meaning 'struck by lightning' – and therefore hallowed, sacred.

And so on, with odysseys, amazons, labyrinths, Adonises etc etc. We can even be under someone's goatskin – αἰγις being just that, a sort of sleeve that Athene shook out and waved at enemies, scaring them into flight.

Answers
Exercise 1
1. The son hates the small child *or vice-versa, as for all these sentences.* 2. The mob loves the devil. 3. The children order the mob. 4. The children do not love the devil. 5. The mobs stop the children.
1. What therefore is the purpose of life? Jesus orders us to love God. 2. What is the work of the lord? 3. The work of the disciples is to have faith. 4. Therefore we must speak out the books of the apostles. 5. If someone writes books, the mob does not speak them. 6. For the apostle writes the book in order that you may have faith. 7. Those therefore having faith are the children of God: for this is the purpose of life. 8. For if someone does the works of the devil, he does not love the lord. 9. This is the command of God, in order that we love each other: for those loving each other love God. For God is love. 10. The beginning of the book is the beginning of the work: but what is the end?
Exercise 2
You were, he spoke, tell!, I/they went, he found, you saw, we were, we said, you went, he saw, I was, you said, you found, I/he

was, I/they saw, they were, you said, he went, we found, you were, I/they said, we went, you found.

ἦλθον, εἴδομεν, εἶπον, ἦν, ἦλθε, ἦσαν, εἶδε, ἦλθον, ἦσθα, εἶπε.

1. I order you to speak. Who was Socrates? I do not know who he was. 2. The disciples of the lord were Matthew, Mark, Luke and John. 3. Jesus replying spoke to the disciples. 4. The Greeks, fighting, came from the sea into the city and found the non-Greeks. 5. Child, I did not find you. Where therefore were you? For I did not see you. 6. What do you want me to do? For I came from the city in order that I may know. Speak, therefore, to me and order me. 7. We spoke to the men, but the men do not reply. For they do not listen. 8. What did your women see? For they came in order that they might see us. 9. I spoke to you, but you came into the house. 10. We do not know where the non-Greeks were: for the non-Greeks came to our city, but we did not see them nor find [them]. 11. Children, what must you do? If I order you to hear the words of your father, listen [to them]. 12. Do not order the disciples to go into the city of the non-Greeks.

Afore ye go

- Have you mastered the forms of the neuter Def Art (**9a-b**)?
- Do you know the new past tenses, exemplified by the five Big Ones ἦν, ἦλθον, εἶπον, εἶδον, ηὗρον (**9d-e**)?
- Have you learnt the nine new words?
- If, not why not?

CHAPTER 10

Middling fine

10a Yes, of course. I know. You just cannot wait for it, can you? Having learnt the aorist indicative *active* verbs, you are dying to know how aorist indicative *middle* verbs go. Time, then, to Reveal All.

Revise first the endings of present indicative middle forms (**5a**), then train the quivering senses on the following new verb and prepare for a pleasant surprise:

10b Aorist indicative middle ἀφικ-ομην 'I came, arrived'

1*s*	ἀφικ-ομην	'I arrived'
2*s*	ἀφικ-ου	'you arrived'
3*s*	ἀφικ-ετο	'he, she, it arrived'
1*pl*	ἀφικ-ομεθα	'we arrived'
2*pl*	ἀφικ-εσθε	'you arrived'
3*pl*	ἀφικ-οντο	'they arrived'

You see how agreeable Greek is? These aorist middle endings are really rather like the present middle endings you met at **5a**. Jolly thoughtful of it.

Vocabulary

Record the following very common aorist middles: ἐγεν-ομην 'I became, happened, was born/made'; ἐπυθ-ομην 'I heard, enquired'; ἠρ-ομην 'I asked'.

Note
• You have not met any of these verbs before, with the exception of ἐγενομην, which comes from γιγνομαι.

Er, come again?

At this point you may up and rap the table and say 'Oi, look, squire, what precisely is going on here? How do we get ἐγενομην from γιγνομαι? Why are we meeting all *new* verbs in this so-called aorist thingy? Why can you not show us how to turn those verbs we have already met and know and love so dearly into this aorist wossit? Verbs like, er (*scrabbles through vocabulary*), ah yes ἀγαπαω and μισεω and um παυω?'

Agreed. All in good time. The fact is that there are one or two nasties hiding under the stones here and I would like them to stay hidden for the moment. They will have to crawl out at some time, and that time will come soon enough.

Meanwhile, gambol innocently about with the aorists you have been given, treating them as brand new vocabulary without connections with anything else. Soon enough, let me assure, there could be weeping and gnashing of teeth (ὁ κλαυθμος και ὁ βρυγμος των ὀδοντων, cf. odontology, Latin *dens* 'tooth').

Exercise 1

Translate into English: ἀφικοντο, ἐπυθου, ἠρομεθα, ἐγενετο, ἀφικεσθε, ἐπυθομεθα, ἠρετο, ἐγενου, ἀφικετο, ἐπυθοντο, ἠρομην, ἐγενομεθα, ηὑρε, εἰπομεν, ἐπυθομην, εἰδες, ἠροντο, ἠλθον, ἐγενοντο.

Translate into Greek: we came, it happened, he enquired, you (*pl*) asked, you (*s*) found, they went, they came, she said, he asked, they became, they saw, we enquired.

Greek's last case: the dative

10c At this point Latinists will be scratching their heads and saying *'last* case?' But what about Latin's well-loved ablative case? Does not Greek have an ablative too? No, is the answer, and a great relief it is too.

The dative case means basically 'to' or 'for'. It is used especially with verbs of speaking *to* someone and giving/showing things *to* someone. Eyeball the following, paying close attention to Def Art:

ὁ Ἰησους εἶπε <u>τῳ μαθητῃ</u>   'Jesus spoke <u>to the disciple</u>'
ὁ Ἰησους εἶπε <u>τοις μαθηταις</u> 'Jesus spoke <u>to the disciples</u>'
ὁ Ἰησους εἶπε <u>τῃ γυναικι</u>   'Jesus spoke <u>to the woman</u>'
ὁ Ἰησους εἶπε <u>ταις γυναιξι</u>   'Jesus spoke <u>to the women</u>'
ὁ Ἰησους εἶπε <u>τῳ τεκνῳ</u>   'Jesus spoke <u>to the child</u>'
ὁ Ἰησους εἶπε <u>τοις τεκνοις</u>   'Jesus spoke <u>to the children</u>'

10d Your conclusions, Sherlock? Precisely:
(i) τῳ, τῃ mark the dative singular. Note the iota subscript.
(ii) τοις, ταις mark the dative plural.
We can thus complete the full Def Art chart, and very pretty it looks too:

	M	F	N
Announcing subject, singular (nom.):	ὁ	ἡ	το
Announcing subject, plural:	οἱ	αἱ	τα
Announcing object, singular (acc.):	τον	την	το
Announcing object, plural:	τους	τας	τα
Announcing 'of', singular (gen.):	του	της	του
Announcing 'of', plural:	των	των	των
Announcing 'to, for' singular (dat.):	<u>τῳ</u>	<u>τῃ</u>	<u>τῳ</u>
Announcing 'to, for' plural:	<u>τοις</u>	<u>ταις</u>	<u>τοις</u>

It is impossible to stress how important this chart is. Def Art gives you the instant key to the forms and functions of all nouns. Know Def Art and you do not need to worry about the following noun: just know its meaning, and Def Art will do the rest for you. If you do not know Def Art by heart already, do so now with the above chart.

> Use the chart!
> Make a start!
> Get Def Art
> Off by heart!

Vocabulary

Record: κηρυττ-ω 'I announce'; λαλε-ω 'I speak'.

Note
• Remember that ἐν 'in' is followed by the dative case. Thus: ἐν τῃ πολει 'in the city'.

LEARN ANCIENT GREEK

Exercise 2

Define the following Def Arts by gender (mfn), case, number (*s*, *pl*) and function, e.g. ὁ = m, nom, *s*, subject: ἡ, τοις, των, τα, τη, τας, τῳ, το, του.

Translate: 1. ὁ Ἰησους ἀφικετο και εἰπε τοις μαθηταις τον λογον του κυριου ἱνα πιστευωσιν. 2. τον λογον του κυριου ὁ Ἰησους τοις μαθηταις εἰπεν. 3. ἀφικετο ὁ Ἰησους και τοις μαθηταις τον λογον του κυριου εἰπεν. 4. ἡ γυνη τῳ υἱῳ λαλει ἐν τῳ οἰκῳ ἡμων. 5. δει τον ἀποστολον κηρυττειν τον λογον τῳ δημῳ ἱνα οἱ ἀνδρες ἀκουωσιν και πιστευωσιν. 6. τί εἰπες τῳ ἀνδρι; τῳ ἀνδρι οὐδεν εἰπον· ἀφικομην γαρ ἐν τη πολει και οὐκ εἰδον τον ἀνδρα. 7. ὁ ἀνθρωπος, ἀποκρινομενος τῳ κυριῳ μου, λεγει ὁτι ὁ Θεος οὐκ ἐστιν. 8. ἐαν τις κηρυττη τη γυναικι ὁτι ὁ Θεος οὐκ ἐστι, οὐδεν λεγει. 9. ὁ λεγων και κηρυττων τῳ δημῳ τον λογον του Θεου ἐχει την ζωην. 10. οὐ βουλομαι παυειν τον ἀποστολον ἀποκρινομενον τοις ἀνθρωποις και λεγοντα τον λογον του κυριου.

10e Now add the datives of the personal pronouns:

ὁ Ἰησους εἰπε (ἐ)μοι, σοι, ἡμιν, ὑμιν 'Jesus spoke to me, to you, to us, to you (*pl*)'.

The complete, collected, first edition person pronouns now look like this:

	'I/me'	'we/us'	'you'	'you' *pl*
Announcing subject, singular (nom.):	ἐγω		συ	
Announcing subject, plural:		ἡμεις		ὑμεις
Announcing object, singular (acc.):	(ἐ)με		σε	
Announcing object, plural:		ἡμας		ὑμας
Announcing 'of', singular (gen.):	(ἐ)μου		σου	
Announcing 'of', plural:		ἡμων		ὑμων
Announcing 'to, for' singular (dat.):	(ἐ)μοι		σοι	
Announcing 'to, for' plural:		ἡμιν		ὑμιν

Vocabulary

Record: μαχ-ομαι 'I fight/with/against' + dative; πειθ-ομαι 'I

103

obey, trust', + dative; πιστευ-ω 'I believe in, have faith in' + dative; ἐστι + dative 'there is to X', 'X has'.

Notes

* μαχομαι, πειθομαι and πιστευω all put their objects not in the acc., but the *dative*, e.g. 'he fights *me*' μαχεται μοι; 'he trusts *you*' πειθεται σοι; 'we believe in *God*' πιστευομεν τῳ Θεῳ (προς τον Θεον also used).
* Note the very common Greek idiom ἐστι μοι/τῃ γυναικι/τοις ἀνθρωποις, lit. 'there is to me/to the woman/to the men', i.e. 'I/the woman/the men have'. For example: ἐστι μοι το βιβλιον 'there is the book to me', 'I have the book'; ἠν τῳ ἀνδρι το τεκνον 'there was the child to the man', 'the man had the child'.

Exercise 3

Translate: 1. ἡ γυνη μοι εἰπεν· εἰπέ μοι, τί εἰπε σοι ἡ γυνη; 2. ὁ ἀνηρ ὑμιν λαλει. 3. ἡμιν κηρυττεις τον λογον. 4. τί σοι εἰπομεν; 5. οὐδεν μοι λεγεις. 6. ὁ ἀνθρωπος ἀποκρινομενος ὑμιν εἰπεν. 7. τί δει με τῳ κυριῳ πιστευειν; 8. μη πειθου τοις κακοις· δει σε τοις ἀγαθοις πειθεσθαι. 9. ὁς ἀν πιστευῃ μοι, πειθεται τοις λογοις μου. 10. το ἐργον των τεκνων ἐστι πειθεσθαι ἡμιν. 11. ἐστι μοι πατηρ ἀγαθος. 12. ἠν τῳ Σωκρατει το δαιμονιον. 13. ἐαν τις την ζωην ἐχειν βουληται, δει τῳ κυριῳ πειθεσθαι. 14. ὁς ἀν μη ἀκουῃ τους λογους ἡμων, οὐ πειθεται ἡμιν. 15. τί μαχεσθε μοι; οὐ γαρ θελω μαχεσθαι ἀλλα πινειν (to drink).

10f Thales

Thales, the first Greek philosopher (*c.* 600 BC), is reported to have said that he possessed three blessings, for which he was grateful to Fortune:

πρωτον (first) ὁτι ἀνθρωπος ἐγενομην και οὐ θηριον (wild beast), εἰτα (next) ὁτι ἀνηρ και οὐ γυνη, τριτον (third) ὁτι Ἑλλην και οὐ βαρβαρος.

The Greek world

Their finest hour

Every society constructs Great Turning Points for itself. The Armada fulfils this function for England, the Boston Tea Party for the United States, and so on. For the Greeks, it was the Persian Wars. These were fought between 490-479 BC and were, for the Athenians at any rate, a powerful test of Cleisthenes' brave new democracy (invented 508 BC).

By 500 BC the Persian Empire stretched from Persia (modern Iran) westwards to embrace Egypt, modern Turkey, Aegean islands like Samos and Lesbos and some areas of northern Greece (in Thrace and Macedonia). Greeks had long been settled on the west coast of modern Turkey and the islands off it, and they did not all take kindly to the Persian advance. Clashes with the Persian invaders were inevitable.

Whatever his motives – to take over Greece? Fire a warning shot? – in 490 BC the Persian king Darius sent an invading force by sea to mainland Greece, which landed at Marathon and was triumphantly driven back into the sea by a combined force of Athenians (including the poet Aeschylus) and Plataeans. The death of Darius and a revolt against Persian rule in Egypt delayed the Persian response, but in 481 the new king, Darius' son Xerxes, personally led a massive combined land-and-sea force to put these Greeks in their place. They crossed the Hellespont and made their way in tandem down through northern Greece.

Greece was not a nation-state, but Athens and Sparta were by far the most powerful *poleis*, and the question was how far they could persuade other *poleis* to co-operate against this threat and under what terms. A Greek alliance was forged of a mere thirty *poleis* (under the aegis of Sparta's league of allies), and a small force under the Spartan king Leonidas was sent to hold up the Persian advance at the narrows of Thermopylae. A heroic resistance was finally defeated. At this the Greeks decided to fall back south, abandon resistance by land and try to destroy the Persian fleet instead, putting their trust in what the Delphic oracle called their 'wooden walls' (interpreted by the Athenian leader Themistocles as their ships). In September 480 off the island of Salamis opposite Athens, the Persian fleet was destroyed. Xerxes returned home, leaving his general Mardonius to fight it out by land, but he was defeated at Plataea in 479 (again, the Spartans were predominant), and the Persian wars ended. It was the Greeks', especially Athens', finest hour.

Wordplay

From history to language

We have seen how the figures of Greek myth contribute to English. So too do the figures and institutions of Greek history.

When we think of ancient Greeks, we usually mean ancient Athenians, but Sparta too makes its contribution to our language. Spartans were renowned for the spareness and rigour of their upbringing (hence 'spartan'). The main reason was that they were heavily out-numbered (perhaps as much as 7-1) by their slave population, οἱ εἵλωται ('the captives'), or 'helots' (another useful word). Spartans therefore concentrated on breeding hardy and courageous males who could defend their own πολις from both internal and external threat. Spartans lived in an area called Λακωνια, and their reputation for keeping talk to a minimum gives us 'laconic'. On one occasion an enemy notified the Spartans that if they invaded Laconia, they (the enemy) would destroy Sparta. 'If' came back the reply.

Back to Athens. An academy is called after an obscure Greek hero Ἀκαδημος (or Ἑκαδημος). In a place dedicated to this Ἀκαδημος, where there also happened to be a public gymnasium, Plato located his school of philosophy, the 'Academy', in the 4th century BC. The Lyceum, meanwhile, was originally the name of Aristotle's 4th-century BC philosophical foundation. This was named after the temple nearby dedicated to Ἀπολλων Λυκειος, 'Apollo the wolf-god'. Lyceums today are generally put to less philosophical use. Δρακων, meanwhile (also Greek for 'snake', cf. 'dragon'), was the name of an Athenian (Draco in English) who in 621 BC constructed the first Athenian law-code, laying down the death penalty for virtually everything (the laws were written in blood rather than ink, the 4th-century orator Demades said). Hence 'draconian'. 'Ostracism' was another Athenian invention. ὀστρακον means 'bit of pot, potsherd'. Every year the Athenian assembly decided whether it wanted to 'ostracize' someone, i.e. banish them from Athens for ten years.

If it did, people wrote the name of their nominee on an ὄστρακον, and the 'winner' was duly banished.

One person the Athenians would doubtless liked to have banished was king Philip of Macedon (northern Greece), father of Alexander the Great. He began a gradual take-over of Greece in the 4th centgury BC, culminating in his victory over the alliance of southern Greek states at Chaeronea in 338 BC, effectively destroying the world of the independent πολις. The great Athenian orator Demosthenes (384-322 BC) tried, in vain, to rally the Greeks against Philip from 351 onwards, directing a series of twelve hostile speeches against him – κατα (against) Φιλιππου. They were subsequently called Φιλιππικοι λογοι, 'Philippic speeches', and a 'philippic' is any hostile verbal attack on someone.

Answers
Exercise 1
They arrived, you enquired, we asked, it/he happened/was born, you came, we enquired, he asked, you became, he came, they enquired, I asked, we became, he found, we said, I enquired, you saw, they asked, I/they went, they became.
ἀφικομεθα, ἐγενετο, ἐπυθετο, ἡρεσθε, ηὑρες, ἡλθον, ἀφικοντο, εἰπε, ἡρετο, ἐγενοντο, εἰδον, ἐπυθομεθα.

Exercise 2
f, nom, s, subject; m/n, dative, pl, 'to/for'; m/f/n, genitive, pl, 'of'; n, nom/acc, pl, subject/object; f, dative, s, 'to/for'; f, acc, pl, object; m/n, dative, s, 'to/for'; n, nom/acc, s, subject/object; m/n, genitive, s, 'of'.

1. Jesus came and spoke to the disciples the word of the lord in order that they might have faith. 2. Jesus spoke the word of the lord to the disciples. 3. Jesus came and spoke the word of the lord to the disciples. 4. The woman speaks to the son in our house. 5. It is necessary for the apostle to announce the word to the people in order that the men may hear and have faith. 6. What did you say to the man? I said nothing to the man: for I arrived in the city and did not see the man. 7. The man, replying to my lord, says that God does not exist. 8. If someone announces to the woman that God does not exist, he says nothing. 9. The one speaking and announcing to the people the word of God has

life. 10. I do not wish to stop the apostle replying to the men and speaking the word of the lord.

Exercise 3

1. The woman spoke to me: tell me, what did the woman say to you? 2. The man speaks to you. 3. You announce the word to us. 4. What did we say to you? 5. You say nothing to me. 6. The man replying spoke to you. 7. Why is it necessary for me to have faith in the lord? 8. Do not obey the wicked: you must obey the good. 9. Whoever has faith in me obeys my words. 10. The work of children is to obey us. 11. I have a good father. 12. Socrates had a divine sign. 13. If anyone wishes to have life, he must obey the lord. 14. Whoever does not hear our words does not obey us. 15. Why do you fight me? For I do not wish to fight but to drink.

10f Thales: First that I was born a human and not a wild beast, then [that I was born] a man and not a woman, third [that I was born] a Greek and not a non-Greek.

Afore ye go

- Make certain you know the new aorist indicative middles like ἀφικομην (**10b**)
- Make sure you have learnt the Def Art Chart at **10d**
- Do you understand the form and function of datives (**10c-e**), including the **10e** vocabulary (ἐστι μοι and verbs with the dative)?
- Learn the seven new words

"You didn't tell me it was only a place."

CHAPTER 11

Taking a breather

11a Half-way home. Let us pause for a rest and consider some interesting features of Greek word order and idiom.

Vocabulary

Record: ἀγω 'I lead'; πεμπ-ω 'I send'; το φως (φωτ-) 'light' (photograph); ὁ κοσμ-ος 'the world' (cosmic); ἡ σκοτι-α 'the darkness'.

1. Ἰησους το φως του κοσμου ἐστιν 'Jesus the light of the world he-is' – 'Jesus [he] is the light of the world'. Main verb at the end in the Greek.
2. το φως του κοσμου ἐστιν 'the light of the world – is? – he is? – she is? – it is?' Since no subject is stated, it could mean 'the light of the world is', i.e. exists, or the subject is 'in the verb', i.e. 'he/she/it is the light of the world'.
3. Ἰησους το του κοσμου φως ἐστιν 'Jesus the of-the-world light he-is'. Same meaning as 1. above, but note the very typical Greek 'bracketing': του κοσμου 'of the world' is bracketed between το and φως 'the...light' so the two are tightly bound together. We get nearly the same effect in English if we say 'Jesus is *the* world's *light*' but that is not really parallel with Greek where two words for 'the' – το and του – come next to each other. This is a very common idiom in Greek indeed.
4. Ἰησους το φως το του κοσμου ἐστιν 'Jesus the light the of the world he-is'. Same meaning again, but note how Greek repeats the το of το φως to bind του κοσμου in with το φως – Jesus is the light, the [that is, light] of the world. Greek uses this 'extension' principle frequently: having announced 'the X', it repeats the 'the' to show that there's a bit more to say about it. Thus: τῳ ἀνδρι τῳ ἐν τῃ θαλαττῃ εἰπεν 'To the man the [man, that is] in the sea, he spoke.'

110

5. ὁ ἀγαπων τον Θεον 'the one-loving God', i.e. 'he who loves God'. All fine and dandy: we know this one.

6. ὁ τον Θεον ἀγαπων 'the-one God [acc.] loving', i.e. same as 5. above but observe the bracketing effect similar to 3. above, with ὁ and τον standing side by side.

7. When Socrates was tried and put to death in 399 BC, a number of his friends offered money to save him (see **The Greek world**, Chapter 18). They included Παραλιος ὁ [του] Δημοδοκου and Ἀδειμαντος ὁ [του] Ἀριστωνος, i.e. 'Paralios the of Demodokos and Adeimantos the of Ariston'. That's right: the word 'son' is missing. It is very common in Greek to express paternity in this way. Thus, for example, Ἰησους ὁ του Ἰωσηφ...

8. ἡ μεν ἀγαθη, ἡ δε κακη ἐστιν 'the [fem. subject] on the one hand good, the [fem. subject] on the other hand evil is', i.e. 'One woman is good, the other is evil'. Note that the one verb ἐστι serves for the two subjects; and observe the idiom ὁ/ἡ/το μεν...ὁ/ἡ/το δε...ὁ/ἡ/το δε 'the one...the other...the other...'. This can of course be plural (οἱ μεν...οἱ δε 'some...others') and in any case e.g. τους μεν ὁρω, τους δε οὐχι 'some [males, acc. *pl*] on the one hand I see, others on the other hand not' – 'I see some, but not others'. **Record**, therefore: ὁ/ἡ/το μεν...ὁ/ἡ/το δε...ὁ/ἡ/το δε 'the one...the other...the other...'.

9. Finally, if you can see no subject in the nominative, the subject will be in the verb, e.g. τους μαθητας τους ἐν τω οἰκω κελευει ἐρχεσθαι 'The disciples [acc., object] the [ones, that is] in the house he/she/it orders to go', i.e. 'he orders the disciples in the house to go'. No subject quoted: therefore subject in the verb.

Exercise 1

Translate into English: 1. οἱ τον Ἰησουν ἀγαπωντες τον Θεον ἀγαπωσιν. 2. τας ἐν τω οἰκω μενουσας οὐχ ὁρωσιν. 3. τον μεν φιλω, τον δε μισω. 4. ὁ μεν του Περικλεους κακος ἐστιν, ὁ δε του Σωκρατους ἀγαθος. 5. δει τας μεν ἐν τη πολει μενειν, τας δε προς την θαλατταν πορευεσθαι. 6. τί γιγνεται; οἱ μεν ἡμιν μαχεσθαι βουλονται, οἱ δε οὐχι. 7. την μεν τον του κυριου λογον λεγουσαν ὁρω, την δε γραφουσαν, την δε οὐδεν ποιουσαν. 8. τα ἐργα τα του Θεου οὐκ ἐστι τα του δαιμονιου.

9. αἱ μεν τῳ πληθει εἰπον, αἱ δε εἰς τον των ἀποστολων οἰκον ἠλθον, αἱ δε τους ἀνδρας τους προς την πολιν ἐρχομενους εἰδον.

The Greek Anthology 5.42
Vocabulary: ἀφελ-ης 'avid, keen (for sex)'; σωφρον- 'modest, chaste'; λιαν 'excessively'; βραδεως 'slowly'; θελω 'I want, desire' i.e. sex; ταχεως 'quickly'.

μισω την ἀφελη, μισω την σωφρονα λιαν.
ἡ μεν γαρ βραδεως, ἡ δε θελει ταχεως.

Anacreonta ('After Anacreon') 21
Anacreon (6th century BC) wrote many light hearted poems about sex and drink, and his poems encouraged many later imitations – of which this drinking song is one. The English poet Robert Herrick was a fan of the *Anacreonta*.

Vocabulary: μελαινα 'black' (agrees with γη); πιν-ω 'I drink'; το δενδρε-ον 'tree'; αὐτην 'it', acc., i.e. the land; θαλασσ-α = θαλαττα; ὁ ἀναυρ-ος 'the torrent'; ὁ ἡλι-ος 'the sun'; ἡ σελην-η 'the moon'; μοι...καὐτῳ 'me myself too'; ὁ ἑταιρ-ος 'friend'; θελ-οντι dat. participle, agreeing with μοι. [I have added Def Art in brackets where necessary.]

ἡ γη μελαινα πινει,
πινει [τα] δενδρεα δ᾽ αὐτην.
πινει [ἡ] θαλασσ᾽ [τους] ἀναυρους,
ὁ δ᾽ ἡλιος [την] θαλασσαν,
τον δ᾽ ἡλιον [ἡ] σεληνη·
τί μοι μαχεσθ᾽, ἑταιροι,
καὐτῳ θελοντι πινειν;

Lightness of being

11b One very useful little word indeed that you have not met yet is the participle of εἰμι 'I am', i.e. 'being'. Before you do – and a charmer he is as well – revise present participles active at **6c**, playing particular attention to the m/f endings in the chart.

112

You have done so? Good. For those endings on their own are the participle forms of εἰμι, 'being', thus:

	M		F	
Nom. s	ὁ	ὤν	ἡ	οὖσα
Nom. pl	οἱ	ὄντες	αἱ	οὖσαι
Acc. s	τον	ὄντα	την	οὖσαν
Acc. pl	τους	ὄντας	τας	οὖσας
Gen. s	του	ὄντος	της	οὔσης
Gen. pl	των	ὄντων	των	οὐσων
Dat. s	τῳ	ὄντι	τη	οὔσῃ
Dat. pl	τοις	οὖσι(ν)	ταις	οὔσαις

11c Thus ὁ ὤν 'the [male] one being', 'the man who is', αἱ οὖσαι 'the [female] ones being', 'the women who are', and so on. **Record** this cheeky chappie: watch out for ὤν, ὀντ-, οὐσ-.

Note word-order possibilities here: ὁ ὤν κακος 'the man being/who is evil' may well appear as ὁ κακος ὤν 'the man evil being', with that typical bracketing effect. One might pop a little phrase in the middle, like ἡ ἐν τῃ πολει οὖσα 'the woman in the city being', 'the woman who is in the city'.

Exercise 2

Translate: 1. ὁ ἀγαθος ὤν οὐκ ἐγενετο κακος. 2. ἀρ' εἰδες την ἐν τῃ θαλαττῃ οὖσαν; 3. μη πειθου ταις κακαις οὖσαις ἀλλα ταις ἀγαθαις. 4. μη πεμπε με, ἐν τῳ φωτι ὀντα, εἰς την σκοτιαν. 5. τας ἐν τῃ σκοτιᾳ οὖσας εἰς το φως ἀγειν βουλομαι. 6. ὁ Ἰησους ἐστιν ὁ ὤν και ὁ ἐρχομενος. 7. δει σε πεμπειν τους ἀποστολους τους ἐν τῃ πολει ὀντας εἰς τον κοσμον. 8. ὃς ἀν μη ἀγῃ εἰς το φως τους ἐν τῃ σκοτιᾳ ὀντας οὐ πειθεται τῳ του Θεου υἱῳ. 9. ὁ Πετρος, μαθητης ὤν, τῳ κυριῳ πιστευει. 10. ὤ Σωκρατες, ἀγαθος ὤν μη ἀδικει τους ἐν τῃ πολει ὀντας.

The Greek world

The invention of history

The history of the Persian Wars is recorded for us by the 'father' of Greek history, Herodotus (Ἡροδοτος). His account, in nine exhilarating books full of moving, hilarious and mind-boggling stories, begins with the history of conflict between East (Asia and beyond) and West (Greece) about women – Jason and Medea, the Trojan War and so on – to show that they had always been at it, and then starts properly by going back some two hundred years before the Persian wars to track the way in which Persian power spread west from Persia (modern Iran) and brought Persians into conflict with the Greeks. As he follows the expansion of Persian power, he describes the customs and habits of the various nations they came into conflict with. The whole of Book 2, for example, is devoted to Egypt, and there are fascinating digressions on the Persians themselves, the Babylonians, the Scythians, and so on. It is not till Book 6 that Herodotus reaches the battle of Marathon.

This combination of war, politics and social customs is the nearest to 'total history' that the Classical world ever came. It is an immense achievement. But there is more to the title 'father of history' than that. History is a Greek word, ἱστορια, meaning 'enquiry, research'. The uniquely important thing about Herodotus is that he is the first historian we know of to be deeply sceptical about accounts of the past. Biblical narratives and Babylonian records, for example, never ask questions or admit doubts or offer more than a single version of events. Herodotus is always saying 'I don't believe this', 'this smells fishy to me,' 'there are three accounts of this event and I find it very difficult to decide which is true'.

Secondly, he is deeply affected by Greek rationalistic tendencies. Though he did see a broad, divinely controlled pattern to the overall direction of events, his impulse is typically Greek – to try to explain human behaviour in human terms without recourse to the supernatural (cf. **The Greek world**, Chapter 4). After all, if the past is to have lessons for us, it can do so only if they are humanly intelligible lessons: we cannot understand the mind of god. But we can have a shot at understanding the mind of men and seeing what makes them tick. The past provides invaluable evidence in this search.

CHAPTER 11

Wordplay

The language of religion

Church vocabulary is filled with Greek words, many bearing little obvious relation to their Greek origins. 'Church', for example, ultimately derives from κυριος, 'lord', through κυριακον δωμα 'house belonging to the lord', which was taken up by Saxons on the continent, who brought it to England, where it emerged as 'cirice' in the language of our ancestors the Anglo-Saxons, out of which 'church' evolved. 'Priest' derives from Greek πρεσβυτερος, 'elder'. This took the same route into continental Saxon, emerging in Anglo-Saxon as 'preost'. 'Devil', from Greek διαβολος 'slanderer', went the same way too, via Anglo-Saxon 'deofol'.

Other derivations are less opaque. This is because they have come through Latin, which preserved the Greek words as faithfully as it could. Thus we find 'apostle' from αποστολος 'sent out'; 'apocalypse' from αποκαλυπτω 'I uncover, reveal'; 'ecclesiastical' from εκκλησια (εκ-καλεω 'I call out, summon, select'), originally the Athenian democratic assembly but used by Latin to mean the church (cf. French *église*, Italian *chiesa*, etc.); 'hymn' from ὑμνος; 'psalm' from ψαλμος; 'bishop' from (amazingly) επισκοπος, 'overseer, superintendent' (old English 'biscop'; cf. 'episcopalian'); 'deacon' from διακονος 'servant'; 'choir' from χορος; 'diocese' from διοικεω 'I manage, administrate'; 'angel' from αγγελος 'messenger'; 'parable' from παραβολη, 'comparison'; 'martyr' from μαρτυς, 'witness'; 'idolatry' from ειδωλολατρεια (ειδωλον 'idol', λατρεια 'service'); 'charity' from χαρις, 'grace', 'reciprocity'; 'baptism' from βαπτισμα, 'dipping'; 'catholic' from καθολικος, 'whole, universal'; 'heresy' from αιρεσις, 'choice'.

Answers
Exercise 1
1. Those who love Jesus love God. 2. They do not see those women waiting in the house. 3. I love the one, but hate the other. 4. The son of Pericles is wicked, the son of Socrates good. 5. It is necessary for some women to stay in the city and others to travel to the sea. 6. What is happening? Some wish to fight us, others not. 7. I see one woman speaking the word of the lord, another

writing, another doing nothing. 8. The works of God are not those of the devil. 9. Some women spoke to the mob, others went into the house of the apostles, others saw the men who were coming into the city.

Greek Anthology: I hate the sex-mad, I hate the excessively modest [woman]./For the one wants it slowly, the other quickly.

Anacreonta: The black earth drinks, trees drink it. The sea drinks the torrents, the sun the sea, the moon the sun. Why fight me, friends, myself wishing to drink too?

Exercise 2

1. The man who was good did not become evil. 2. Did you see the woman who was in the sea? 3. Do not trust women who are evil but good. 4. Do not send me, being in the light, into darkness. 5. I want to lead women who are in the darkness into the light. 6. Jesus is the one who is and the one to come. 7. It is necessary for you to send the apostles who are in the city into the world. 8. Whoever does not lead those who are in the darkness into the light does not obey the son of God. 9. Peter, being a disciple, has faith in the lord. 10. O Socrates, being good do not wrong those who are in the city.

Afore ye go

- Make sure you know ὤν οὖσα 'being' (**11c**)
- Are you confident about the 'bracketing' and 'extension' principles of Greek word order (**11a**, 3 and 4) and ὁ μεν...ὁ δε (**11a**, 8)?
- Learn the five new words

CHAPTER 12

Augmenting imperfections

12a Dark threats were uttered about nasties lurking beneath stones back at **10b**, but they are not about to crawl out yet. Let me just re-emphasise: the aorist tenses (plain pasts, 'I -ed') that you have met so far in **9** and **10** are one-offs. Let me remind you what they were:

Aorist active:	ἠλθ-ον	'I/they went/came'
	ηὑρ-ον	'I/they found'
	εἰπ-ον	'I/they said, spoke'
	εἰδ-ον	'I/they saw'
Aorist middle:	ἀφικ-ομην	'I arrived/came'
	ἐγεν-ομην	'I became, was born/ made, happened'
	ἐπυθ-ομην	'I heard, enquired'
	ἠρ-ομην	'I asked'

There they are, in all their glory. They are fantastically common in Greek, but they have no lessons to tell us, no deep insights to impart. You learn them and move on.

The imperfect enjoyment

12b The tense we meet for the first time now is the imperfect indicative active and middle. It means, broadly, 'I was -ing, I used to -, I began to -'. It gives a picture of an action continuing, being repeated, or beginning in the past.

Switch off the telly, pour a stiff one, adjust the focus and see what conclusions you can draw from the following. You will be pleasantly surprised:

Imperfect indicative active of παυ-ω 'I stop'

1s	ἐ-παυ-ον	'I was stopping'
2s	ἐ-παυ-ες	'you were stopping'
3s	ἐ-παυ-ε(ν)	'he, she, it was stopping'
1pl	ἐ-παυ-ομεν	'we were stopping'
2pl	ἐ-παυ-ετε	'you were stopping'
3pl	ἐ-παυ-ον	'they were stopping'

12c The rules? Precisely!
(i) We take our old chum the present stem παυ- , already an all-time favourite.
(ii) You stick ἐ- in front of it, giving you ἐπαυ- . This ἐ- job is called the 'augment'.
(iii) Then you tack on a series of strangely familiar looking endings – blow me down, Watson, are they not the same as that odd collection of aorists we met back in **9e**? Indeedy, as they say, doody. Very useful. But note 1s and 3pl both end in -ον.

Thus, for example, ἐ-λεγ-ον 'I was/they were saying', ἐ-μεν-ον 'I was/they were waiting, ἐ-γραφ-ον 'I was/they were writing' and so on and on and on and on...

Note
These imperfects may share the same endings as the aorist (plain past) we revised at **12a**, but the meanings are different. Those aorists (one-offs) mean 'I -ed'; the imperfects you can now construct for yourself for any verb you like mean 'I was -ing'.

Vocabulary

Record: διωκ-ω 'I pursue, chase'; φερ-ω 'I carry, bear, endure'; φευγ-ω 'I flee, run away'.

Exercise 1

Translate, twice where necessary (note – we revise datives, 'to', here as well): ἐπεμπε, ἐδιωκες, ἐφευγομεν, ἐφερετε, ἐκηρυττον ἡμιν, ἐγιγνωσκεν, ἐπεμπομεν, ἐδιδασκετε, ἐκελευες, ἐλεγον τοις μαθηταις, ἐμενε, ἐπιστευετε τῳ κυριῳ.

Translate: you (*pl*) were chasing, they used to flee, you (*s*) were saying, I was enduring, she was sending, they began to teach, we were ordering, he began to have faith, you (*pl*) used to wait, she was announcing, you (*pl*) were sending.

Starting a decree

When the Athenian assembly decided on a course of action, this was the formula with which the decree began – lots of lovely imperfects, naming who was in charge at the time when the decree was passed. For the βουλη, see **The Greek world** in Chapter 7. The πρυτανεις were a small sub-division of the βουλη, on duty 24 hours a day for reception and initial discussion of all business.

Note: ἐδοξεν 'it seemed good to', 'it was decreed by'; ἡ βουλ-η 'the *boule*'; πρυτανευ-ω 'I serve as prytanes'; γραμματευ-ω 'I serve as secretary'; ἐπιστατε-ω 'I preside'.

ἐδοξεν τη βουλη και τω δημω, W (one of the tribes) ἐπρυτανευε, X (name) ἐγραμματευε, Y (name) ἐπεστατει, Z (name) εἰπε...

Further contracts

12d But now, ten thousand curses, we remember those contract verbs with their horrible α- and ε-stems. Do we feel the contractions coming on again? Yes we do, but there's no need to groan and pant like that. The contraction rules are the same as for the present (see **3b** and **4b**). Observe:

Imperfect indicative active of νικα-ω 'I conquer'

1*s*	ἐνικα-ον	becomes	ἐνικ-ων 'I was conquering'
2*s*	ἐνικα-ες	becomes	ἐνικ-ας 'you were conquering'
3*s*	ἐνικα-ε	becomes	ἐνικ-α 'he, she, it was conquering'
1*pl*	ἐνικα-ομεν	becomes	ἐνικ-ωμεν 'we were conquering'
2*pl*	ἐνικα-ετε	becomes	ἐνικ-ατε 'you were conquering'
3*pl*	ἐνικα-ον	becomes	ἐνικ-ων 'they were conquering'

12e Imperfect indicative active of φιλε-ω, 'I love'

1s	ἐφιλε-ον becomes	ἐφιλ-ουν 'I was loving'
2s	ἐφιλε-ες becomes	ἐφιλ-εις 'you were loving'
3s	ἐφιλε-ε becomes	ἐφιλ-ει 'he, she, it was loving'
1pl	ἐφιλε-ομεν becomes	ἐφιλ-ουμεν 'we were loving'
2pl	ἐφιλε-ετε becomes	ἐφιλ-ειτε 'you were loving'
3pl	ἐφιλε-ον becomes	ἐφιλ-ουν 'they were loving'

Exercise 2

Translate, twice where necessary: ἐποιουν, ἐλαλει τῳ μαθητῃ, ἐτηρουμεν, ἐνικας, ἐδοκειτε ἡμιν, ἐποιει, ἐλαλουν, ἐδοκεις ἐμοι, ἐτηρει, ἐνικων.

Translate: they were loving, he used to keep, you (pl) were talking, she was conquering, they used to seem, we were making, they were keeping.

12f Now the excitement begins to mount. Pant, gasp, what happens to all those heavenly middle verbs in the imperfect? Any chance they follow the same rules, i.e. ἐ- (the augment) + present stem + middle endings like those funny aorist middle thingies at **10b**? You may peep out from behind your fingers now and SHAZAM! Correct! Perpend:

Imperfect indicative middle of πορευ-ομαι 'I travel'

1s	ἐ-πορευ-ομην	'I was travelling'
2s	ἐ-πορευ-ου	'you were travelling'
3s	ἐ-πορευ-ετο	'he, she, it was travelling'
1pl	ἐ-πορευ-ομεθα	'we were travelling'
2pl	ἐ-πορευ-εσθε	'you were travelling'
3pl	ἐ-πορευ-οντο	'they were travelling'

Exercise 3

Translate: ἐγιγνετο, ὑμιν ἐμαχοντο, ἐβουλεσθε, ἐπειθομεθα σοι, ἐφαινου ἡμιν, ἐγιγνοντο, ἐπορευομεθα, ἐμαχετο, ἐβουλοντο, ἐφαινεσθε μοι, ἐγιγνου, ἐπειθετο μοι.

Translate: I was becoming, he used to fight, they were wishing, he was appearing, they were travelling, you (*pl*) were fighting, you (*s*) began to travel, he used to wish.

Vowels

12g Those of a suspicious frame of mind will have gradually spotted something, i.e. that the following verbs have not featured in any of the exercises:

ἀγαπαω, ἀδικεω, ἀκουω, ἐθελω, ἀγω and ὁμολογεω.

How can this be? Old friends all, now shunned as if possessed of some horrible disease. What is going on? Now pay attention:

(i)   observe the initial letter of all these rejected verbs. Correct – vowels.
(ii) then remember that all imperfect verbs begin with ἐ-, the 'augment'.

Aha! You mean something special happens to verbs beginning with a vowel when you want to augment them? Got it in one.

Basically, verbs that *already begin with a vowel* augment themselves by *lengthening this vowel*. Thus:

1. Verbs beginning ἐ- and ἀ- augment themselves by turning ἐ- or ἀ- to ἠ.
   Thus: ἠ-γαπ-ων 'I was loving'; ἠ-δικ-ουν 'I was harming'; ἠ-κου-ον 'I was hearing'; ἠ-θελ-ον 'I was wishing'; ἠγ-ον 'I was leading'.
2. Verbs beginning o- augment themselves by turning o- to ω-.
   Thus: ὠ-μολογ-ουν 'I was agreeing'.
3. Record an exception: ἐχ-ω 'I have' forms its imperfect as εἰχ-ον 'I was having'.

Vocabulary

Record: ἀρχ-ομαι 'I begin'; εὐχ-ομαι 'I pray'; εὑρισκ-ω 'I find'.

Exercise 4

Translate, twice where necessary: ἠγες, ἠγαπατε, ἠδικουν,

ἤκουες, εἶχον, ὡμολογειτε, ἤρχετο, ηὔχοντο τοις θεοις, εἴχετε, ηὑρισκετε, ἤθελον, ἠγαπωμεν, εἴχομεν, ἠκουετε, ἠδικεις, ἤρχοντο, ηὔχετο τῳ κυριῳ, ἤγετε, ηὕρισκον, ἤκουε, ἠθελομεν, ὡμολογουν, ἠγαπας, ηὐχομεθα ταις γυναιξιν, ἠδικειτε, εἶχεν.

Translate: you (s) were wishing, I used to do wrong, they were having, he was hearing, we used to agree, I was praying, she was loving, they were beginning, she began to find [see **12b**], we used to have, they were hearing, you (pl) used to pray, they were leading.

The Greek world

Empire and culture

The Persian Wars were instrumental in the development of the Athenian maritime empire and therefore of democracy and of the vision we have of the 'glory that was Greece'.

Though the Spartan land army had been mainly responsible for repelling the Persians, it was the Athenian fleet of triremes (warships) that had won the victory at Salamis, and Athens decided to capitalise on it. A large find of silver at Laurium in southern Attica financed an expanded navy; Athens rebuilt its defensive walls (destroyed by the Persians); and headed up a league of maritime allies mainly from the western coast of Turkey and the Aegean islands, determined never to let Persia attack again. This Delian league, founded in 478 BC (its head-quarters were on the island of Delos), gradually turned itself into an empire, with Athens demanding tribute from its allies in money or ships and imposing garrisons where necessary. It slowly spread its power into mainland Greece too – where, inevitably, its interests would clash with the other great power in the land, Sparta.

This was the source of Athens' wealth and power during its heyday in the 5th century BC. It was this money that financed the Parthenon – Pericles' concept, and a powerful statement about Athenian greatness and the power of Athene. Pericles also reformed the democracy, acknowledging that power now lay not with the middle-class hoplite land-forces, but with the poor, who manned and rowed the fleet and ensured that Athens remained firmly on top. This is fifth-century Classical Athens, the world of Socrates, Aeschylus, Sophocles, Euripides, Herodotus, Thucydides, Pericles, Aristophanes, Plato...has ever so brief a period exerted such radical influence for so long?

Wordplay

Game words

The Olympic games were named in honour of Olympian Zeus, king of the gods and champion of competition (see **The Greek world**, Chapter 3). They were held nowhere near Mt Olympus, but near Elis, in the north-western Peloponnese. Founded in 776 BC, they became in time a focus for Greeks from all over the Mediterranean, who made their way there to honour Zeus and enjoy the five-day festival of sport. Greeks adored competition, but adored winning even more (the image of the games as a festival of amateur sportsmanship is pure invention). Games were held in hundreds of other venues, but Olympia was the most prestigious and guaranteed the victors fame and fortune (the actual prize for winning was a wild olive-wreath, but financial rewards were widely available elsewhere). There were no records or prizes for coming second. Winning was all.

Our sporting vocabulary is filled with Greek ideas and words. The Big Four games – at Olympia, Delphi, Nemea and Isthmia – were known as the περιοδος ('circuit'), and at Delphi a wreath of δαφνη (laurel, whence 'laurels') was the prize. Competitions were held in the σταδιον. ἀθλον means 'prize, contest' and an ἀθλητης competed for it, practising hard beforehand in the γυμνασιον (γυμνος 'naked'). νικη was what they were after – not the footwear, but 'victory'. The πενταθλος went in for the pentathlon (πεντε 'five'), comprising sprint, standing jump, javelin, δισκος and wrestling. Other cultures invented the ἑπταθλον (ἑπτα 'seven') and δεκαθλον (δεκα 'ten'). The nastiest contest was probably the παγκρατιον (παν 'all', κρατος 'power'), in which only biting and gouging were forbidden, but it was not rated as dangerous as boxing.

Incidentally, there was no such ancient race as the μαραθων – that was invented for the refounding of the games in Athens in 1896, in memory of Phidippides' heroic run from Athens to Μαραθων to fight the Persians and back to Athens to report victory (though the tale has many different versions).

Answers
Exercise 1
He was sending, you were pursuing, we were fleeing, you were carrying, I/they were announcing to us, he was recognising, we were sending, you were teaching, you were ordering, I/they were speaking to the disciples, he was staying, you were having faith in the lord.

ἐδιωκετε, ἐφευγον, ἐλεγες, ἐφερον, ἐπεμπε, ἐδιδασκον, ἐκελευομεν, ἐπιστευε, ἐμενετε, ἐκηρυττε, ἐπεμπετε.

Inscription: It was decreed by the Council and People, W was serving as prytanes, X was secretary, Y was presiding, Z said...

Exercise 2
I/they were making, he was speaking to the disciple, we were guarding, you were conquering, you were seeming to us, he was making, I/they were speaking, you were seeming to me, he was guarding, I/they were conquering.

ἐφιλουν, ἐτηρει, ἐλαλειτε, ἐνικα, ἐδοκουν, ἐποιουμεν, ἐτηρουν.

Exercise 3
He was becoming, they were fighting you, you were wishing, we were obeying you, you were seeming to us, they were becoming, we were travelling, he was fighting, they were wishing, you were seeming to me, you were becoming, he was obeying me.

ἐγιγνομην, ἐμαχετο, ἐβουλοντο, ἐφαινετο, ἐπορευοντο, ἐμαχεσθε, ἐπορευου, ἐβουλετο.

Exercise 4
You were leading, you were loving, I/they were harming, you were hearing, I/they were having, you were agreeing, he was beginning, they were praying to the gods, you were having, you were finding, I/they were wishing, we were loving, we were having, you were hearing, you were harming, they were beginning, he was praying to the lord, you were leading, I/they were finding, he was hearing, we were wishing, I/they were agreeing, you were loving, we were praying to the women, you were harming, he was having.

ἠθελες, ἠδικουν, εἰχον, ἠκουε, ὡμολογουμεν, ηὐχομην, ἠγαπα, ἠρχοντο, ηὑρισκε, εἰχομεν, ἠκουον, ηὐχεσθε, ἠγον.

"Funny, with me it's spiders."

Afore ye go

- Ensure you know the new imperfect indicative active at **12b** and imperfect indicative middle at **12f**
- Check that you are happy with the contracted imperfect forms at **12d-e**
- Do you understand the principles of augmentation – ἐ- or lengthening an initial vowel – at **12c, g**?
- Revise the six new words

CHAPTER 13

Personalising the Word

13a John 1.1-10

Vocabulary

Record: αὐτ- 'him'; δια or δι', 'through, because of'; μαρτυρε-ω 'I bear witness'; περι 'about, concerning'.

ἐν ἀρχῃ ἠν ὁ Λογος, και ὁ Λογος ἠν προς [with] τον Θεον, και Θεος ἠν ὁ Λογος. οὑτος [this] ἠν ἐν ἀρχῃ προς τον Θεον. παντα [everything] δι' αὐτου ἐγενετο, και χωρις [apart from] αὐτου, ἐγενετο οὐδεν which was made. ἐν αὐτῳ ζωη ἠν, και ἡ ζωη ἠν το φως των ἀνθρωπων. και το φως ἐν τῃ σκοτιᾳ φαινει [shines] και ἡ σκοτια αὐτο [it, acc.] οὐ κατελαβεν [overwhelmed]. ἐγενετο ἀνθρωπος sent from God, whose name was John. οὑτος [he] ἠλθεν εἰς μαρτυριαν, ἱνα μαρτυρησῃ περι του φωτος, ἱνα παντες [everyone] πιστευσωσιν δι' αὐτου. οὐκ ἠν ἐκεινος [that man, i.e. John] το φως, ἀλλ' ἱνα μαρτυρησῃ περι του φωτος. ἠν το φως το ἀληθινον [true], which enlightens every ἀνθρωπον, ἐρχομενον εἰς τον κοσμον. ἐν τῳ κοσμῳ ἠν, και ὁ κοσμος δι' αὐτου ἐγενετο, και ὁ κοσμος αὐτον οὐκ ἐγνω [recognised]...και ὁ Λογος σαρξ [flesh] ἐγενετο.

Getting personal yet again

13b Time now to get a grip on the personal pronouns 'he, she it': αὐτος '(s)he, it'; οὑτος '(s)he, it; this man'; ἐκεινος '(s)he, it; that man'.

Warning: As you let your gaze wander down the page, you may feel your brain turning to spaghetti hoops. But, honest, you will have to learn virtually nothing except the Greek words above, with Def Art attached to them. It is just all being spelt out in full for reference's sake.

As I said, think of dear old Def Art and now (forgetting

meaning for the moment) fasten the fascinated gaze on especially the *endings* of:

	'he'	'this (man)'	'that (man)'
Nom. singular masculine:	αὐ-τος	οὑ-τος	ἐκειν-ος
Acc. singular masculine:	αὐ-τον	του-τον	ἐκειν-ον
Gen. singular masculine:	αὐ-του	του-του	ἐκειν-ου
Dat. singular masculine	αὐ-τῳ	του-τῳ	ἐκειν-ῳ

You see? Look how the first syllables – αὐ-, (τ)ου-, ἐκειν- – are followed by Def Art, or something like it. Think therefore:

αὐ- + Def Art   'he, she, it'
οὑ- and του- + Def Art   'he, she, it, this (man)'
ἐκειν- + Def Art minus τ: 'he, she, it, that (man)'

As usual, Def Art will give you case, number, gender and so on: but you have to look at the *end* of the word for Def Art to emerge and work its magic.

13c Here are the charts in full. Remember that on its own:

αὐτος means 'he'
οὑτος means 'he/this man'
ἐκεινος 'he/that man'
(or e.g. 'she', 'him', 'her', 'them' etc. depending on case, number and gender)

e.g. οὑτος ἐκεινον νικα 'this man/he defeats that man/him'
ἐκεινη ταυτην φιλει 'that woman/she loves this woman/her'
ἐκειναι τουτους μισουσι 'those women/they hate these men/them'.

αὐ-τος 'he',	αὐ-τη, 'she'	αὐ-το, 'it'
M	F	N
Singular		
Nom. αὐ-τος	αὐ-τη	αὐ-το
Acc. αὐ-τον	αὐ-την	αὐ-το
Gen. αὐ-του	αὐ-της	αὐ-του
Dat. αὐ-τῳ	αὐ-τη	αὐ-τῳ

Plural

Nom.	αὐ-τοι	αὐ-ται	αὐ-τα
Acc.	αὐ-τους	αὐ-τας	αὐ-τα
Gen.	αὐ-των	αὐ-των	αὐ-των
Dat.	αὐ-τοις	αὐ-ταις	αὐ-τοις

Exercise 1

Translate: 1. ὁ Ἰησους ὁ του Θεου υἱος ὢν ἀποκρινομενος αὐτῃ εἶπεν. 2. το βιβλιον αὐτου οὐκ ἐφιλει. 3. τον αὐτων λογον ἐκηρυττομεν. 4. οἱ βαρβαροι οἱ ἀγαθοι ὀντες αὐτους προς την γην ἐδιωκον. 5. ὁ Ἰησους αὐτους ἐκελευε μενειν και μη φευγειν. 6. την αὐτων ἐντολην οὐκ ἐτηρειτε. 7. τον λογον τον του κυριου αὐταις ἐλεγεν. 8. το βιβλιον αὐτῃ οὐκ ἐστιν· οὐκ ἰσμεν που ἐστι το αὐτης βιβλιον.

13d οὑ-τος 'he, this man', αὑ-τη, 'she, this woman', του-το, 'it, this thing'

	M	F	N
Singular			
Nom.	οὑ-τος	αὑ-τη	του-το
Acc.	του-τον	ταυ-την	του-το
Gen.	του-του	ταυ-της	του-του
Dat.	του-τῳ	ταυ-τῃ	του-τῳ
Plural			
Nom.	οὑ-τοι	αὑ-ται	ταυ-τα
Acc.	του-τους	ταυ-τας	ταυ-τα
Gen.	του-των	του-των	του-των
Dat.	του-τοις	ταυ-ταις	του-τοις

Notes
- Think οὑ-, του-, αὑ-, ταυ- + Def Art
- τουτο 'this thing' and ταυτα 'these things' are very common in Greek.

Exercise 2

Translate: 1. οὑτος, μαθητης ὢν, ἐλεγεν ἡμιν. 2. τουτον μεν ἐφιλουν, ταυτην δε ἐμισουν. 3. τουτο μεν κακον ἐστι, ταυτα δε

129

ἀγαθα. 4. τί ἐστι τουτο; 5. τίνες εἰσιν οὑτοι οἱ ἐν τῃ θαλαττῃ ὀντες; 6. ταυτας ἐβουλομην εἰς τον οἰκον ἐρχεσθαι. 7. ἐδιωκον τουτους εἰς την πολιν φευγοντας. 8. οὑτοι οἱ ἐκ της πολεως φευγοντες οὐκ ἠλθον προς τουτον. 9. οὑτος μεν ἀφικετο προς ταυτας, αὑται δε οὐκ ἐμενον ἀλλ' ἐφευγον. 10. τί εἰπεν αὑτη τουτῳ; οὐ γαρ βουλεται οὑτος ἀποκρινεσθαι ταυτῃ.

13e ἐκειν-ος 'he, that man', ἐκειν-η, 'she, that woman', ἐκειν-ο, 'it, that thing'

	M	F	N
Singular			
Nom.	ἐκειν-ος	ἐκειν-η	ἐκειν-ο
Acc.	ἐκειν-ον	ἐκειν-ην	ἐκειν-ο
Gen.	ἐκειν-ου	ἐκειν-ης	ἐκειν-ου
Dat.	ἐκειν-ῳ	ἐκειν-ῃ	ἐκειν-ῳ
Plural			
Nom.	ἐκειν-οι	ἐκειν-αι	ἐκειν-α
Acc.	ἐκειν-ους	ἐκειν-ας	ἐκειν-α
Gen.	ἐκειν-ων	ἐκειν-ων	ἐκειν-ων
Dat.	ἐκειν-οις	ἐκειν-αις	ἐκειν-οις

Exercise 3

Translate: 1. ἐλαλει μεν ἐκειναις, ἐκεινους δε ἐδιωκεν. 2. δει ἡμας εὐχεσθαι μεν ἐκειναις, φευγειν δε ἀπ' ἐκεινων. 3. τί οὐν ἐστιν ἐκεινο; οὐ γαρ οἰδα. 4. ἀποκρινομενος ἐκεινοις ἠλθεν. 5. οὐκ ἐγιγνωσκομεν το βιβλιον ἐκεινων. 6. ἐθελομεν εἰδεναι τίς ἐστιν ἐκεινη. 7. ὁ ἐκεινων πατηρ ἐκεινους ἠδικει. 8. ἐκεινοι μεν ἐδιωκον, ἐκεινοι δε ἐφευγον. 9. τουτ' ἐκεινο!

13f Now peruse the following:

ἐκεινος ὁ οἰκος ἐστιν ἀγαθος 'that [the] house is good'
γραφω ταυτην την ἐπιστολην 'I am writing this [the] letter'
ἐπεμπον τουτους τους υἱους 'I was sending these [the] sons'

You see what is happening? When οὑτος/ἐκεινος is at once followed by Def Art, it means 'This/ that, ah here is Def Art, so

I am now going to define it more closely (*extension*), this/that house, letter, son, large sliced cottage loaf/whatever' (cf. **11a**.4).
So: οὗτος ὁ 'this X', ἐκεινος ὁ 'that X'.

Vocabulary

Record: δια, δι' + genitive, 'because of'; ζητε-ω 'I seek, look for'; καλε-ω 'I call'; περι + genitive 'around, concerning'.

Exercise 4

Translate: οὗτος ὁ μαθητης ἐκεινην την γυναικα ἐζητει. 2. ἐγω μεν γαρ τουτους τους ἀνδρας καλω, συ δε ἐκεινας τας γυναικας καλεις. 3. οὗτοι οὖν οἱ βαρβαροι περι ταυτης της πολεως ἐπορευοντο. 4. δια οὖν τουτων των Ἑλληνων ἐνικωμεν ἐκεινην την πολιν. 5. δια ἐκεινου του πληθους ἐδει [past of δει] ἡμας ἀπο της πολεως ἐρχεσθαι. 6. οὗτοι μεν ἐπεμπον τουτους τους ἀνδρας εἰς την θαλατταν, ἐκεινοι δε ἐκαλουν ἐκεινας τας γυναικας εἰς την πολιν.

The Greek world

Old gods

The monotheistic (μονος 'alone, single') Christian tradition assumes that 'God is love'. Perhaps the best way to begin thinking about Greek gods, who were certainly not love, is to envisage them as powers, like gravity. They did not require belief, let alone love – just acknowledgement. So too does gravity. Walk along a cliff top and fail to acknowledge it, and you are dead. But you can refuse to love it and refuse to believe in it all your life, and it will make no difference – as long as, in certain critical circumstances, you acknowledge it.

The Greek for 'acknowledge' is νομιζω, 'I treat as one would a νομος', where νομος means 'custom, law, habit'. You treat gods, in other words, in the way you have always treated them. That means ritual, most of all, sacrifice (Latin *sacrifico* – 'I make sacred'). This can range from a ἑκατομβοιον (hecatomb – ἑκατον '100', βους 'oxen') on the most magnificent state occasions – one of the few occasions when Greeks would eat meat – to a cake left on a house altar. But whatever the offering, it was made sacred, removed from human use and made over to the gods.

Prayers were made standing, with hands raised to the gods above, or lowered to the gods below. A typical prayer addresses the god, names him (must get the right one) and identifies his powers; thanks him for or reminds him of past favours ('if ever you...'); makes the request; and finally promises future favours. There is a strong whiff of tit-for-tat about the relationship between men and gods.

Unlike the Christian religion, there were no divine books or divine revelations. There was no such thing as theology. Priests were there simply to oversee public rituals: they had, for example, no moral functions or counselling obligations.

Wordplay

Divine vocabulary

Gods present all sorts of linguistic challenges. The most common god to swear by was Ἡρακλῆς, for he was the only man to have become a god and was therefore especially sympathetic to men's plight. The word looks as if it means the glory κλεος of the goddess Ἡρα, but given that she hated him (he was a son of Zeus by Alcmena) and imposed the twelve labours on him, this looks difficult.

Ζευς on the other hand is linguistically easy. He has the stem Δι- and the same name as the Indic sky god *Dyaus pita* (cf. Latin *Jupiter=Diespiter* 'father of the day' and *dies, divinus, Diana*). He is a sky-god, god of weather ('cloud-gatherer' and 'loud-thunderer' in Homer) and of the bright light of day. Latin *diurnus* 'daily' became, through French, our 'journal'.

His wife Ἡρα, goddess of marriage, may be connected with ὡρα, *hora*, the hour or season (i.e. right time for marriage). Ποσειδων is god of powerful natural forces like the sea, earthquakes and horses. Ποσει- looks like 'lord', and it would be very helpful if -δων could be connected with δα/γα and mean 'earth' – but it cannot. Ἀφροδιτη was goddess of sex (homo- and heterosexual) – you appealed to her for help in matters sexual. Much she appreciated it too – a god was honoured when humans indulged his or her specialities. Greeks derived her name from ἀφρος 'foam' because she was born from the semen of the castrated Uranus which mixed with the waves of the sea, but this is pure Greek invention. Ἄρτεμις oversaw hunting, childbirth and virginity – which seems odd. But then Ἀπολλων was god of music, plague and healing. If you are acquainted with the one, you must also be acquainted with the other – they are two sides of the same coin. Both their names are etymologically obscure. Ἑρμης (ἑρμα means 'boundary-stone') was god of borders: he carried messages across them, transported the dead down to Hades and helped thieves transgress them. Διονυσος was god of life and transformation, whether engendered by drink, acting or moving from life to death. The Δι- stem points to a connection with Zeus, but the rest is quite obscure.

The fact that some of these names are so hard to derive from Greek argues very strongly indeed that, like Zeus, they are not original Greek inventions. They have been taken over from other cultures and adapted to Greek ways.

Answers
Exercise 1
1. Jesus being the son of God replying spoke to her. 2. He did not like his book. 3. We announced their word. 4. The barbarians who were brave were chasing them towards the land. 5. Jesus was ordering them to stay and not to flee. 6. You were not keeping their command. 7. He was speaking the word of the lord to them (women). 8. She does not have a book: we do not know where her book is.

Exercise 2
[Note: he/this man, she/this woman, these, and so on, are variables here] 1. He, being a disciple, was speaking to us. 2. I/they loved him, but hated her. 3. This is bad, but these things are good. 4. What is this? 5. Who are these who are in the sea? 6. I was wanting these women to go into the house. 7. I/they was pursuing those who were fleeing into the city. 8. These who were fleeing out of the city did not go to him. 9. He came towards these women, but they were not waiting, but began fleeing. 10. What did she say to him? For he does not wish to reply to her.

Exercise 3
[Note: he/that man, she/that woman, those, and so on, are variables here] 1. While he was speaking to those women, he was pursuing those men. 2. It is necessary for us to pray to those

women, but to escape from those women. 3. What, therefore, is that? For I do not know. 4. Replying to those men he went. 5. We did not recognise their book. 6. We want to know who that woman is. 7. Their father did them wrong. 8. They were pursuing, but they were fleeing. 9. This [is] that! That's it!

Exercise 4

1. This disciple was seeking that woman. 2. For I am calling these men, but you are calling those women. 3. Therefore these non-Greeks were travelling around this city. 4. Therefore because of these Greeks we were conquering that city. 5. Because of that mob it was necessary for us to go from the city. 6. These men were sending these men into the sea, but those men were calling those women into the city.

Afore ye go

- Make sure you have mastered the various words for 'he, she, it, this person, that person' – αὐ-τος, οὑ-τος and ἐκειν-ος – in form and meaning at **13b-e**
- Make sure that you are alert to οὑ-τος ὁ and ἐκειν-ος ὁ meaning 'this' and 'that'
- Learn the five new words

CHAPTER 14

Passive reflections

14a So far we have used six prepositions:

εἰς 'into'
πρoς 'towards'
followed by the accusative

ἀπo 'away from'
ἐκ 'out of'
δια 'because of'
περι 'around, concerning'
followed by the genitive.

These prepositions are often attached to the front of verbs (as a 'prefix', cf. 'suffix', something attached to the end), and this will alter a verb's meaning, sometimes only very slightly, sometimes quite a lot, e.g.

> ἠλθον 'I went', ἀπηλθον 'I went away'
> πεμπω 'I send', ἀποπεμπω 'I send away', shading into 'I divorce'!
> ἐρχομαι 'I come', προσερχομαι 'I come towards, I approach'

14b Note, however, an important technical point. The 'augment' (the ἐ- attached to the stem of the verb to form the imperfect, e.g. ἐ-λεγον 'I was saying') *remains* attached to the *stem* of the verb even when the verb has a prefix. Observe:

ἐπεμπον 'I was sending': προσ-επεμπον 'I was sending to', ἀπ-επεμπον 'I was sending away', δι-επεμπον 'I was sending through', ἐξ-επεμπον 'I was sending out'.

135

Note

• See how ἀπ(o) and δι(α) lose their last vowel before the augment, and how ἐκ changes to ἐξ before a vowel.

Exercise 1

Place ἀπο, δια, προς and ἐκ in front of the following verb stems: φαινομαι, οἰδα, ἐρχομαι, εἰδον.

Here are some imperfect verbs, with prefix: what would their dictionary form be (i.e. 1s present)? E.g. ἐξεδιδασκε comes from ἐκδιδασκω:

προσηγαπα, διηκουομεν, ἐξεπιστευες, διεκελευετε, ἐξεμισει, προσεμαχοντο.

Present and imperfect indicative passive 'I am being -ed' and 'I was -ed'

14c Do I sense an in-drawing of breath? A faint scream of 'O crikey, we've laboured through all the active voices ("I am -ing") – now we've got a whole load of ghastly passive voices to learn as well ("I am being -ed")'?

Take it easy. Relax, with smoooooth Classics. Rustle the newspaper a bit. Take the dog for a stroll. Then come back and have a look at the present indicative passive of παυ-ω and pour yourself a large congratulatory drink:

Present indicative passive of παυ-ω, 'I am being stopped'

1s	παυ-ομαι	'I am being stopped'
2s	παυ-ῃ	'you (s) are being stopped'
3s	παυ-εται	'he, she, it is being stopped'
1pl	παυ-ομεθα	'we are being stopped'
2pl	παυ-εσθε	'you (pl) are being stopped'
3pl	παυ-ονται	'they are being stopped'

There! You see what has happened? I knew you'd be pleased. You have simply taken the active verb and tacked your old friends the middle endings like those of ἐρχομαι (**5a**) on to it.

So: an active verb (one ending in -ω) becomes passive by

changing the -ω endings to -ομαι endings. Thus, e.g. διωκω 'I pursue', διωκ-ομαι 'I am being pursued' – and so on.

Note

- There will be the usual contract rules to watch out for – but they are the same as ever (see **3b** and **4b**).
- Middles remain quite unaffected by all this, of course, since the -ομαι endings are their normal endings. Translate the middles as you have always done, thoroughly active without any passive undertones at all, e.g. πορευονται 'they travel'. The important thing is to know the verb is middle in the first place.

Exercise 2

Turn the following present actives into present passives and translate, e.g. παυει – παυεται 'he is being stopped': διωκουσι, ἀγομεν, λεγει, πεμπεις, κηρυττετε, κελευουσι, ἀκουομεν, εὑρισκει.

Translate (watch it – a few highly active middle indicatives lurking here): πεμπονται, ποιειται, νικωμαι, ἀγαπωμεθα, ἀδικεισθε, μαχονται, γιγνωσκεται, λεγομεθα, διδασκονται, γραφεται, ἀποκρινεσθε, τηρουμεθα, φιλεισθε, ὁρωνται, πορευονται, ζητουμεθα.

Translate: he is being sent, we are being taught, it is being said, they are being pursued, you (*pl*) are being ordered, it is being announced.

14d Now, you are saying to yourselves with that iron logic typical of all who study ancient Greek, if the present passives are formed by using the endings of the present middle, are the imperfect passives formed by using the endings of the imperfect middle? Judge for yourselves, Aristotles all:

Imperfect indicative passive of παυ-ω 'I stop'

1s	ἐ-παυ-ομην	'I was being stopped'
2s	ἐ-παυ-ου	'you were being stopped'
3s	ἐ-παυ-ετο	'he, she, it was being stopped'
1pl	ἐ-παυ-ομεθα	'we were being stopped'

137

2*pl* ἐ-παυ-εσθε   'you were being stopped'
3*pl* ἐ-παυ-οντο   'they were being stopped'

The answer, as you can see, is 'yes' (compare **12f**).

But before we leap confidently onto our imperfect passive exercise machines, here is another very common preposition:

ὑπο, ὑπ᾽, ὑφ, meaning 'by' (a person)

e.g. ὑπο του ἀνδρος 'by the man', ὑπο των γυναικων 'by the women', ὑπ᾽ ἐμου 'by me', ὑφ᾽ ὑμων 'by you'. Note that it is followed by the genitive. **Record** it.

I introduce it here for obvious reasons: passive verbs beg for 'the agent', i.e. the person *by whom* the action is being done. Thus παυομαι ὑπο τουτου, 'I am being stopped *by him*'; ἐπαυετο ὑπο ταυτης 'he was being stopped *by her*'. Watch out for it, therefore, in the next exercise.

Exercise 3

Turn the following imperfect actives into imperfect passives and translate, e.g. ἐπαυομεν – ἐπαυομεθα 'we were being stopped': ἐκελευε, ἐκηρυττομεν, ἐδιωκον, ἐλεγετε, ἐδιδασκες, ἐπεμπε.

Translate: ἠδικειτο ὑπο σου, ὑπ᾽ ἐμου ἐπεμπεσθε, ἠγαπωντο ὑπο του Θεου, το βιβλιον ὑπ᾽ ἐκεινου του ἀποστολου ἐγραφετο, ἐδιδασκομεθα ὑπ᾽ ἐκεινων, ὑπο των γυναικων ἐζητουμην, ὑπο τουτων των βαρβαρων ἐνικωντο οἱ Ἑλληνες, ὁ λογος ὑπο των μαθητων ἐλεγετο.

Translate (the odd non-passive middle here): it was being announced, we were being ordered, they were being taught, he was fighting, they were being said, you (*pl*) were being sent, I was being heard, we were being recognised, he was travelling.

Present participles passive

14e And what, you say stretching happily, about present participles passive? We remember that present participles active ('-ing') were formed by adding
  m. -ων (-οντ-)

f. -ουσ-α

to the present stem (**6c**):

e.g. παυ-ων παυ-ουσα 'stopping', διωκ-ων διωκ-ουσα 'pursuing'.

You are surely not going to tell me that you form present participles passive ('being -ed') by adding (yawn) the middle participle ending (-ομενος η ον) to the present stem (**6a**)?

Sorry. That's exactly what I am going to tell you. Thus:

παυ-ομεν-ος η ον 'being stopped', διωκ-ομεν-ος η ον 'being pursued', etc.

Exercise 4

Form the nom. present passive participle, m/f/n, of the following verbs and translate, e.g. ἀγω – ἀγομεν-ος η ον 'being led': κηρυττω, κελευω, ἐχω, λεγω, γιγνωσκω, γραφω.

Translate and name the case, e.g. ἡ παυομενη 'the woman being stopped', nom: οἱ διωκομενοι, τας πεμπομενας, των διδασκομενων, τους ὁρωμενους, τοις ζητουμενοις, την μισουμενην, του νικωμενου, τον φιλουμενον.

Present infinitives passive

14f Further (stifle) I suppose present infinitive passives are formed by adding the present infinitive middle ending (**7a**) to the present stem? So that while παυ-ειν means 'to stop', παυ-εσθαι means 'to be stopped'? And διωκ-εσθαι 'to be pursued'? And so on (nod)?

παυ-ειν 'to stop'   παυ-εσθαι 'to be stopped'

You see? I'm afraid it's true. Divinely dull, isn't it? Anyway, slap yourselves a few times round the cheeks, stick a few pins in the thighs, prop up the eyelids with a brace of matchsticks, and have a go at the next exercise.

Exercise 5

Turn the following active infinitives into passive infinitives and translate, e.g. κελευειν – κελευεσθαι 'to be ordered': ἀγειν, διδασκειν, ἀκουειν, γραφειν, λεγειν.

Translate (watch it – passive and lethally active middle infinitives are mixed up here): νικασθαι, ἐρχεσθαι, φιλεισθαι, μαχεσθαι, μισεισθαι, ζητεισθαι, γιγνεσθαι, ἀδικεισθαι, ἀποκρινεσθαι, πεμπεσθαι, πορευεσθαι.

Revision Exercise 6

Translate: 1. ἐκεινοι οἱ βαρβαροι, διωκομενοι ὑπο τουτων των Ἑλληνων, ἀπηλθον ἱνα μη νικωνται. 2. το τεκνον μου οὐκ ἐβουλετο διδασκεσθαι ὑπο του πατρος. 3. οἱ τον Θεον ἀγαπωντες ὑπο του Θεου ἠγαπωντο. 4. οἱ ἀποστολοι οἱ ἀγαπωμενοι ὑπο του Θεου ἐπιστευον εἰς αὐτον. 5. δει τουτους τηρεισθαι ὑφ' ἡμων ἱνα μη φευγωσιν. 6. ἐβουλομεθα ἐκεινο το βιβλιον ὑπο σου γραφεσθαι. 7. ὁ λογος ὁ ὑφ' ὑμων κηρυττομενος ἠκουετο ὑπο τουτου του πληθους ἱνα πιστευῃ τῳ Θεῳ. 8. οἰδατε ὁτι χρη τους καλουμενους ὑπο του κυριου ἡμων πεμπεσθαι εἰς το κοσμον ἱνα μαρτυρωσιν περι του φωτος.

The Greek world

Delphic utterances

Greeks are presented as a highly rational people. What then do we make of oracles, like the Delphic oracle? Rational people do not believe in them, surely?

Let us clear up two misconceptions. First, certain Greek thinkers were rational. That does not mean every Greek was. Second, whether you 'believe' in oracles depends on what you think oracles should be able to do. Our vision of oracles as an infallible means of foretelling the winner of the 3.30 at Gosforth Park may be appealing, but common sense tells us it cannot be right. Yet the Delphic oracle was enormously successful. Tens of thousands of Greeks consulted it over hundreds of years. If it was all a fraud, it is hard to believe it would have lasted so long.

We need to clear some ground. For example, one should distinguish between mythical and genuine oracles. Mythical oracles (e.g. predicting that Oedipus would kill his father and marry his other) tend to be fantastical and are just that: mythical (and fantastical). They are simply not the sort of oracle for which solid evidence survives. By far the majority of oracles for which we have such evidence (e.g. inscriptions recording them) are not asked to foretell the future but to give advice, mostly on religious matters, e.g. cult practices, which god to consult on any issue, ritual pollution and so on. Such questions were regularly posed by e.g. cities intending to set up a colony abroad. The oracle, then, is essentially a form of counselling service.

That some oracles did give advice about 'the future', however, is probably historically the case. But Greeks were well aware that gods could not be interpreted with 100% success by humans. After all, the response came from the god – Apollo – to his mèdium, the Pythia, whose reply was interpreted by priests, and might then need further interpretation still. The chances of misunderstanding were high. Greeks, reasonably, were not worried by a degree of ambiguity in response to a difficult question. Thus, when Socrates receives an oracle from Delphi (surely historical) that 'no one is wiser than Socrates' he is utterly baffled by it: it cannot be what the god means. So he sets out to interpret it.

No Greek, then, would have questioned the value of an oracle which gave a riddling answer. When the Greeks were told by the oracle to trust in their wooden walls against the Persians, and Themistocles said that meant, metaphorically, their ships, no one would have been worried in the slightest had Themistocles been proved wrong (see **The Greek world**, Chapter 10). What can you expect of humans trying to understand gods? The argument is as watertight today as it was then.

There is a wonderful story in Herodotus of the Lydian king Croesus deciding to check the validity of Greek oracles by sending to all of them and asking what he had done on a particular day at a particular time. He had in fact cut up a tortoise and a lamb and boiled them together in a bronze cauldron with a bronze lid. Delphi, naturally, got it right ...

Wordplay

Number crunching

Numbers 1-10 in Greek go: εἱς, δυο, τρεις, τετταρες, πεντε, ἑξ, ἑπτα, ὀκτω, ἑννεα, δεκα. The comparison with Latin is interesting: *unus, duo, tres, quattuor, quinque, sex, septem, octo, novem, decem*. Then take German, from which English derives: *ein, zwei, drei, vier, fünf, sechs, sieben, acht, neun, zehn*.

The obvious similarities between many of the numbers in the three languages cannot be coincidence. As we know, Greek, Latin and German do not derive from each other. So the reason for the connection must be that all three languages derive from a common source – known as Indo-European, because Sanskrit also joins in the fun (see **Wordplay**, Chapter 1).

But what about those numbers where there seem to be few similarities? Take, for example, Greek πεντε and Latin *quinque*. How can they be the same?

Well, at least they both have two syllables. But then look more closely. Greek has -εν- and Latin -*in*-, and both numbers end in *e*. The problem surely comes with Greek π and τ being represented by Latin *qu*. But when we examine other connections between Greek and Latin, this looks like a common link. Greek for 'who?' τίς, Latin for 'who?' *quis*; Greek for four τετταρες, Latin *quattuor*; Greek for 'and' τε, Latin *que*. Then take π: Greek 'I follow' ἑπομαι, Latin *sequor*; Greek 'I leave' λειπω, Latin *linquo* – and so on. In other words, πεντε and *quinque* are the same words, however different they may look at first sight.

One can play the same trick with ἑξ and ἑπτα, *sex* and *septem*. We immediately conclude that a rough breathing 'h' in Greek can become *s* in Latin – and indeed it can. We have already seen the phenomenon with ἑπομαι, Latin *sequor*. Now try Greek ἁλς, Latin *sal* (salt); Greek ἡμι-, Latin *semi*; Greek ὑς, Latin *sus* (pig), Greek ἑρπω, Latin *serpo* (I crawl), Greek ὑπερ, Latin *super*, etc.

Wonderful thing, language – and linguistics.

Answers
Exercise 1
ἀποφαινομαι, διαφαινομαι, προσφαινομαι, ἐκφαινομαι, ἀποιδα, διοιδα, προσοιδα, ἐξοιδα, ἀπερχομαι, διερχομαι, προσερχομαι, ἐξερχομαι, ἀπειδον, διειδον, προσειδον, ἐξειδον. προσαγαπαω, διακουω, ἐκπιστευω, διακελευω, ἐκμισεω, προσμαχομαι.

Exercise 2
διωκονται they are being pursued; ἀγομεθα we are being led; λεγεται it is being said; πεμπῃ you are being sent; κηρυττεσθε

you are being announced; κελευονται they are being ordered; ἀκουομεθα we are being heard; εὑρισκεται it is being found.

They are being sent, it is being made, I am being conquered, we are being loved, you are being wronged, they fight, he is being recognised, we are being said, they are being taught, it is being written, you reply, we are being kept, you are being loved, they are being seen, they travel, we are being sought.

πεμπεται, διδασκομεθα, λεγεται, διωκονται, κελευεσθε, κηρυττεται.

Exercise 3

ἐκελευετο he was being ordered; ἐκηρυττομεθα we were being announced; ἐδιωκομην or ἐδιωκοντο I/they were being pursued; ἐλεγεσθε you were being said; ἐδιδασκου you were being taught; ἐπεμπετο he was being sent.

He was being wronged by you; you were being sent by me; they were being loved by God; the book was being written by that apostle; we were being taught by those men/women; I was being sought by the women; the Greeks were being defeated by these non-Greeks; the word was being spoken by the disciples.

ἐκηρυττετο, ἐκελευομεθα, ἐδιδασκοντο, ἐμαχετο, ἐλεγοντο, ἐπεμπεσθε, ἠκουομην, ἐγιγνωσκομεθα, ἐπορευετο.

Exercise 4

κηρυττομενος η ον being announced, κελευομενος η ον being ordered, ἐχομενος η ον being had, λεγομενος η ον being said, γιγνωσκομενος η ον being known, γραφομενος η ον being written.

The men being pursued nom; the women being sent acc; of those being taught gen; the men being seen acc; to those being sought dat; the woman being hated acc; of the man being conquered gen; the man being loved acc.

Exercise 5

ἀγεσθαι to be led, διδασκεσθαι to be taught, ἀκουεσθαι to be heard, γραφεσθαι to be written, λεγεσθαι to be said.

To be conquered, to go, to be loved, to fight, to be hated, to be sought, to become, to be wronged, to reply, to be sent, to travel.

Exercise 6

1. Those non-Greeks, being pursued by these Greeks, departed in order that they might not be conquered. 2. My child did not wish to be taught by the father. 3. Those loving God were loved by God. 4. The apostles who were loved by God trusted in him.

5. It is necessary for these men to be guarded by us in order that they should not flee. 6. We wanted that book to be written by you. 7. The word which was announced by you was being heard by this mob in order that it might believe in God. 8. You know that those called by our lord must be sent into the world in order that they might witness concerning the light.

Afore ye go

- There should (*cough*) be nothing new to learn here. What is new is conceptual – being able to distinguish between verbs with active and passive forms, and therefore active and passive meanings (and remembering that middle verbs are unaffected by all this)
- Fine in theory. Make sure you know the form and meaning of the present passive indicative (**14c**), infinitive (**14f**) and participle (**14e**); and the form and meaning of the imperfect indicative passive (**14d**)

CHAPTER 15

Sacred and secular love

John 3.16-21

15a Time for some seriously healthy chunks of Greek to translate:

Note: ἠγαπησαν 'they loved'; ἠγαπησεν 'he loved'; κριν-ω 'I judge'; ἡ κρισ-ις 'the judgement'; πας ὁ + participle 'everyone -ing, everyone who -es'; το σκοτ-ος 'the darkness'.

οὑτως [so] γαρ ἠγαπησεν ὁ Θεος τον κοσμον, ὡστε [that] τον Υἱον τον μονογενη [only-begotten] ἐδωκεν [he gave], ἱνα πας ὁ πιστευων εἰς αὐτον μη ἀποληται [be destroyed] ἀλλ᾽ ἐχη [την] ζωην αἰωνιον [eternal]. οὐ γαρ ἀπεστειλεν [sent] ὁ Θεος τον Υἱον εἰς τον κοσμον ἱνα κρινη τον κοσμον, ἀλλ᾽ ἱνα σωθη [be saved] ὁ κοσμος δι᾽ αὐτου. ὁ πιστευων εἰς αὐτον οὐ κρινεται. ὁ μη πιστευων ἠδη [already] κεκριται [has been judged], ὁτι μη πεπιστευκεν [he has believed] εἰς το ὀνομα [name] του μονογενους Υἱου του Θεου. αὑτη δε ἐστιν ἡ κρισις, ὁτι το φως ἐληλυθεν [has come] εἰς τον κοσμον και ἠγαπησαν οἱ ἀνθρωποι μαλλον [rather] το σκοτος ἠ [than] το φως. ἠν γαρ αὐτων πονηρα [wicked] τα ἐργα. πας γαρ ὁ φαυλα [evil deeds acc.] πρασσων [doing] μισει το φως και οὐκ ἐρχεται προς το φως, ἱνα μη ἐλεγχθη [be judged] τα ἐργα αὐτου. ὁ δε ποιων την ἀληθειαν ἐρχεται προς το φως...

Poems from *The Greek Anthology*

15b Poetry! Hankies out? No, actually. *The Greek Anthology* is a collection of 'epigrams', short Greek poems composed between *c*. 650 BC and 900 AD. They cover a huge range of topics – from sex to parties, drink, education, politics (and even grammar). They are arch and clever.

They also scan. Mark the following basics of Greek scansion.

It all looks utter madness, but when you read the poems and see the help there, you will see what I am getting at:

1. In Greek, *every syllable* counts for the purpose of scansion: and a syllable will scan long or short – *tum* or *ti*. Thus παυω has two syllables, scanning *tum-tum*; φιλεω has three syllables scanning *ti-ti-tum*; φιλουμεν scans *ti-tum-ti*, etc.
2. In the metre of these poems, the longs and shorts form themselves into two shapes: the dactyl, long-short-short (*tum-ti-ti*), and spondee, long-long (*tum-tum*). Thus, in this metre, you will find assortments of *tum-ti-ti* and *tum-tum*.

Marking longs and shorts over Greek is the devil of a job. I have therefore underlined the longs. All others are short. Remember: count *every* syllable. You should bounce along, *tum-ti-ti*-ing and *tum-tum*-ing to your heart's delight, like cavalry galloping over a tin bridge.

Warning: just because I have marked a vowel long does not mean it was *pronounced* long. φιλος, for example, should I so mark it, would still be pronounced with a short 'o'. It is just 'long' for the sake of the metre. Think in terms of underlying rhythm rather than vowel-length.

Vocabulary (for all these poems)

Note: ἀληθης 'true'; δυναμαι 'I am able, I can' (dynamite); δυο 'two'; ὁ ἐρως (ἐρωτ-) 'passion, lust, love' (erotic); ἠν = ἐαν 'if'; ὁ θησαυρ-ος 'the treasure' (thesaurus); τα κακα 'evils'; ἡ Κυπρις (Κυπριδ-) 'Cypris, Venus, Love'; μεγας 'great' (mega); μον-ος 'sole, only' (mono-); ὁ πλουτ-ος 'the wealth' (plutocrat); το πυρ 'the fire' (pyre); ὁ φιλ-ος 'friend'; ἡ ψυχ-η 'the soul, spirit, life' (psychology).

5.50 The Fire of Love

Here is a simple paraphrase: δυο κακα ἐστι μοι – ἡ πενιη (poverty) και ὁ ἐρως. οἰσω (I shall endure) το μεν (the one) κουφως (easily); οὐ δυναμαι φερειν το πυρ της Κυπριδος. Now for the Greek:

καὶ πενίη [poverty] καὶ ἐρῶς δυο μοι κακα. καὶ το μεν οἰσω
κουφῶς, πυρ δε φερειν Κυπριδος οὐ δυναμαι.

Scan: Tum ti ti, tum ti ti, tum ti ti, tum ti ti, tum ti ti, tum-tum
Tum-tum, tum-ti-ti, tum/tum-ti-ti, tum-ti-ti/tum.

12.60 Theron, my all

Paraphrase: ἐαν [=ἠν] εἰσορω [ἐσιδω] τον Θηρωνα, τα παντα
[everything, acc. pl) ὁρω. ἐαν δε τα παντα ὁρω [=βλεψω], ἀλλα
μη τον Θηρωνα [τονδε=τουτον], τἀμπαλιν [again] οὐδεν ὁρω.

> ἠν ἐσιδω Θηρωνα, τα πανθ᾽ ὁρω. ἠν δε τα παντα
> βλεψω, τονδε δε μη, τἀμπαλιν οὐδεν ὁρω.

Scan: Tum-ti-ti, tum-tum, tum-ti-ti, tum-ti-ti, tum-ti-ti, tum-tum
Tum-tum, tum-ti-ti, tum/tum-ti-ti, tum-ti-ti/tum.

12.103 On friends and enemies

It was a commonplace of Greek thought that one helped one's
friends and harmed one's enemies.

Paraphrase: οἰδα [+ infinitive, = 'know how to'] φιλειν τους
φιλουντας [φιλεοντας is the uncontracted form]. οἰδα [=
ἐπισταμαι, cf. epistemology], ἐαν τις με ἀδικη, μισειν. εἰμι γαρ
οὐκ ἀδαης [inexperienced in] ἀμφοτερων [both].

> οἰδα φιλειν φιλεοντας. ἐπισταμαι, ἠν μ᾽ ἀδικη τις,
> μισειν. ἀμφοτερων εἰμι γαρ οὐκ ἀδαης.

Scan: tum-ti-ti, tum-ti-ti, tum-ti-ti, tum-ti-ti, tum-ti-ti, tum-tum
Tum-tum, tum-ti-ti, tum/ tum-ti-ti, tum-ti-ti/tum.

More on friends:

10. 39 θησαυρος μεγας ἐστ᾽ ἀγαθος φιλος.
10.117 γνησιος [true] εἰμι φιλος, και τον φιλον ὡς [as] φιλον οἰδα.

10.41 True wealth

πλοῦτος ὁ τῆς ψυχῆς πλοῦτος μονος ἐστιν ἀληθης.

Notice, incidentally, anything about the patterns of the above metres?

(i) The long line has six feet (hence, *hexameter*). The first four feet can be any mixture of *tum-ti-ti* and *tum-tum*; the last two are always *tum-ti-ti tum-tum* in that order.

(ii) The second, shorter line has the first two feet dactyl or spondee, then one syllable; the second two feet are always two dactyls *tum-ti-ti tum-ti-ti*, then one syllable.

Two times two-and-a-half = five. Hence *pentameter*.

Hexameter + pentameter = elegiac couplet. *So* romantic.

Adjectives

15c Adjectives describe things: they are words like 'good, bad, indifferent, great, brill, fab' and so on. If the thing they describe is acc. m. *s*, say, the adjective will be acc. m. *s*; if the things are dat f. *pl*, the adjective too will be dat f. *pl*.

In other words, an adjective has to be all things to all men, women and neuters – so it must have male, female and neuter forms, in all cases, singular and plural. And lo, it does. Think of Def Art. That is an adjective. It has male, female and neuter forms, in all cases, singular and plural.

But how do these adjective wossits decline? Very many of them decline almost exactly like Def Art. Think of our old chum ἐκειν-ος at **13e**. He is the model for a vast range of adjectives, of which we take καλ-ος η ον 'fine, beautiful, good' as typical. Note the three forms quoted: the first m., the second f., the third n. Now direct the mighty 20-20 vision at the following paying, as ever, close attention to the end of the word:

	καλ-ος	καλ-η	καλ-ον
	M	F	N
Singular			
Nom.	καλ-ος	καλ-η	καλ-ον
Acc.	καλ-ον	καλ-ην	καλ-ον
Gen.	καλ-ου	καλ-ης	καλ-ου

Dat. καλ-ῳ   καλ-ῃ   καλ-ῳ
Plural
Nom. καλ-οι   καλ-αι   καλ-α
Acc. καλ-ους   καλ-ας   καλ-α
Gen. καλ-ων   καλ-ων   καλ-ων
Dat. καλ-οις   καλ-αις   καλ-οις

15d See? Almost identical to Def Art and ἐκεινος. On precisely the same pattern you will find: ἀγαθ-ος η ον 'good'; κακ-ος η ον 'bad, evil'; φιλ-ος η ον 'dear, friendly'.

As you would expect, add some form of Def Art to any of these, and you have 'the one who is, the X person', e.g. ὁ φιλος 'the friend', οἱ ἀγαθοι 'good people/men', ἡ καλη 'the beautiful woman', το καλον 'the beautiful thing', 'the good', 'the fine' (as an abstract concept); τα καλα 'good/fine things' (on these neuters see further below).

Note: adjectives whose stem ends in ι- or ρ- or ε- e.g. δικαι-ος 'just' and πονηρ-ος 'wicked', replace η with α in the f. *s*, e.g. δικαι-α δικαι-αν δικαι-ας δικαι-ᾳ.

Vocabulary

Record: ἡ ἀδικι-α 'the injustice, crime'; ἀπαγ-ω 'I arrest'; βοα-ω 'I shout'; δηλ-ος η ον 'clear, evident'; δικαι-ος α ον 'just, lawful, right'; ἡ δικ-η 'the judgement, trial'; ζα-ω 'I live'; ὁ θανατ-ος 'the death' (euthanasia); καθευδ-ω 'I sleep'; μον-ος η ον 'sole, alone'; ὁ νομ-ος 'the law' (economy); ὁ παις (παιδ-) 'the child' (paediatrics); πραττ-ω 'I make, do, act, fare'; ῥᾳδι-ος α ον 'easy'; φιλ-ος η ον 'dear, (be)loved, friendly, one's own' (-phile); φοβε-ομαι 'I fear' (phobia).

Note
• ζαω 'I live' conjugates in the present: ζω ζῃς ζῃ ζωμεν ζητε ζωσι(ν); infinitive 'to live' ζην

Neuters

15e Sniff at the following:
δηλον ἐστιν ἡμιν ὁτι ὁ ἀνηρ φευγει 'it is clear to us that the man is fleeing'

149

CHAPTER 15

οὐ ῥᾳδιον ἐστι μοι καθευδειν 'it is not easy for me to sleep'
φιλον ἦν σοι ταυτα πραττειν 'it was dear to you to do these
things'

Why 'it'? Answer: because the adjectives δηλον, ῥᾳδιον and
φιλον are *neuter*. Watch out for this very common usage.
Also inspect the following:

δικαια πραττω 'I do just things', 'I act justly'
καλον λεγω 'I speak finely'
ὁ Σωκρατης το δικαιον και το καλον φιλει 'Socrates loves
   justice and beauty'
το καλον φιλον ἐστι, το δ' οὐ καλον οὐ φιλον ἐστιν 'virtue
   (moral beauty) is dear, the not-virtue is not dear', 'virtue
   is precious, its opposite is not'
το καλον ἐστιν ἀγαθον 'virtue/the fine is good'

Neuter adjectives, then, have a range of possibilities:

(i)   with Def Art, they turn the adjective into a noun, e.g. το
      δικαιον 'justice'
(ii) on their own, they can act as adverbs ('-ly'), e.g. δικαια
      'justly'

Exercise 1

Translate: 1. ἀρα δηλον ἐστιν ὁτι ἡ ἐντολη των θεων δικαια ἦν;
2. δηλον ἐστιν ὁτι μονοι οἱ του Θεου νομοι δικαιοι ἦσαν. 3.
την οὖν των ἀνδρων ἀδικιαν οὐ φοβουμαι, ἀλλα την των θεων
δικην· το γαρ δικαιον φιλον ἐστι τοις θεοις. 4. [τα] δικαια οὖν
πραττειν ἐβουλοντο οὑτοι οἱ ἀνδρες· ταυτα γαρ πραττοντες τον
θανατον οὐκ ἐφοβουντο. 5. δηλον ἐστιν ἡμιν ὁτι οὐκ ἦν ῥᾳδιον
την των θεων δικην φευγειν. 6. οἱ μεν τον ἀνδρα διωκοντες
αὐτον ἀπαγειν ἠθελον, ὁ δε ἐφευγε βοων ὁτι δικαιον οὐκ ἐστιν·
ἐφοβειτο γαρ τον θανατον. 7. οὐκ ἐστι ῥᾳδιον ὑμιν [τα] δικαια
πραττειν· οὐ γαρ βουλεσθε ἀπαγεσθαι ὑπο τουτων των κακων
ἀνδρων. 8. οὐκ ἦν ῥᾳδιον τω παιδι καθευδειν· ἐβοων γαρ οἱ
ἀνδρες. 9. εἰπέ μοι, τί ζῃς; τί βουλη ζην; οὐ γαρ δικαια
πραττεις. 10. φιλον ἐστιν δικαια πραττειν, φιλον οὐκ ἐστι
κακα πραττειν. 11. ἐγω μεν ζω το ἀγαθον φιλων, συ δε ζῃς

150

κακα πραττων. 12. μη καθευδε· δει γαρ σε, δικαια πραττοντα, ἀπαγειν τον ἀνδρα. 13. μη βοα, ὠ ἀνθρωπε· καθευδειν γαρ βουλεται ὁ παις ὁ ἐν τῳ οἰκῳ ὠν. 14. ὁ ἀγαθος και δικαιος ὠν οὐ πειθεται τῳ κακῳ ὀντι. 15. [Sappho] ἐστι μοι καλη παις...Κλεις ἀγαπατα (beloved). 16. [Sappho] παρα (along, by) δ᾽ ἐρχετ(αι) (ἡ) ὡρα, ἐγω δε μονη καθευδω. 17. [Euripides: Alcestis, who has agreed to die for her husband, leaves her children] Ὠ τεκν᾽, ὀτε ζην χρη μ᾽, ἀπ-ερχομαι κατω (below).

The Greek world

Periclean Athens

The most important statement about what the Athenian empire meant to Athens was made by Pericles in his famous 'Funeral Speech', commemorating those who had died in battle in 431 BC, and recorded (or rather, interpreted?) for us by the historian Thucydides. Here are some extracts from it:

'Our constitution does not copy the laws of neighbouring states; we are rather a pattern to others than imitators ourselves. Our administration favours the many instead of the few; this is why it is called democracy. As for our laws, they afford equal justice to all in their private differences; as for social standing, advancement in public life falls to reputation for capacity, class considerations not being allowed to interfere with merit. Nor again does poverty bar the way: if a man is able to serve the state, he is not hindered by the obscurity of his condition ....

We cultivate refinement without extravagance and knowledge without effeminacy; wealth we employ more for use than show, and place the real disgrace of poverty not in owning to the fact but in declining to struggle against it. Our public men have, besides politics, their private affairs to attend to, and our ordinary citizens, though occupied with the pursuits of work, are still fair judges of public matters; for, unlike other nations, we regard him who takes no part in these duties not as unambitious but as useless. We Athenians are able to judge or reflect on events correctly, and instead of looking on discussion as a stumbling-block to action, we think it an indispensable preliminary to any wise action at all.

In short, I say that as a city we are the school of Hellas; while

I doubt if the world can produce a man who, where he has only himself to depend on, is equal to many emergencies and graced by so happy a versatility, as the Athenian ... the admiration of present and succeeding ages will be ours, since we have not left our power without a witness, but have show it by mighty proofs; and far from needing a Homer for our panegyrist, or other of his craft whose verses might charm for the moment only for the impression which they gave to melt at the touch of fact, we have forced every sea and land to be the highway of our daring, and everywhere, whether for evil or good, have left imperishable monuments behind us.'
(Richard Crawley, modified)

Wordplay

From halves to half-wits

Some more useful number words. ἡμι- is the Greek prefix meaning 'half': thus ἡμισφαιριον, ἡμιθεος, a demigod, ἡμιανθρωπος, a half-man, ἡμιμεθης, half drunk, and so on. μονος means 'single' – whence mono-cycle, monotone, etc. – and πρωτος means 'first', whence proton, protein (πρωτειος, of the first quality), prototype, protocol (πρωτοκολλον, the first 'page', κολλημα, of a papyrus-roll).

δις/δι- 'twice' gives e.g. diode, dioxide, cf. διχα 'in two' (dichotomy, τομος 'cut'). δευτερος means 'second' (Deuteronomy, deuterium, the second heaviest hydrogen isotope) and τρι- and τριτος 'third', 'tripod' (τριπους (tripod-), tricycle, τριπολις, a league of three cities, cf. Tripoli). τετρα- 'four times' gives e.g. tetrahedron, tetraethyl.

Moving up the scale, ἑκατον is Greek for 100 (ἑκατομπεδος 'a hundred feet long'), often shortened to 'hect-', as in hectare, hectolitre; and χιλιοι means 1000, whence kilo-.

And on a completely different tack, try ἰδιος. English 'idiot', of course, but the Greek means 'private, personal, one's own, peculiar' – keeping oneself to oneself. In the highly politicised world of ancient Athens, anyone who was an ἰδιος and kept himself to himself was regarded as rather odd (see what Pericles says above about those who take no part in public life). The whole point of living was to engage with others, especially politically, to work up friends and make alliances. An idiograph is a signature. 'Idiosyncrasy' is the mixing (κρασ-) together (συν) of personal traits.

Meaning 'one's own' in a different sense is φιλος. This is etymologically connected with Latin *suus*, 'one's own'. φιλος (verb φιλεω) is usually translated 'dear, friendly', but it means 'dear' in the sense that one loves what is one's own, and makes common cause with one's own, i.e. one's friends, φιλοι. The antonym of φιλος is ἐχθρος, 'personal enemy', and that is the point. Greeks divided their acquaintances into φιλοι and ἐχθροι, and did all in their power to help the one and harm the other – as you have seen from the poems in this chapter. 'Love' and 'dear' and 'friendly' do not quite catch that sharp sense of personal alliance with those who can benefit you.

Answers

John 3.16-21: consult your New Testament.

The Greek Anthology: 5.50 Both poverty and passion are two evils for me. I shall endure the one easily; I cannot endure the fire of Cypris. 12.60 If I see Theron, I see everything. If I see everything, but not him, again I see nothing. 12.103 I know how to love those who love [me]. I know, if someone wrongs me, how to hate. For I am not inexperienced in both. 10.39 A good friend is a great treasure. 10.117 I am a true friend, and I know a friend as a friend. 10.41 Wealth of the soul is the only true wealth.

Exercise 1

1. Is it clear that the command of the gods was just? 2. It is clear that only the laws of God were just. 3. Therefore I do not fear the injustice of men, but the judgement of the gods: for justice is dear to the gods. 4. Therefore these men were wishing to act justly: for doing these things, they did not fear death. 5. It is clear to us that it was not easy to flee the judgement of the gods. 6. Those pursuing the man wanted to arrest him, but he fled, shouting that it was not just: for he feared death. 7. It is not easy for you to act justly: for you do not wish to be arrested by these evil men. 8. It was not easy for the child to sleep: for the men were shouting. 9. Tell me, why do you live? Why do you want to live? For you do not act justly. 10. It is friendly to act justly, it is not friendly to do evil. 11. I live loving the good, but you live doing evil. 12. Do not sleep: for it is necessary for you, acting justly, to arrest the man. 13. Do not shout, fellow: for the child

153

who is in the house wishes to sleep. 14. The man who is good and
just does not trust the man who is evil. 15. I have a beautiful
child ...beloved Kleis. 16. The hour goes by, but I sleep alone. 17.
Children, when it is necessary for me to live, I go off below.

Afore ye go

- There is a lot of new, important vocabulary here. Make
  certain you master the sixteen words in the vocabulary section
- The adjective formation at **15c** should not be difficult, but the
  use of the neuter adjective at **15e** (turning adjectives into
  concepts, e.g. 'the good' or adverbs, e.g. 'justly') is very common in Greek

CHAPTER 16

Last tense moments

16a By way of revision. We have already met:

(i) the present tense active/middle ('I am -ing', like παυ-ω
(**2a**) and ἐρχ-ομαι (**5a**)) and passive ('I am being -ed' like
παυ-ομαι (**14c**));

(ii) the imperfect tense active/middle ('I was -ing', like ἐ-παυ-
ον (**12b**) and ἐ-πορευ-ομην (**12f**)) and passive ('I was
being -ed' like ἐ-παυ-ομην (**14d**));

(iii) and an oddball assortment of aorists active/middle ('I
-ed') which we have treated as one-offs (like ἠλθ-ον, εἰδ-
ον, εἰπ-ον, ηὑρ-ον (**9e**), ἀφικ-ομην, ἐγεν-ομην, ἠρ-ομην,
ἐπυθ-ομην (**10b**)).

Now extract the magnifying glass, smoothly nudge the brain
into overdrive, and submit the following to an intensive Einste-
inian analysis:

1. From παυ-ω:	ἐ-παυ-σ-α	'I stopped'
2. From ἀκου-ω:	ἠ-κου-σ-α	'I heard'
3. From λεγ-ω:	ἐ-λεξ-α (= ἐ-λεγ-σ-α)	'I said'
4. From φιλ-ε-ω:	ἐ-φιλ-η-σ-α	'I loved'
5. From ἀγαπ-α-ω:	ἠ-γαπ-η-σ-α	'I loved'

Your conclusions? Hmm.

(i) We have the initial augment ἐ- (see 1) or a lengthened
first vowel (see 2, 5). We are therefore dealing with a
past tense. Correct.

(ii) The translations ('I -ed', see all) suggest it is this aorist
thingy. Correct.

(iii) After the stem we have a σ (correct, 1 and 2) which can
combine with a consonant to form a new letter (see 3,
λεγ – λεγσ – λεξ). Correct.

155

(iv) Contract verbs lengthen the contract vowel (α/ε – η) before the σ. Correct (4, 5).

(v) And finally, the 1*s* 'I' ends in α. Correct.

The aorist

16b Excellent. A model answer. Gallop to the top of the class. This is none other than (fanfare of trumpets) the usual formation of the aorist indicative active, or plain past, 'I -ed'. Here it is in all its naked splendour:

Aorist indicative active of παυ-ω 'I stop'

1*s*	ἐ-παυσ-α	'I stopped'
2*s*	ἐ-παυσ-ας	'you stopped'
3*s*	ἐ-παυσ-ε(ν)	'he, she, it stopped'
1*pl*	ἐ-παυσ-αμεν	'we stopped'
2*pl*	ἐ-παυσ-ατε	'you stopped'
3*pl*	ἐ-παυσ-αν	'they stopped'

Notes
- The key to the regular aorist is (a) augment (b) stem in -σ-α. Look out for delicious added σα! You know it makes σα-nse!
- Observe what *regularly* happens to verbs ending in consonants like the following when they form the aorist:

γραφ-ω	ἐγραφσ-	= ἐγραψ-α	'I wrote'
πεμπ-ω	ἐπεμπσ-	= ἐπεμψ-α	'I sent'
διδασκ-ω	ἐδιδασκσ-	= ἐδιδαξ-α	'I taught'
διωκ-ω	ἐδιωκσ-	= ἐδιωξ-α	'I chased'
λεγ-ω	ἐλεγσ-	= ἐλεξ-α	'I said'
κηρυττ-ω	ἐκηρυττσ-	= ἐκηρυξ-α	'I announced'
πραττ-ω	ἐπραττσ-	= ἐπραξ-α	'I did, acted, fared'

- Make a special note of the following irregular aorists:
  μενω ἐμειν-α 'I waited' (α, but no yummy σ)
  ἐθελω ἠθελησ-α 'I wished, wanted'
- Remember: those non-σα aorists we have met already (see **16a**(iii)) are to be treated as special cases, having nothing to do with our nice σα aorists *as far as formation goes*. The non-σα's form one way: the σα's form the other. *Vive la différence.*

Exercise 1

Translate: ἐμισησαν, ἐπιστευσε, ἐποιησαμεν, ἠδικησας, ἐπεμψαν, ἐτηρησεν, ἐπραξε, ἠγαπησαν, ἐζητησα, ἐγραψατε, ἐλαλησαμεν, ἐμεινε, ὡμολογησα, ἐνικησαν, ἐκηρυξαμεν, ἠθελησας, ἐλεξαν, ἐβοησας.

Translate (plain -σα verbs): I ordered, we stopped, they had faith, you (s) stopped, he ordered, you (pl) had faith.

Translate (contract verbs: lengthen contract vowel + σ-α): he loved (two different verbs), we hated, you (s) sought, they conquered, he made, they shouted.

Translate (requiring change of consonant – check *Notes* above): they taught, he chased, I announced, we waited, you (pl) sent, she wrote, he wished, they fared.

Infinite riches

16c Aorists also have their own aorist infinitives. Eye the following beadily:

παυσ-αι	'to stop'
ἀκουσ-αι	'to hear'
ἀγαπησ-αι	'to love'
γραψ-αι	'to write'
πεμψ-αι	'to send'
διωξ-αι	'to pursue'
πραξ-αι	'to do, fare'

16d What is happening? Two things, the first of very great importance indeed, namely, viz., i.e. and to wit:
(i) the disappearance of nice augment. Look! Not ἐπαυσ- but plain παυσ-; not ἠκουσ- but plain ἀκουσ-, and so on.
(ii) in order to form the aorist infinitive active, as well as removing nice augment, we have to add vitamin-packed -ι to the aorist stem σα (or whatever form it takes – ψα-, ξα- etc.,) making -σαι (-ψαι, -ξαι, etc.).
But what does it all mean? We thought e.g. the present infinitive παυ-ειν meant 'to stop'. How come the aorist infinitive παυσαι means 'to stop' as well?

157

What the aorist infinitive means

16e Well, (cough), I could say 'who cares?' See an infinitive, present or aorist, translate it 'to –', and go on your way whistling a happy tune. But we are ancient Greeks. We have an unquenchable curiosity. Right.

It's all a matter of aspect. Pretend you are an ancient Greek. You are learning English. You find that παυω means 'I stop, I am stopping, I do stop'. You would be justified in saying 'Oi, look, squire, παυω does us perfectly well in Greek. Why does English need three forms of the present?'

Well, we would reply, thinking fast, it's all a matter of um aspect – the way you *look* at the action: the simple fact expressed in 'I stop', the sense of the action going on or continuing in 'I am stopping', and the abruptly emphatic 'I do stop'.

So with the present and aorist infinitive in Greek. The present infinitive suggests something going on (the Greek would probably use it to translate e.g. I order you *to obey* your father at all times); the aorist infinitive something happening just once (I order you *to close* the door, now, pronto, smartish).

Thus, to exaggerate somewhat: βουλομαι φιλειν σε means 'I wish to keep on loving you the whole night throu-ou-ough'; βουλομαι φιλησαι σε means 'how about a quick peck?'

But for our purposes, we can just translate present and aorist infinitives as 'to – ' and that's it.

Exercise 2

Translate (mixed aorist infinitives and aorist indicatives! Ouch):
λαλησαι, κελευσαι, ἐκελευσα, τηρησαι, ἀγαπησαι, ἠγαπησας, ἀκουσαι, ἐγραψαν, διωξαι, ἐβοησαμεν, ζητησαι, ἐζητησε, ἐπραξας, μειναι, κηρυξαι, ἠδικησεν.

Translate (mixed aorist indicatives and imperfect indicatives! Ooooh): ἠκουες, ἠγαπας, ἠκουσας, ἠγαπησας, ἠδικησαν, ἠθελεν, ἐλεγον, εἰπον, ἐκαλουμεν, ἐνικων, ἐνικησατε, ἐκελευεν, ἐκελευσεν, ἐπεμψαν, ηὑρον.

The sheep and the dog

The women of the household are complaining to their master

Aristarchus that while they work hard, he does nothing to earn his bread. Socrates suggests he tell them the story of the sheep and the dog – the sheep complaining that they supply wool, lambs and cheese, but have to feed themselves, while dog, who supplies nothing, gets fed – and its moral.

Vocabulary

ὁ κυων κυν- 'the dog'; ὁτε 'when'; φωνηεντ- 'able to speak'; το ζῳ-ον 'animal'; ἡ οἰς 'the sheep'; ὁ δεσποτ-ης 'master'; τα ἐρια 'the wool'; ὁ ἀρν- 'the lamb'; ὁ τυρ-ος 'the cheese'; διδως 'you give'; ὁς 'who'; παρεχ-ω 'I provide'; παντα 'everything'; ναι μα Δια 'yes, by Zeus'; σωζ-ω 'I keep safe, protect, save'; οὐτε ... οὐθ' 'neither ... nor'; κλεπτ-ω 'I steal'; ὁ λυκ-ος 'the wolf'; ἁρπαζ-ω 'I seize'; ἀσφαλως 'in safety'; νεμ-ομαι 'I feed'; τα προβατ-α 'the sheep'.

και ὁ Σωκρατης ἐλεξεν· Οὐ λεγεις αὐταις τον του κυνος λογον; ὁτε φωνηεντα ἠν τα ζῳα, ἡ οἰς προς τον δεσποτην εἰπεν·

Ἡμεις μεν τα ἐρια και τους ἀρνας και τον τυρον σοι παρεχομεν, συ δε ἡμιν οὐδεν διδως· ἀλλα τῳ κυνι, ὁς οὐδεν σοι παρεχει, διδως παντα.

ὁ κυων οὐν ἠκουσε και ἐλεξε·

Ναι μα Δια· ἐγω γαρ εἰμι ὁ ὑμας σωζων. ὑμεις οὐν οὐτε ὑπ' ἀνθρωπων κλεπτεσθε οὐθ' ὑπο λυκων ἁρπεσθε, ἀλλα ἀσφαλως νεμεσθε και οὐδεν φοβεισθε.

οὑτος οὐν ἠν ὁ λογος ὁ λεγομενος ὑπο του κυνος· τα δε προβατα ἠκουσε και ὡμολογησεν. και συ, ὠ Ἀρισταρχε, ἐκειναις λεγε, ὁτι συ τηρεις αὐτας και οὐκ ἀδικουνται και ἀσφαλως ζωσιν, τηρουμεναι ὑπο σου.

Adapted from Xenophon, *Memorabilia*, Book 2, 7.

The Greek world

The Peloponnesian War

In 431 BC, the inevitable happened: Athens came into conflict with its most powerful rival, Sparta. As the Athenian historian Thucydides says in his brilliant account of the war, it was 'the growth of Athenian power and the fear which this caused in

Sparta' that triggered it. The Peloponnesian War, as it is known, lasted 27 years. Concerned by the legendary might of the Spartan army, Athens withdrew its people from all over Attica within the city's insurmountable long walls. When a plague immediately hit Athens, removing a third of its inhabitants including Pericles, the suffering was terrible. But the walls went down to the sea, and Athens' fleet was invincible. No matter what the Spartans did by way of ravaging the countryside round about, the fleet both kept the city supplied and maintained the pressure on Sparta's allies.

A brief truce was declared in 421 BC, but war soon broke out again, and in 415 BC Athens launched an expedition to take resource-rich Sicily. It ended in disaster in 413 BC, the Athenian fleet completely wiped out. Athens rallied bravely, but surrendered in 404 BC. Their walls were destroyed, and the democracy replaced with a vicious oligarchy, known as the Thirty Tyrants (Plato's relation Critias was its leader).

The oligarchy in fact did not last long, and in 403 BC a slightly modified democracy was restored. But things were stirring in the north. Philip of Macedon, in expansionist mood, and with an invincible army at his back armed with vicious 19 foot long pikes, was looking to move south. The orator-politician Demosthenes attempted to rally the ever-squabbling Greek states against him, to no avail. In 338 BC Philip was master of Greece. He was assassinated in 336 BC (and buried in a magnificent tumulus discovered only in the 1970s). His son was Alexander the Great, whose even more expansionist plans for empire-building took him as far east as India, before he returned to die in Babylon (modern Iraq) in 323 BC, his plans for conquering the west still brewing.

Wordplay

Delphic maxims

On the temple of Apollo at Delphi were carved three Greek maxims. Two are very famous indeed: γνωθι σεαυτον, 'know yourself' (γνωθι is an imperative form of γιγνωσκω and you will recognise σε 'you': αὐτον here means 'self') and μηδεν ἀγαν 'nothing in excess' (for μηδεν, cf. οὐδεν).

To know oneself was to know what one could and could not

"But it could be argued, in a manner of speaking, that, after all, and not to make too much of a point of it, one could perhaps hazard a guess. . ."

do. It was to acknowledge one was human, to stay within normal, human limits. μηδεν ἀγαν preached the same message. Only gods could go to excess. If humans did, disaster would surely follow. Since Greeks were, as we have seen, a fiercely competitive people, sanctions of this sort were needed if society was not to tear itself apart. Greeks were constantly preaching σωφροσυνη – 'moderation, prudence, temperance, discipline, chastity', the very opposite of the 'harm your enemy' ethos so commonly expressed in Greek literature. But in a world where everyone wanted to be top of the squash ladder, there had to be moral constraints.

One sort of behaviour which invited disaster was ὑβρις. This is commonly taken to mean 'pride', but its basic meaning is 'physical assault' and its developed meaning 'the desire to humiliate'. No Greek could take humiliation. Nor could any god – especially from a human grown to think himself equal to a god.

The third, forgotten saying on the temple of Apollo, by the way, was ἐγγυη· παρα δ᾽ ἀτα, 'a pledge/bond: alongside [goes] disaster'. Work that one out.

Answers
Exercise 1
They hated, he had faith, we made, you wronged, they sent, he kept, he did, they loved, I sought, you wrote, we talked, he waited, I agreed, they conquered, we announced, you wished, they said, you shouted.

ἐκελευσα, ἐπαυσαμεν, ἐπιστευσαν, ἐπαυσας, ἐκελευσε, ἐπιστευσατε.

ἠγαπησε/ἐφιλησε, ἐμισησαμεν, ἐζητησας, ἐνικησαν, ἐποιησε, ἐβοησαν.

ἐδιδαξαν, ἐδιωξε, ἐκηρυξα, ἐμειναμεν, ἐπεμψατε, ἐγραψε, ἠθελησε, ἐπραξαν.

Exercise 2
To speak, to order, I ordered, to keep, to love, you loved, to hear, they wrote, to pursue, we shouted, to seek, he sought, you did, to wait, to announce, he wronged.

You were hearing, you were loving, you heard, you loved, they wronged, he was wishing, I/they were saying, I/they said, we were calling, I/they were conquering, you conquered, he was ordering, he ordered, they sent, I/they found.

The sheep and the dog

And Socrates said 'Do you not tell them the story of the dog? When animals could speak, the sheep said to the master "We provide wool and lambs and cheese for you, but you give us nothing. But to the dog, who provides nothing for you, you give everything."

'The dog therefore heard and said "Yes, by Zeus. For I am the one that keeps you safe. You therefore are not stolen by men nor are you seized by wolves, but you feed safely and you fear nothing."

'This therefore was the story spoken by the dog. The sheep heard and agreed. You too, Aristarchus, say to the women that you guard them and they are not harmed and live safely, being guarded by you.'

Afore ye go

- Aorists, aorists, aorists – doncha love 'em? It would be wise to. Note in particular that the σα aorists are the standard. Those non-standard, non-σα, aorists we have already met (**16a**(iii)) are the oddballs.

CHAPTER 17

Mass participlation

17a So, as we saw last time, aorist indicative actives have infinitives. Well, I never. Do they by any chance have participles as well? Sure do: with delicious added σα as you would expect.

Remember those li'l ol' present participles active – like ὁ μενων 'the male waiting', ἡ μενουσα 'the female waiting', οἱ μενοντες 'the males waiting' and so on? Nope? Don't blame you one little bit. It was all a thousand years ago back at **3c** and **6c**.

Anyway, when you've checked **6c** take a look at the aorist participles active. As you see, you take (yawn) the aorist stem (no augment but yummy σα) and:

Masculine
ὁ παυσ-ας   'the man stopping' (subject)
τον παυσ-αντ-α   'the man stopping' (object)

So παυσας, stem παυσαντ- gives us the m. forms of the aorist participle 'stopping'. On the same pattern, we can construct e.g.

ἀκουσας, ἀκουσαντ-   'hearing'
ἀγαπησας, ἀγαπησαντ- 'loving'
γραψας, γραψαντ-   'writing'

Feminine
ἡ παυσασ-α   'the woman stopping' (subject)
την παυσασ-αν   'the woman stopping' (object)

So παυσασ-α, stem παυσασ- gives us the f. forms. Compare e.g.

ἀκουσασ-α   'hearing'
ἀγαπησασ-α   'loving'
γραψασ-α   'writing'

Notes

• As with the infinitives, the distinction between present and aorist participles is one of aspect (**16e**): present indicating continuity, aorist indicating that it just happened. Observe:

ἡ φιλουσα με 'the woman who keeps on loving me'
ἡ φιλησασα με 'she who gives me a quick peck'

• That said, the aorist participle does often shade into meaning 'having -ed'. Thus:

φιλησασα με ἀπηλθεν 'having kissed me, she went off'

But if you were to say in English 'kissing me, she went off' it would be perfectly acceptable. For all forms, see **Grammatical Summary 23**.

Exercise 1

Define the case and translate, e.g. των παυσαντων gen. pl., 'of the men stopping': τον διωξαντα, τας πεμψασας, των κηρυξαντων, τοις λεξασι, οἱ φιλησαντες, τῳ λαλησαντι, της ἀδικησασης, ταις πιστευσασαις, ὁ μεινας, τους ζητησαντας, οἱ βοησαντες.

Translate: 1. οἱ οὖν ἀποστολοι, λεξαντες τον λογον τον του κυριου, εἰς τον οἰκον ἀφικοντο. 2. δει γαρ τουτους τους ἀνδρας, διωξαντας ἐκεινην την γυναικα, ἀπαγειν αὐτην. 3. ὁ Σωκρατης ἐκελευσεν ἡμας, δικαια πραξαντας, τον θανατον μη φοβεισθαι. 4. αἱ μεν διδαξασαι ἐκεινους τους παιδας ἐκαθευδον, αἱ δε ἀπηλθον προς την πολιν. 5. οἱ Ἑλληνες ἐβουλοντο πειθεσθαι τοις την πολιν και τους νομους ἀδικησασιν. 6. οἱ τους ἀνδρας τηρησαντες ἐκαθευδον. 7. δει αὐτους, γραψαντας τουτο το βιβλιον, κηρυξαι τῳ κοσμῳ τον του κυριου λογον. 8. δικαιοι ἠσαν οἱ νομοι οἱ των πιστευσαντων εἰς τον κυριον. 9. δει ὑμας ἀκουσαι και, ἀκουσαντας, πειθεσθαι. 10. τί δει με δικαια πραξαι; οὐ γαρ βουλομαι ζην. ἐαν γαρ τις ζην βουληται, δει αὐτον τοις νομοις πειθεσθαι.

Middle and off

17b OK, the last hurdle. Yes, there are active aorist indicatives, infinitives and participles. And yes, you have guessed it in one. There are middle ones too.

For the last time, therefore, eyes down for a full house of aorist middles. And no odds are being taken on whether they have augments and super protein-enriched σα. Of course they do.

Hint: take at peek at **12f** first to raise the spirits.

Aorist indicative middle of πορευ-ομαι 'I travel'

1s	ἐ-πορευσ-<u>αμ</u>ην	'I travelled'
2s	ἐ-πορευ<u>σ</u>-ω	'you travelled'
3s	ἐ-πορευ<u>σ</u>-ατο	'he, she, it travelled'
1pl	ἐ-πορευ<u>σ</u>-<u>αμ</u>εθα	'we travelled'
2pl	ἐ-πορευ<u>σ</u>-ασθε	'you travelled'
3pl	ἐ-πορευ<u>σ</u>-αντο	'they travelled'

So e.g. εὐχομαι 'I pray' ηὐ<u>ξ</u>-<u>αμ</u>ην 'I prayed'; φοβε-ομαι 'I fear', ἐφοβ-η-<u>σ-αμ</u>ην 'I feared'.

Note
* Does this remind you of anything? Look again at the imperfect indicative middle at **12f**. The endings are almost the same, except (of course) for energy-packed σα.

17c Observe the following slight irregularities in aorist formation:

μαχομαι 'I fight'   ἐμαχεσ-<u>αμ</u>ην 'I fought'
ἀποκρινομαι 'I reply'   ἀπεκριν-<u>αμ</u>ην 'I replied'
                          (note position of augment – see **14b** – and lack of σ but presence of α)

Vocabulary

Record: ἀδικ-ος 'unjust'; βουλευ-ομαι 'I advise as a council

(βουλη) member' [n.b. do not confuse with βουλ-ομαι 'I wish'];
διακωλυ-ω 'I prevent'; οἱ δικαστ-αι 'the jury men, judges';
μεγαλ- 'great, large, weighty'; μετα, μετ', μεθ' (+ gen.) 'with';
οὐδεποτε 'never'; παρεχ-ω 'I provide'; πειθω (aor. ἐπεισ-α) 'I
persuade'; το τεκμηρι-ον 'evidence'; ὑπερ (+ gen.) 'for, on behalf
of'; ψηφιζ-ομαι (aor. ἐψηφισ-αμην) 'I vote'.

Exercise 2

Translate: οἱ δικασται ἐψηφισαντο μεθ' ὑμων, τα ἀδικα
ἐβουλευσαντο, οὐδεποτε ἐμαχεσασθε, ἀπεκρινατο,
ἐψηφισαμεθα μετα τουτου, ἐβουλευσω ὑπερ του δικαιου και
των νομων, οὐδεποτε ἀπεκριναντο οἱ δικασται, ἐμαχεσατο,
ηὐξαμεθα, ἐφοβησατο.

Translate these mixed aorists and imperfects and boomps-a-
daisy (ooooh! Vicious!): οὐδεποτε ἀπεκριναμην, ἀπεκρινομην,
ηὐξατο, ηὐχετο, ἐμαχομεθα, ἐμαχεσαμεθα, ἐβουλευεσθε ὑπερ
της πολεως, ἐβουλευσασθε, ἐβουλεσθε (watch it!) ἀκουσαι,
οὐδεποτε βουλεσθε (watch it even more) ψηφισασθαι ὑπερ του
δικαιου, ἐψηφισατο μεθ' ἡμων, ἐψηφιζοντο, οὐδεποτε ἐφοβου
τον θανατον, ἐφοβησω.

Exercise 3

Here is part of Socrates' *Apology* (Ἀπολογια Σωκρατους), an
ἀπολογια meaning 'defence speech'. Here he argues that the
man who wishes to fight for what is right had better remain a
private citizen, and recounts an experience of his while serving
as member of the council (βουλη) that nearly led to his death.
The speech has been adapted.

Def Art has been inserted occasionally in [square brackets] to
help case identification.

Ὦ ἀνδρες δικασται, ἐαν τις [των] ἀνθρωπων ἐθελη
ἐναντιουσθαι (to oppose + dat.) ὑμιν και τω πληθει, και
διακωλυειν [τα] πολλα (many) ἀδικα ἐν τη πολει γιγνεσθαι, οὐ
σωθησεται (he will come out of it alive). ἀλλα δει τον
μαχομενον ὑπερ του δικαιου ἰδιωτευσαι (to remain a private
citizen) και μη δημοσιευσαι (guess! Cf. δημος). ὁ γαρ
ἰδιωτευσας γαρ και μη δημοσιευσας σωθησεται.

[τα] μεγαλα τεκμηρια ὑμιν παρεχειν ἐθελω, οὐ λογους ἀλλ᾽ ἐργα. δει οὐν ὑμας ἀκουσαι, ἱνα ἀκουσαντες γιγνωσκητε ὁτι οὐδεποτε οὐδεν (=anything) ποιησαι ἐβουλευσαμην παρα (contrary to) το δικαιον, φοβουμενος (τον) θανατον.

[Socrates now recounts the time he was serving on the council. After the disastrous battle of Arginusae, when a storm blew up and the Greek admirals did not pick up their dead, the people decided to condemn the admirals *en bloc* rather than give them individual trials. This, says Socrates, was illegal, so:] τοτε (then) ἐγω μονος ὑμων ἐβουλευσαμην μηδεν (nothing, cf. οὐδεν) ποιησαι παρα (against) τους νομους, και ἐναντια (against) ἐψηφισαμην. ὑμεις μεν οὐν, βοωντες και κελευοντες, ἠθελησατε ἀπαγειν με, ἐγω δε μετα του νομου και του δικαιου ἠθελησα διακινδυνευειν (run the ultimate risk) μαλλον ἠ (rather than) μεθ᾽ ὑμων μη δικαια βουλευεσθαι, φοβουμενος τον θανατον. και τοτε (at that time) ἡ πολις ἐδημοκρατειτο. ἐπειδη (when) δε (ἡ) ὀλιγαρχια ἐγενετο....

But the oligarchy is another story. For the background, see **The Greek world**, Chapter 16.

The Greek world

Aristophanic comedy

However grim life must have been for the Athenians cooped up in the city during the Peloponnesian War, festivals of the gods still had to be observed – ritual was all. Perhaps the festivals Athenians enjoyed most of all were the dramatic festivals, the Lenaea in January and the Dionysia in March/April, when they could see the latest offerings of their top comedians and tragedians.

Greeks, as we have seen, loved competing, and the plays that had been selected in the previous year by the official in charge competed against each other for the coveted dramatic prizes. Comedians submitted one comedy at a time, tragedians three tragedies plus a satyr play. Unless a touring company took them round the regions, they were played once only, at the festival: that was it.

Athens' star comedian was Aristophanes. We have plays of his spanning the period 425-388 BC, and while the early ones are rumbustious, knockabout and full of often cynical and obscene reference to the local political scene and its politicians, the last plays are considerably quieter and less personal or political in tone. This, surely, has something to do with the demise of radical democracy in Athens.

Aristophanes' plays tend to be about the triumph of the little man against powerful forces – mainly political, but also intellectual and artistic (particularly the latest trends and fashions). For example, in *Clouds* he attacks Socrates (423 BC), in *Women at the Thesmophoria* Euripides (411 BC). His most famous play is *Lysistrata* (411 BC), where the women led by Lysistrata combine a sex-strike with the capture of the treasury on the acropolis of Athens to force the Athenians and Spartans to make peace. Perhaps his most strikingly inventive plot is *Acharnians* (425 BC, another 'peace' play), when the farmer Dikaiopolis, fed up with living in Athens away from his farm and desperate for peace, make his own, personal peace-treaty with the Spartans – and can thus go back to his old way of life. Certainly his filthiest and most vicious play is *Knights* (424 BC), in which the powerful politician Cleon, whom Aristophanes loathed, is given a treatment which no censor would allow on stage today.

Wordplay

The language of science

The Greek language has loaded English with scientific terminology, particularly medical. This is because Greeks invented rational medicine, i.e. explaining disease without recourse to the supernatural (the 5th century BC doctor Hippocrates is the big name here). Being unscientific and knowing nothing of viruses or bacteria or how the body really worked, Greek doctors produced diagnoses that were usually complete nonsense, but it is the principle that counts. On the credit side, they were very good at prognosis – observing the course of a disease and learning to predict what turn it would take next.

The suffix '-itis', for example, indicates inflammation, and ἀρθρον means 'joint', νεφρον 'kidney', ἐντερα 'insides', ἡπατ-'liver', ῥιν- 'nose', δερμα 'skin'. The suffix '-oma' indicates a tumour or swelling, and is added to μελαν- 'black', ὀστε- 'bone', αἱματ- 'blood'. '-osis' indicates a diseased condition, and is added to ψυχη 'soul', νευρ- 'nerve', θρομβ- 'lump, clot'.

'-path' derives from Greek πασχω 'I suffer' and indicates someone who suffers from or treats a disease. Combine it with ψυχη, ὀστεο-, ὁμοιο- ('the same'). '-pathy' indicates 'disease of' or 'treatment for disease of', whence νευρο- ('nerve') and ὑδρο- ('water'). '-tomy' indicates cutting, from Greek τομος 'slice', and '-ectomy' a cutting out (ἐκ), to go with e.g. ὑστερα 'womb'.

Reckon also with λευκος 'white', πληγ- 'struck', σωμα 'body', θεραπ- 'cure', while ῥεω means 'flow', whence all the -rrhea/rrhoea words (διαrrhoea flows 'through' you).

Answers
Exercise 1
Acc., the man pursuing; acc., the women sending; gen., of the men announcing; dat., to the men speaking; nom., the men loving; dat., to the man speaking; gen., of the woman wronging; dat., to the women having faith; nom., the man waiting; acc., the men seeking; nom., the men shouting.
1. Therefore the apostles, having spoken the word of the lord, came into the house. 2. It is necessary for these men, having pursued that woman, to arrest her. 3. Socrates ordered us, acting justly, not to fear death. 4. The women who had taught those children were asleep, but the [other] women departed towards the city. 5. The Greeks wanted to trust those who had harmed the city and the laws. 6. Those who had guarded the men were asleep. 7. It is necessary for them, having written this book, to announce the word of the lord to the world. 8. The laws of those trusting in the lord were just. 9. It is necessary for you to hear and, having heard, to obey. 10. Why must I act justly? For I do not want to live. If someone wants to live, he must obey the laws.
Exercise 2
The judges voted with you; they advised injustice; you never fought; he replied; we voted with him; you advised on behalf of justice and the laws; the judges never replied; he fought; we prayed; he feared.
I never replied; I was replying; he prayed; he was praying; we were fighting; we fought; you were advising on behalf of the city; you advised; you were wishing to hear; you never wish to vote

on behalf of justice; he voted with us; they were voting; you were never fearing death; you feared.

Exercise 3

Gentlemen jurors, if someone of men wishes to oppose you and the mob, and to prevent many injustices happening (lit. 'to happen') in the city, he will not come out of it alive. But it is necessary for the man fighting on behalf of justice to remain a private citizen and not enter public life. For he who remains a private citizen and does not enter public life will come out of it alive.

Powerful evidence I wish to provide for you – not words, but actions. It is therefore necessary for you to listen, in order that, having listened, you may know that I never advised [you] to do anything contrary to justice, fearing (i.e. because I feared) death.

Then I alone of you advised to do nothing against the laws and I voted against. You therefore, shouting and ordering, wanted to arrest me, but I wanted to run the ultimate risk with the law and with justice, rather than not advise justly with you, fearing death. And then the city was under a democracy. But when the oligarchy happened ....

Afore ye go

- Revise your aorist participles active (-σας (σαντ-), σασ-α) **(17a)**
- Revise your aorist middle actives (σα + μην, etc.) **(17b)**
- Learn the twelve new words

171

CHAPTER 18

The final nail (but in whose coffin?)

18a Of course you are keen to hurry on to the finishing post.
What rich rewards lie just round the corner! But just be patient
for a little longer. We must dance an old, but by now delightfully
predictable, routine just once more.

Do aorist middle verbs, like their aorist active counterparts,
have infinitives and participles? Are they based on the σα-rich
aorist middle stem (with no augment)? Are they an absolute
piece of cake?

As well ask if the Pope is a Catholic. Yes, yes and yes (or, to
put it in Greek, which, unlike Latin, does have a word for it, ναι,
ναι, και ναι).

Aorist middle infinitives

18b Cast a cold eye on the following and draw conclusions:

Aor. indic. middle		Aor. infin. middle	Meaning
ἐπορευσ-αμην	'I travelled'	πορευσ-ασθαι	'to travel'
ἐμαχεσ-αμην	'I fought'	μαχεσ-ασθαι	'to fight'
ηὐξ-αμην	'I prayed'	εὐξ-ασθαι	'to pray'
ἀπεκριν-αμην	'I replied'	ἀποκριν-ασθαι	'to reply'

Gorrit? Aorist middle infinitives = aorist middle stem (no augment) + -ασθαι. Note our friend -σθαι, the sign of the middle
infinitive (cf. **7a**).

Vocabulary

Record: ἀπολογε-ομαι 'I defend myself'; διανοε-ομαι 'I plan,
realise'; καταψηφιζ-ομαι 'I condemn'.

172

CHAPTER 18

Exercise 1

Translate: 1. ἠθελησα βουλευσασθαι περι των νομων. 2. οὐ
ῥᾳδιον ἠν σοι μαχεσασθαι και μη φοβησασθαι. 3. τί οὐκ
ἐβουλου ψηφισασθαι ὑπερ του Σωκρατους; 4. τους φευγοντας
ἐκελευσε μαχεσασθαι. 5. ἐδει τους ἐν τη θαλαττη ὀντας
εὐξασθαι τοις θεοις. 6. δηλον μοι ἐστιν ὁτι χρη τον μεν
Σωκρατη ἀπολογησασθαι περι του βιου, τους δε δικαστας
καταψηφισασθαι αὐτου. 7. μη κελευε με ἀδικα διανοησασθαι.

Aorist middle participles

18c Cast another c.e. on the f. and draw conkers:

Aor. indic. middle		Aor. participle middle	Meaning
ἐπορευσ-αμην	'I travelled'	πορευσ-αμεν-ος -η -ον	'travelling'
ἐμαχεσ-αμην	'I fought'	μαχεσ-αμεν-ος -η -ον	'fighting'
ηὐξ-αμην	'I prayed'	εὐξ-αμεν-ος -η -ον	'praying'
ἀπεκριν-αμην	'I replied'	ἀποκριν-αμεν-ος -η -ον	'replying'

If you are still awake, aorist middle participles = aorist middle
stem (no augment) + αμεν-ος -η -ον. Note our friends σα and
-μεν-ος, the sign of the middle participle (see e.g. 6a).

Exercise 2

Identify case and translate: τῳ ψηφισαμενῳ, των εὐξαμενων,
της φοβησαμενης, οἱ μαχεσαμενοι, τους βουλευσαμενους, τοις
καταψηφισαμενοις, τῳ ἀπολογησαμενῳ, την διανοησαμενην.

Aorist revision

18d Sign of the aorist: σα.

Aor. indic. act.	Aor. infin. act.	Aor. participle act.
ἐ-παυσ-α	παυσ-αι	παυσας (παυσαντ-), παυσασ-α
'I stopped'	'to stop'	'stopping'

173

Aor. indic. mid. Aor. infin. mid. Aor. participle mid.

ἐ-πορευσ-αμην   πορευσ-ασθαι   πορευσ-αμεν-ος -η -ον
'I travelled'   'to travel'   'travelling'

Socrates' ἀπολογια: his response to being condemned to death

Vocabulary

Record vocabulary marked with an asterisk *.

*οὐτε...οὐτε 'neither...nor'; τοτε 'then'; ἀνελευθερος 'ignoble, unworthy of a free man'; *νυν 'now'; μεταμελει μοι 'it is a source of regret to me'; *οὑτως 'in this way'; *ἀπολογε-ομαι (*here agrees with* μοι); πολυ μαλλον 'much more'; ὡδε 'thus'; τεθναναι 'to die'; ἡ 'than'; ἐκεινως 'in that [other] way' (i.e. ignobly); *ὁ πολεμ-ος 'the battle'; ἀλλον οὐδενα 'anyone else' (*acc.*); *παν ποιων 'doing everything'; θανατον *is object of* ἀποφευγῃ; και γαρ 'what's more'; ἡ μαχ-η 'battle'; *πολλακις 'often'; ἀφεις 'throwing away'; τα ὁπλα 'the weapons'; ἱκετευω 'supplicate'; ἀλλ-ος 'other'; ἡ μηχαν-η 'the device, means'; *ἑκαστ-ος 'each'; *ὁ κινδυν-ος 'the danger'; ὡστε 'so as to'; *τολμα-ω 'I dare'; *χαλεπ-ος 'difficult'; χαλεπωτερος 'more difficult'; πολυ 'much'; ἡ πονηρι-α 'wickedness, wrong'; θαττον θανατου 'quicker than death'; θε-ω 'I run'; βραδυς 'slow'; πρεσβυτης 'old man'; του βραδυτερου 'the slower', i.e. death; ἑαλων 'I have been caught'; *ὁ κατηγορ-ος 'the accuser'; δεινος 'smart'; ὀξ-υς 'quick'; του θαττονος 'the quicker'; ἡ κακι-α 'wickedness'.

When the death penalty is passed, Socrates wryly observes that if the jury had waited a little longer, he would have died of natural causes anyway. He goes on to address those who voted for death, arguing that he was condemned for not sucking up to them enough and going into the sort of pathetic pleading routines they were used to. He continues:

Ἀλλ' οὐτε τοτε ἠθελησα πραξαι οὐδεν ἀνελευθερον, οὐτε νυν μοι μεταμελει οὑτως ἀπολογησαμενῳ, ἀλλα πολυ μαλλον βουλομαι ὡδε ἀπολογησαμενος τεθναναι ἡ ἐκεινως ζην. οὐτε γαρ ἐν δικῃ οὐτ' ἐν πολεμῳ οὐτ' ἐμε οὐτ' ἀλλον οὐδενα δει τουτο ποιειν, ἱνα ἀποφευγῃ παν ποιων [τον] θανατον. και γαρ ἐν ταις μαχαις πολλακις δηλον γιγνεται ὁτι τον θανατον τις βουλεται ἐκφευγειν, ἀφεις τα ὁπλα και ἱκετευων τους διωκοντας. και [αἱ] ἀλλαι μηχαναι πολλαι εἰσιν ἐν ἑκαστοις τοις κινδυνοις ὡστε διαφευγειν [τον] θανατον, ἐαν τις τολμα παν ποιειν και λεγειν. ἀλλ᾽ οὐ χαλεπον ἐστι [τον] θανατον ἐκφευγειν, ἀλλα πολυ χαλεπωτερον [ἐκφευγειν την] πονηριαν. θαττον γαρ θανατου θει. και νυν ἐγω, βραδυς ὠν και πρεσβυτης, ὑπο του βραδυτερου ἑαλων, οἱ δε κατηγοροι, δεινοι ὀντες και ὀξεις, ὑπο του θαττονος, της κακιας. και νυν ἐγω μεν shall go found guilty by you of death, οὑτοι δε found guilty ὑπο της ἀληθειας of wickedness and injustice. I shall stick by my punishment, and they by theirs.

The end of Socrates' ἀπολογια

Vocabulary

εὐελπιδας 'hopeful, confident'; τελευτα-ω 'I die'; *οὐδε 'nor, and … not'; ἀμελε-ω 'I neglect'; *το πραγμα (πραγματ-) 'affair, business, matter'; *δια + acc., 'because of'; οὐδαμου 'nowhere'; ἀποτρεπ-ω 'I turn aside, divert'; το σημει-ον 'the sign'; πανυ 'at all'; χαλεπαιν-ω 'I feel angry with (+ dat. – the dat. being the previous τοις … τοις); *καιτοι 'and yet'; ταυτη τη dat., meaning 'with'; ἡ διανοι-α 'the plan, intention'; κατηγορε-ω 'I accuse'; οἱ-ομαι 'I think, suppose, believe to – ' (i.e. that they were -ing); βλαπτ-ω 'I harm' (i.e. harm me); ἠδη 'already'; ἡ ὡρ-α 'fine'; ὁποτερ-οι 'whichever'; ἐπι 'to'; ἀμεινον 'better'; ἀδηλον 'it [is] unclear'; παντι 'to everyone'; πλην ἡ 'except'.

Socrates addresses the jury, arguing that a good man has nothing to fear in life or death. The 'sign' is his δαιμονιον, a sort of divine conscience, which he claims always turned him away from any wrong path. These are his closing words.

Ἀλλα ὑμας χρη, ὠ ἀνδρες δικασται, εὐελπιδας εἰναι προς τον θανατον, και διανοεισθαι ὁτι οὐκ ἐστιν [τω] ἀνδρι ἀγαθω κακον οὐδεν, οὐτε [τω] ζωντι οὐτε τελευτησαντι, οὐδε ἀμελειται ὑπο [των] θεων τα τουτου πραγματα. But what has happened to me now has not happened by accident (ἀπ᾽ αὐτοματου), but it is clear to me that it is better for me to die and be finished with this business. δια τουτο ἐμε οὐδαμου ἀπετρεψεν το σημειον, και ἐγω τοις κατεψηφισαμενοις μου και τοις κατηγοροις οὐ πανυ χαλεπαινω. καιτοι οὐ ταυτῃ τῃ διανοιᾳ κατεψηφιζοντο μου και κατηγορουν, ἀλλ᾽ οἰομενοι βλαπτειν. This was blameworthy of them.

(Socrates now tells the jury to admonish his children 'as I admonished you' if they grow up to believe anything is more important than goodness. και ἐαν ταυτα ποιητε, ἐγω και οἰ υἰοι will have justice at your hands.)

ἀλλα ἠδη [ἐστιν ἡ] ὡρα ἀπερχεσθαι, ἐμοι μεν προς θανατον, ὑμιν δε προς βιον. [οἰ] ὁποτεροι δε ἡμων ἐρχονται ἐπι ἀμεινον πραγμα, ἀδηλον [ἐστι] παντι πλην ἠ τῳ θεῳ.

The Greek world

Why are we here?

Socrates was executed in 399 BC. He is a figure of very great importance in the history of thought. Early Greek philosophers – natural scientists would be a better description – were mainly interested in how the world began and what it consisted of (see **The Greek world**, Chapter 4). Socrates changed the whole direction of philosophy, turning the spotlight on man and asking the crucial question – how best can we lead our lives? For him life was a constant search to answer that question – ὁ ἀνεξεταστος βιος οὐ βιωτος ἀνθρωπῳ, 'the unexamined life [is] not to-be-lived by man', he famously said.

Socrates never wrote a word. His life and work are recorded for us first-hand by his ardent admirer Plato. Plato constructed his own philosophy on Socratic foundations, but since he uses Socrates as his mouthpiece in almost all his work, it is quite difficult to decide where the real Socrates ends and Plato begins. But one can perhaps say three things about Socrates' work.

First, he felt that ἀρετη ('goodness, expertise, success') was the key to life. Only a good man could be a happy man. But how did one define goodness – since if one could not define it, one would not recognise it when one met it? This is the central Socratic paradox, and led to his famous sayings 'goodness is knowledge' and 'no one does wrong willingly' (since goodness is so advantageous, leading to happiness as it does, that once you know what it is, you will always do it).

Second, to help solve the problem, Socrates invented dialectic technique – the question and answer method. He used this in encouraging those he met to attempt to define ἀρετη – by gathering examples of it and seeing what all the examples had in common (the inductive method). His questioners, naturally, never succeed, but the process of question and answer at least clarifies the problems.

Third, Socrates never claimed to be a teacher of anything: indeed his only recognisable 'mission statement' was that he knew he knew nothing (one would love to see a modern university adopting it). But he became a highly controversial figure for his relentless questioning of everyone and everything, and eventually he was charged with introducing new gods and corrupting the young – though his friendship with Critias, hated leader of the Thirty Tyrants, cannot have helped his cause (see **The Greek world**, Chapter 16). He was found guilty and executed.

Xenophon's *Memorabilia* and Aristophanes' comedy *Clouds* (423 BC) are also contemporary evidence for Socrates' life – presenting a rather different picture from Plato's.

Answers
Exercise 1
1. I wanted to advise about the laws. 2. It was not easy for you to fight and not be afraid. 3. Why were you not wishing to vote on behalf of Socrates? 4. He ordered those fleeing to fight. 5. It was necessary for those who were in the sea to pray to the gods. 6. It is clear to me that Socrates must defend himself concerning his life, but the jurors condemn him. 7. Do not order me to plan injustice.
Exercise 2
Dat., to/for him voting; gen., of them praying; gen, of her fearing; nom,. the men fighting; acc., the men advising; dat., to/for the men condemning; dat., to/for the man defending himself; acc. the woman planning/realising.
Socrates' ἀπολογια
But neither then did I wish to do anything [nothing] ignoble, nor now is it a source of regret to me [for] having defended myself in this way, but much more I want to die defending myself in this way than to live in that way. For neither in a trial nor in war neither I nor anyone [no one] else ought to do this, in order that he may escape death, doing everything [i.e. do every-

177

thing to escape death]. What's more, in battles often it becomes clear that someone wishes to escape death, abandoning his weapons and supplicating the pursuers. And there are many other devices in each danger so as to escape death, if someone dares to do and say everything. But it is not difficult to escape death, but much more difficult [to escape] wickedness. For it runs faster than death. And now I, being slow and old, have been caught by the slower, but my accusers, being smart and quick [have been caught] by the quicker, wickedness. And now I on the one and...they on the other ... by the truth.

The end of Socrates' ἀπολογια

But it is necessary for you, gentlemen of the jury, to be confident towards [in the face of] death and to realise that there is not for the good man any [no] evil, neither [for him] living nor dying, nor are his affairs neglected by the gods ... Because of this the sign nowhere diverted me, and I do not feel angry at all at those condemning me and the accusers. And yet they did not condemn and accuse me with this intention, but thinking to [that they were] harm me...and if you do these things, I and my sons ... But already [it is] time to depart, for me to death, for you to life. Whichever of us is going to a better business, is unclear to everyone except the god.

CHAPTER 19

From death to life

The end of the Syracusan expedition, 413 BC

Vocabulary

*ἐπειδη 'when'; *ἡ ἡμερ-α 'the day'; ἡ στρατι-α 'the army'; ὁ
συμμαχ-ος 'the ally'; προσκει-μαι 'I harass'; *πανταχοθεν 'from
all sides'; *βαλλ-ω 'I throw (missiles at)'; κατακοντιζ-ω 'I shoot
down'; ἐπειγ-ομαι 'I hurry'; *ὁ ποταμ-ος 'the river'; ἁμα μεν ...
ἁμα δε 'at the same time...at the same time'; βιαζ-ομαι 'I am
pressured'; ἡ προσβολ-η 'the attack'; οἱ ἱππ-εις 'the cavalry';
*ἀλλ-ος 'other'; ὁ οχλ-ος 'the mass (of soldiers)'; ἡ ταλαιπωρι-α
'the distress'; *ὡς 'as'; ἐπ' αὐτῳ 'on it' (the river); ἐσπιπτ-ω 'I fall
in'; οὐδενι κοσμῳ 'in no order'; πας τις 'every one'; αὐτος 'himself'; πρωτος 'first'; διαβηναι 'to cross'; ὁ πολεμι-ος 'the enemy';
ἐπικει-μαι 'I press hard'; ἡ διαβασ-ις 'the crossing'; ἀθρο-ος 'all
together'; ἀναγκαζ-ω 'I compel'; χωρε-ω 'I advance'; ἐπιπιπτ-ω 'I
fall on' + dat.; *ἀλληλ-οι 'each other'; καταπατε-ω 'I trample
down'; ἀνωθεν 'from above'; πιν-ω 'I drink'; ἀσμεν-ος 'happy';
κοιλ-ος 'hollow, bottom of'; ἐν σφισιν αὐτοις 'among themselves'; ταρασσ-ω 'I entangle'; ἐπικαταβαντ-ες 'coming down';
μαλιστα 'particularly'; σφαζ-ω 'I slaughter'.

In the long drawn out war between Athens and Sparta (the
Peloponnesian War, 431-404 BC), the Athenians in 415 sent a
major expeditionary force to Sicily, hoping to use its wealth in
the conflict. It turned into a disaster . The Athenian fleet was
destroyed in the battle in the harbour in Syracuse, and the
remnants of the army had to retreat south by land. Here, led by
Nikias, it reaches the river Assinaros, and a nightmare slaughter ensues.

Νικιας δ᾽, ἐπειδη [ἡ] ἡμερα ἐγενετο, ἠγε την στρατιαν. οἱ
δε Συρακοσιοι και οἱ συμμαχοι προσεκειντο, πανταχοθεν

179

βαλλοντες και κατακοντιζοντες. και οἱ Ἀθηναιοι ἠπειγοντο προς τον Ἀσσιναρον ποταμον, ἁμα μεν βιαζομενοι ὑπο της πανταχοθεν προσβολης [των] ἱππεων πολλων και του ἀλλου ὀχλου, thinking it would be easier for them if they crossed the river, ἁμα δ᾽ ὑπο της ταλαιπωριας και their desire to drink. ὡς δε γιγνονται ἐπ᾽ αὐτῳ, ἐσπιπτουσιν οὐδενι κοσμῳ, ἀλλα πας τις αὐτος πρωτος διαβηναι βουλομενος, και οἱ πολεμιοι ἐπικειμενοι, χαλεπην την διαβασιν ἐποιουν. [οἱ] ἀθροοι γαρ ἀναγκαζομενοι χωρειν, ἐπεπιπτον ἀλληλοις και κατεπατουν, and some were immediately killed on their own spears and weapons, others got tangled up and swept away. On the other side of the river stood the Syracusans (it was steep and rocky) and they ἐβαλλον ἀνωθεν τους Ἀθηναιους, [τους] πινοντας τους πολλους ἀσμενους, και ἐν κοιλῳ τῳ ποταμῳ ἐν σφισιν αὐτοις ταρασσομενους. και οἱ Πελοποννησιοι, [οἱ] ἐπικαταβαντες, τους ἐν τῳ ποταμῳ μαλιστα ἐσφαζον. And the water was immediately fouled, but was drunk none the less all bloody with mud and was fought over by many.

Thucydides, *History of the Peloponnesian War* 7.84.

The death of Julius Caesar, Ides of March 44 BC

Vocabulary

ἐπισκωπτ-ω ʻI joke'; ὁ μαντ-ις ʻthe prophet'; φυλασσ-ομαι ʻI watch out for'; δητα ʻthen'; το μαντευμα ʻthe oracle'; ἠ ʻor'; ἐδεδιεις ʻyou feared'; *παρ-ειμι ʻI am present'; τοσουτον μονον ʻonly this much'; ναι ʻyes'; *οὐδεπω ʻnot yet'; παρεληλυθεν ʻit has passed'; μυθολογε-ω ʻI chat'; ἱκετευ-ω ʻI plead with'; ὑποπτευ-ω ʻI suspect'; ὁ καιρ-ος ʻthe right time'; το ἱματι-ον ʻthe toga'; ὁ ὠμ-ος ʻthe shoulder'; καθειλκυσ-α ʻI ripped'; το σημει-ον ʻthe sign'; προσπιπτ-ω ʻI attack' + dat.; κατετρωσα ʻI wounded'; *εἰπ-ειν ʻto speak'; τι ʻanything'; *δυνα-μαι ʻI am able, can'.

Here is Cassius Dio's account of the death of Julius Caesar on 15 March 44 BC. Dio's *Roman History* was composed from c. AD 200 till his death in AD 229.

ὁ Καισαρ, ἐπισκωπτων προς τον μαντιν τον κελευσαντα αὐτον φυλασσεσθαι την ἡμεραν ἐκεινην, εἰπεν ʻπου δητα σου τα μαντευματα; ἠ οὐχ ὁρᾳς ὁτι ἡ ἡμερα ἠν [which] ἐδεδιεις

παρεστι, και ἐγω ζω;' και ἐκεινος τοσουτον μονον, ὡς λεγουσι, ἀπεκρινατο ὁτι 'ναι παρεστιν, οὐδεπω δε παρεληλυθεν.'
(The conspirators now gather round him in a body and...)
οἱ μεν ἐμυθολογουν, οἱ δε ἱκετευον αὐτον, ἱνα μη ὑποπτευσῃ. ἐπειδη ὁ καιρος ἐγενετο, προσηλθε τις αὐτῳ, και το ἱματιον αὐτου ἀπο του ὡμου καθειλκυσε. τουτο ἠν το σημειον. προσεπιπτον αὐτῳ ἐκεινοι πανταχοθεν και κατετρωσαν αὐτον. και δια του πληθους αὐτων ὁ Καισαρ οὐτε εἰπειν οὐτε πραξαι τι ἐδυνατο, but veiled his face and was despatched with many blows. This is the truest account, though some say that when Brutus struck him a heavy blow, Caesar said to him και συ, τεκνον;

Cassius Dio, *Roman History* 44.19

A fable: it is stupid to pity the pitiless

Vocabulary

*ὁ γεωργ-ος 'the farmer'; λαβων 'taking'; *ὁ ἐχ-ις 'the snake'; ἐκπνε-ω 'I die'; το ψυχ-ος 'the cold'; θαλπ-ω 'I warm'; ἡπλωθη 'it stretched out'; προσφυς 'attaching itself to' + dat.; ἡ χειρ 'the hand'; δακων 'biting'; ἀνιητως 'incurably'; ἐκτειν-ω 'I kill, stretch X out'; θνησκ-ω 'I die'; ὁ μυθος 'the word'; ἀξιος 'worthy of' + gen.; ἡ μνημ-η 'recall, memory'; πασχ-ω 'I suffer'; οἰκτειρας 'having pitied'; πονηρ-ος 'wicked, evil'.

Babrius (2nd century AD?) collected Aesop's fables and turned them into verse. Here a farmer takes pity on a snake. The first version is in a normal Greek prose order, with added Def Arts etc., the second in its original poetic form.

ὁ γεωργος, λαβων τον ἐχιν ἐκπνεοντα ὑπο του ψυχους, ἐθαλπεν αὐτον. ἀλλ᾽ ἐκεινος ὁ ἐχις ἡπλωθη, προσφυς τῃ χειρι, και δακων ἀνιητως ἐκτεινεν [αὐτον]. ὁ γεωργος, θνησκων, εἰπεν [τον] μυθον ἀξιον [της] μνημης· 'δικαια πασχω, οἰκτειρας τον πονηρον.'

Scansion

The rhythm is 'blank tum-ti-tum', where blank can be tum or ti, repeated twice; then 'blank tum-tum-tum': thus 'blank tum-ti-tum/blank tum-ti-tum/blank tum-tum-tum' (see **15b** for principles of scansion).

ἐχιν γεωργος ἐκπνεοντ᾽ ὑπο ψυχους
λαβων ἐθαλπεν. ἀλλ᾽ ἐκεινος ἡπλωθη
τῃ χειρι προσφυς και δακων ἀνι-ητως
ἐκτεινεν...
θνῃσκων δε μυθον εἰπεν ἀξιον μνημης
'δικαια πασχω, τον πονηρον οἰκτειρας.'
Babrius, *Fable* 143.

Zeus, father – and mother? – of the gods

Vocabulary

ἀκαιρον 'the wrong time'; *ἐξεστιν 'it is permitted to' + dat.; ἰδειν 'to see'; το παρον 'the present'; μων 'surely not?'; συν-ειμι 'I am with, make love to' + dat.; ἑτεροιον τι 'something rather different'; ἐνδον 'inside'; *μαλακως ἐχ-ω 'I feel poorly'; ποθεν 'from what cause?'; δειν-ος 'terrible'; *αἰσχυν-ομαι 'I feel ashamed'; ὁ θει-ος 'uncle'; *τετοκεν 'he has given birth'; ἀρτιως 'recently'; ἀπαγε 'get away!'; ἀνδρογυνος 'hermaphrodite'; ἡ γαστηρ 'the stomach'; ἐπεσημαν-α 'I indicated'; ὁ ὀγκ-ος 'the swelling'; εὐ 'well'; το ἐμβρυ-ον 'the embryo'; *ἡ κεφαλ-η 'the head'; (ἐξ) ἐτεκεν 'he bore'; αὐθις 'again'; *ὡσπερ 'as if, like'; τοκαδα [acc.] 'for breeding, broody'; το μηρ-ον 'the thigh'; κυ-ω 'I carry'; το βρεφ-ος 'the child'; τριτος 'third'; ὁ μην 'the month'; ἡ ὠδιν-η 'birth pains'; [το] ὑδωρ 'the water'; το τραυμα 'pain, hurt'; λεχοι 'for a woman who has just given birth'.

Lucian was born about AD 125 in Samosata, a town in the Roman province of Syria. He was a brilliant satirist. The background to the first passage is as follows: Zeus' mistress Semele, demanding to see Zeus in his full majesty, has been destroyed by the fire of his thunderbolts. But Zeus rescues the embryo of the god Dionysus, with whom she was pregnant, and sews it into his thigh until it is ready to be born.

Here the god Ποσειδων has come to see Zeus, but Ἑρμης, on guard outside his room, puts him off. Ποσειδων tries to guess what he is up to.

182

CHAPTER 19

Hera is Zeus's wife; Ganymede his male cup-bearer (and catamite); Zeus bore Athene from his head.

ΕΡΜ: ἄκαιρον ἐστιν. οὐκ ἐξεστιν σοι ἰδειν αὐτον ἐν τῳ παροντι.
ΠΟΣ: μων τῃ Ἡρᾳ συνεστιν;
ΕΡΜ: οὐκ, ἀλλα ἑτεροιον τι ἐστιν.
ΠΟΣ: οἰδα. ὁ Γανυμηδης ἐνδον.
ΕΡΜ: οὐδε τουτο. ἀλλα μαλακως ἐχει.
ΠΟΣ: ποθεν, ὠ Ἑρμη; δεινον γαρ τουτο λεγεις.
ΕΡΜ: αἰσχυνομαι εἰπειν.
ΠΟΣ: ἀλλα οὐ χρη αἰσχυνεσθαι προς ἐμε, θειον ὀντα.

Hermes now reveals the truth.

ΕΡΜ: τετοκεν ἀρτιως, ὠ Ποσειδον.
ΠΟΣ: ἀπαγε, τετοκεν ἐκεινος; τίς ὁ πατηρ; οὐ γαρ φαινεται ἀνδρογυνος εἰναι. ἀλλα ἡ γαστηρ οὐκ ἐπεσημανεν [τον] ὀγκον.
ΕΡΜ: εὐ λεγεις; οὐ γαρ ἐκεινη εἰχε το ἐμβρυον.
ΠΟΣ: οἰδα. ἐκ της κεφαλης ἐτεκεν αὐθις ὡσπερ την Ἀθηναν. τοκαδα γαρ την κεφαλην ἐχει.
ΕΡΜ: οὐκ, ἀλλα ἐν τῳ μηρῳ ἐκυει το της Σεμελης βρεφος...νυν τριτος ἐστιν ὁ μην, και ἐξετεκεν αὐτο, και ἀπο των ὠδινων μαλακως ἐχει. νυν ἀπερχομαι ἱνα φερω [το] ὑδωρ αὐτῳ προς το τραυμα και τα ἀλλα ὡσπερ λεχοι.

Lucian, *Dialogues of the gods* 12.

The Greek world

Greeks under the Romans

'Who came first, the Greeks or the Romans?' is a favourite question, and 'the Greeks' is the right answer (though it is worth pointing out that the centre of future Rome was occupied from 1000 BC and that Rome traditionally became a republic in 508 BC, the same year that Cleisthenes invented democracy in Athens). But it may come as a surprise to find yourself reading Greek literature dated AD. Surely Rome ruled the roost by then?

It certainly did. Greece had become a province of Rome in the 2nd century BC, and after Rome conquered Britain in AD 43, its empire stretched from Britain to Syria, from Germany to Egypt and North Africa. But the point is that, however politically powerful Rome was, the Greek language was still the common language of the Mediterranean (which explains why the *New Testament* was originally written in Greek, not Latin) and Greek was the foreign language that all educated Romans learnt. It was the language of culture. Further, Athens in particular and Greece in general were seen as *the* place for top Romans to complete their education: they all went to 'university' there, as it were. Parallels in the modern world between the 'Roman' USA and the 'Greek' UK have some truth to them in this respect.

So Greek literature does not end with the demise of democracy and classical Athens in the 4th century BC. Far from it. Greeks continued churning the stuff out wherever they lived in the Mediterranean. Greeks in Alexandria in Egypt were especially prolific. When Alexander the Great died (323 BC – see **The Greek world** Chapter 16), the Greeks he had left in charge of his empire promptly turned themselves into kings. Πτολεμαιος made himself king of Egypt (Ptolemy) and at once decided to turn its capital Alexandria into a cultural centre to rival Athens. He poured state funding into the Museum (science) and Library (the arts) and attracted the best Greek scholars and writers from all over the Mediterranean to work there. Indeed, it was scholars working in the Library who produced definitive texts of all classical Greek literature – from which our texts derive today.

While the Roman empire survived, so did Greek language and culture. Lucian, Cassius Dio, the *New Testament* and the epigrams we read earlier are all products of the post-classical Greek world under Roman rule. Indeed, we owe the very survival of Greek literature to the Romans. What happened when the Roman empire collapsed awaits the last chapter.

Answers
Syracuse
When day came, Nikias led the army. The Syracusans and allies harassed them, hurling missiles and shooting down [on them] from all sides. And the Athenians hurried towards the river Assinaros, at the same time being pressured by the attacks from all sides of the many cavalry and the rest of the crowd of

soldiers, and at the same time by distress...As they came upon
it, they fell in in no order, but each one wishing to cross first
himself and the enemy pressing hard made the crossing difficult. Being compelled to advance all together, they fell on each
other and trampled [each other] down...they were throwing
missiles at the Athenians from above, who were – the majority
– drinking happily, and tangled up with each other in the bottom
of the river. And the Peloponnesians, coming down, slaughtered
those in the river particularly.

Julius Caesar

Caesar, joking at the prophet who had ordered him to guard
against that day, said 'Where then [are] your oracles? Or do you
not see that the day which you feared is here, and I live?' And
he, as they say, replied only this much 'Yes, it is here, but it has
not yet passed.'

Some were chatting, others were pleading with him, in order
that he might not suspect. When the right moment came, someone approached him and ripped his toga off his shoulder. This
was the sign. They attacked him from all sides and wounded
him. And because of the mob of them Caesar was unable to say
or do anything ...'you too, child'.

A fable

A farmer, taking a snake which was dying of cold, warmed [it].
But that snake stretched out, attaching itself to his hand, and
biting [him] incurably laid him low. The farmer, dying, uttered
a word worthy of recall: 'I suffer justly, taking pity on a wretch'.

Lucian

Her: It is not the right time. It is not permitted for you to see him
at the moment. *Pos*: Surely he's not with Hera? *Her*: No, but
something like it. *Pos*: I know. Ganymede's inside! *Her*: Nor this
[either]. But he's feeling poorly. *Pos*: For what reason, Hermes?
For this [is] a terrible [thing] you're saying. *Her*: I'm ashamed to
say. *Pos*: But you must not be ashamed before me, being your
uncle.

Her: He has just given birth, Poseidon. *Pos*: Get away! He's given
birth? Who's the father? He doesn't *appear* to be a hermaphrodite. But his stomach did not indicate a swelling. *Her*: You speak
correctly. For it did not contain the embryo. *Pos*: I know. He bore
[it] from his head again, like Athene. He's got a broody head.
Her: No, but he carried the son of Semele in his thigh ... it's the

185

third month now, and he has given birth to it, and is feeling poorly from labour pains. Now I'm going in order that I may carry water to him for the pains and for everything else, as if for a woman who has just given birth.

CHAPTER 20

Eternal truths

In Zeus's Prayer HQ

Here from the satirist Lucian again the philosopher Menippus
describes how Zeus deals with prayers – many of which are
contradictory.

Vocabulary

το χωρι-ον 'the place'; ἐνθα 'where'; *καθεζ-ομαι 'I sit'; *ἡ εὐχ-η
'the prayer'; ἐπι 'at, beside'; ἀφελων 'removing'; *παρεχω 'I provide, offer'; ἑαυτον 'himself' (acc.); πανταχοθεν της γης 'from all
over the world'; διαφορ-ος 'different'; ποικιλ-ος 'varied';
τοι-οσ-δε 'like this'; *γενοιτο μοι 'may it come about for me to X
(infin.)/for X (acc.) to Y (infin.)'; βασιλευ-ω 'I am king'; το
κρομμυ-ον 'the onion'; φυναι 'to grow'; το σκοροδ-ον 'the garlic';
ταχεως 'quickly'; ἀποθανειν 'to die'; στεφθηναι τα Ὀλυμπια 'to
be crowned in the Olympics'; των πλεοντων; 'of those sailing'; ὁ
βορεας 'the north wind'; ἐπιπνεω 'I blow'; ὁ νοτ-ος 'the south
wind'; ὁ γεωργ-ος 'the farmer'; αἰτεω 'I ask for'; ὁ ὑετ-ος 'the
rain'; ὁ γναφευς 'the potter'; ὁ ἡλι-ος 'the sun'; ἀκριβως 'precisely'; ἐξεταζ-ω 'examine, test'; παντα 'all, every one' (acc.);
ὑπισχνε-ομαι 'promise, answer'; ὁ ἑτερ-ος 'the one, the other';
ἐδωκε 'granted'; ἀνανευ-ω 'I refuse' [this is a quotation from
Homer's *Iliad*, a hexameter (see **15b**)]

Ἀφικομεθα εἰς το χωριον ἐνθα ἐδει αὐτον καθεζομενον
ἀκουσαι των εὐχων. There were rows of openings, rather like
the mouths of wells, each with a lid (το πωμα), and beside each
was a golden throne. καθεζομενος οὖν ὁ Ζευς ἐπι της πρωτης
[i.e. opening] και ἀφελων το πωμα, παρειχε τοις εὐχομενοις
ἑαυτον. ηὐχοντο δε πανταχοθεν της γης [τα] διαφορα και
ποικιλα. αἱ εὐχαι ἠσαν τοιαιδε 'ὠ Ζευ, γενοιτο μοι
βασιλευσαι', 'ὠ Ζευ, γενοιτο μοι τα κρομμυα φυναι και τα

187

σκοροδα', 'ὦ θεοι, γενοιτο μοι τον πατερα ταχεως ἀποθανειν',
'γενοιτο μοι νικησαι την δικην', 'γενοιτο μοι στεφθηναι τα
Ὀλυμπια'. των δε πλεοντων ὁ μεν [τον] βορεαν ηὔχετο
ἐπιπνευσαι, ὁ δε [τον] νοτον, ὁ δε γεωργος ᾐτει [τον] ὑετον, ὁ δε
γναφευς [τον] ἡλιον.

ἀκουων δε ὁ Ζευς, και την εὐχην ἑκαστην ἀκριβως
ἐξεταζων, οὐ παντα ὑπισχνειτο,
    ἀλλ' [το] ἑτερον μεν ἐδωκε [ὁ] πατηρ, [το] ἑτερον δ' ἀνενευσεν.

The Bread [ἀρτ-ος] of Life

The people ask Jesus how they can work the works of God. This
is Jesus' reply.

Vocabulary

*Ἀπεκριθη 'he replied'; εἰς ὁν 'in [the one] whom'; ἀπεστειλεν
'he sent'; τί... σημειον 'what sign'; ἰδωμεν 'we may see'; ἐργαζ-
ομαι 'work, do'; το μαννα 'the manna'; *ἐφαγον 'they ate'; *ἡ
ἐρημ-ος 'the desert'; *καθως 'as'; γεγραμμεν-ος 'written'; *ὁ
οὐραν-ος 'the heaven'; ἐδωκεν 'he gave'; *φαγειν 'to eat'; ὁ
Μωυσης 'Moses'; δεδωκεν 'he gave'; διδωσιν 'he gives'; ἀληθιν-ος
'true'; *καταβαιν-ω 'I come down'; διδους 'giving'; παντοτε 'always'; δος 'give!'; *οὐ μη 'never'; πειναση 'he will hunger'; διψησει 'he will thirst'; πωποτε 'ever'; ἑωρακατε 'you have seen';
*ἀναστησω 'I shall resurrect, raise up'; *ἐσχατ-ος 'last'; πας
'everyone'; θεωρε-ω 'I see'; *αἰωνι-ος 'eternal'; *γογγυζ-ω 'murmur, grumble'; οἱ Ἰουδαι-οι 'the Jews'; *καταβας 'descending';
οὑ 'of whom, whose'; πως 'how?'; καταβεβηκα 'I have come
down'; οὐδεις 'no one'; ἐλθειν 'to come'; ἑλκυση 'draw, drag,
attract'; *κἀγω = και ἐγω; παρα 'from' + gen.; μαθων 'learning';
*ἀπεθανον 'they died'; *φαγη 'may eat'; ἀποθανη 'may die';
*ζησει 'he will live'; *ὁ αἰων 'eternity'; ὁν 'which'; δωσω 'I shall
give'; *ἡ σαρξ, σαρκ- 'the flesh'; δουναι 'to give'; φαγητε 'you
eat'; πιητε 'you drink'; *το αἱμα 'the blood'; ἑαυτοις 'yourselves';
*τρωγ-ω 'I eat'; *πιν-ω 'I drink'; *ἀληθης 'true'; βρωσις 'food';
ποσις 'drink'; ἀπεστειλεν 'he sent'; ἡ συναγωγ-η 'the syna-
gogue'; Καφαρναουμ 'Capernaum'; σκληρος 'difficult, harsh'.

Ἀπεκριθη ὁ Ἰησους και ειπεν αὐτοις 'τουτο ἐστι το ἐργον του
Θεου, ἱνα πιστευητε εἰς ὁν ἀπεστειλεν ἐκεινος.'

εἰπον οὐν αὐτῳ 'τί οὐν ποιεις συ σημειον, ἱνα ἰδωμεν και
πιστευσωμεν σοι; τί ἐργαζῃ; οἱ πατερες ἡμων το μαννα ἐφαγον
ἐν τῃ ἐρημῳ, καθως ἐστι γεγραμμενον, Ἀρτον ἐκ του οὐρανου
ἐδωκεν αὐτοις φαγειν.'

εἰπεν οὐν αὐτοις ὁ Ἰησους ' Ἀμην ἀμην λεγω ὑμιν, οὐ ὁ
Μωυσης δεδωκεν ὑμιν τον ἀρτον ἐκ του οὐρανου, ἀλλ᾽ ὁ Πατηρ
μου διδωσιν ὑμιν τον ἀρτον ἐκ του οὐρανου τον ἀληθινον. ὁ
γαρ ἀρτος του Θεου ἐστιν ὁ καταβαινων ἐκ του οὐρανου και
[την] ζωην διδους τω κοσμῳ.'

εἰπον οὐν προς αὐτον 'κυριε, παντοτε δος ἡμιν τον ἀρτον
τουτον.'

εἰπεν αὐτοις ὁ Ἰησους 'ἐγω εἰμι ὁ ἀρτος της ζωης. ὁ
ἐρχομενος προς ἐμε οὐ μη πειναση και ὁ πιστευων εἰς ἐμε οὐ
μη διψησει πωποτε. ἀλλ᾽ [ἐγω] εἰπον ὑμιν ὁτι και ἑωρακατε με
και οὐ πιστευετε. All that the Father giveth me shall come to
me; and him that cometh to me I shall in no wise cast out. For I
came down from heaven, not to do my own will, but the will of
him that sent me [*το θελημα του πεμψαντος με]. τουτο δε
ἐστιν το θελημα του πεμψαντος με, that of all which he hath
given me I should lose nothing, ἀλλ᾽ ἀναστησω αὐτο ἐν τῃ
ἐσχατῃ ἡμερα. τουτο γαρ ἐστι το θελημα του Πατρος μου, ἱνα
πας ὁ θεωρων τον Υἱον και πιστευων εἰς αὐτον ἐχῃ ζωην
αἰωνιον, και ἀναστησω αὐτον ἐν τῃ ἐσχατῃ ἡμερα.'

ἐγογγυζον οὐν οἱ Ἰουδαιοι περι αὐτου ὁτι εἰπεν ' ἐγω εἰμι
ἀρτος ὁ καταβας ἐκ του οὐρανου', και ἐλεγον 'οὐχ οὑτος ἐστιν
Ἰησους ὁ υἱος Ἰωσηφ, οὑ ἡμεις οἰδαμεν τον πατερα και την
μητερα; πως νυν λεγει ὁτι " ἐκ του οὐρανου καταβεβηκα";'

ἀπεκριθη Ἰησους και ειπεν αὐτοις 'μη γογγυζετε μετ᾽
ἀλληλων. οὐδεις δυναται ἐλθειν προς ἐμε ἐαν μη ὁ Πατηρ ὁ
πεμψας με ἑλκυση αὐτον, κἀγω ἀναστησω αὐτον ἐν τῃ
ἐσχατῃ ἡμερα. It is written in the prophets "And they shall all
be taught by God". πας ὁ ἀκουσας παρα του Πατρος και μαθων
ἐρχεται προς ἐμε. Not that any man hath seen the Father, save
he which is of God, he hath seen the father. ἀμην ἀμην λεγω
ὑμιν, ὁ πιστευων ἐχει ζωην αἰωνιον. ἐγω εἰμι ἀρτος της ζωης.
οἱ πατερες ὑμων ἐφαγον ἐν τῃ ἐρημῳ το μαννα, και ἀπεθανον.
οὑτος ἐστιν ὁ ἀρτος ὁ ἐκ του οὐρανου καταβαινων, ἱνα τις ἐξ
αὐτου φαγῃ και μη ἀποθανη. ἐγω εἰμι ἀρτος ὁ ζων ὁ ἐκ του

οὐρανου καταβας. ἐαν τις φαγῃ ἐκ τουτου του ἀρτου, ζησει εἰς τον αἰωνα. και ἀρτος ὁν ἐγω δωσω ἡ σαρξ μου ἐστιν ὑπερ της του κοσμου ζωης.'

ἐμαχοντο οὐν προς ἀλληλους οἱ Ἰουδαιοι λεγοντες 'πως δυναται οὑτος ἡμιν δουναι την σαρκα φαγειν;'

εἰπεν οὐν αὐτοις ὁ Ἰησους 'ἀμην ἀμην λεγω ὑμιν, ἐαν μη φαγητε την σαρκα του Υἱου του ἀνθρωπου και πιητε αὐτου το αἱμα, οὐκ ἐχετε ζωην ἐν ἑαυτοις. ὁ τρωγων μου την σαρκα και πινων μου το αἱμα ἐχει ζωην αἰωνιον, κἀγω ἀναστησω αὐτον ἐν τῃ ἐσχατῃ ἡμερᾳ. ἡ γαρ σαρξ μου ἀληθης ἐστι βρωσις, και το αἱμα μου ἀληθης ἐστι ποσις. ὁ τρωγων μου την σαρκα και πινων μου το αἱμα ἐν ἐμοι μενει κἀγω ἐν αὐτῳ. καθως ἀπεστειλεν με ὁ ζων Πατηρ κἀγω ζω δια τον Πατερα, και ὁ τρωγων με κἀκεινος ζησει δι' ἐμε. οὑτος ἐστιν ἀρτος ὁ ἐκ οὐρανου καταβας, οὐ καθως ἐφαγον οἱ πατερες και ἀπεθανον. ὁ τρωγων τουτον τον ἀρτον ζησει εἰς τον αἰωνα.'

ταυτα εἰπεν ἐν συναγωγῃ διδασκων ἐν Καφαρναουμ. πολλοι οὐν ἀκουσαντες ἐκ των μαθητων αὐτου εἰπον 'σκληρος ἐστιν οὑτος ὁ λογος. τίς δυναται αὐτου ἀκουειν;'

John 6.29-60

Antigone's defence

Antigone has buried her brother Polyneices in open defiance of her uncle, King Creon. She is caught doing the deed, and brought before the king.

Creon here begins his interrogation of her and Antigone makes her famous statement about the gods' unwritten laws. The text first appears in simple prose order; then in Sophocles' original verse.

Vocabulary

μηκος 'at length'; συντομως 'briefly'; ἠδησθα 'you knew'; κηρυχθεντα 'things announced, edict'; ἠδη 'I knew'; μελλ-ω 'I am likely to'; ἐμφαν-ης 'clear, plain'; δητα 'yet'; τολμα-ω 'I dare'; ὑπερβαιν-ω 'I transgress'; *ὁ-δε 'this'; τι 'at all'; ξυνοικος 'living with', + gen.; κατω 'below'; ὁριζ-ω 'lay down, define'; τοι-οσ-δε 'such'; ᾠμην 'I considered'; σ-ος 'your'; κηρυγμα 'edict'; *γε 'at any rate'; θνητ-ος 'mortal'; σθεν-ω 'I have power' τοσουτον 'so

190

much'; ὥστε 'as to'; ὑπερδραμειν 'to override'; ἀγραπτ-ος 'unwritten'; κάσφαλη = και ἀσφαλη 'unfailing, secure'; τα νομιμα 'laws'; τι 'merely'; κἀχθες = και ἐχθες 'yesterday'; ἀει 'always'; ποτε 'ever'; κοὐδεις = και οὐδεις 'no one'; ὁτου 'what source'; 'φανη = ἐφανη 'they appeared'.

Prose version

ΚΡΕΩΝ: συ δ᾽ εἰπε μοι μη μηκος, ἀλλα συντομως, [ἀρα] ᾐδησθα [τα] κηρυχθεντα μη πρασσειν ταδε;
ΑΝΤΙΓΟΝΗ: ᾐδη. τί δ᾽ οὐκ ἐμελλον; ἡν γαρ ἐμφανη.
ΚΡΕΩΝ: και δητ᾽ ἐτολμας ὑπερβαινειν τουσδε νομους;
ΑΝΤΙΓΟΝΗ: [ὁ] γαρ Ζευς οὐκ ἡν ὁ κηρυξας ταδε μοι τι. οὐδ᾽ ἡ Δικη ἡ ξυνοικος των κατω θεων ὡρισεν τοιουσδε νομους ἐν ἀνθρωποισιν. οὐδε ᾠμην τα σα κηρυγμαθ᾽, ὀντα γε θνητα, σθενειν τοσουτον ὡστε δυνασθαι ὑπερδραμειν [τα] ἀγραπτα κάσφαλη νομιμα [των] θεων. ταυτα [τα νομιμα] γαρ ζῃ οὐ νυν τι γε κἀχθες, ἀλλ᾽ ἀει ποτε, κοὐδεις οἰδεν ἐξ ὁτου [ταυτα τα νομιμα] 'φανη.

Scansion

The rhythm is 'blank tum-ti-tum', where blank can be tum or ti, repeated three times: thus 'blank tum-ti-tum/blank tum-ti-tum/blank tum-ti-tum'. Line ten does something tricky with the first four syllables, all short.

This is the iambic trimeter, the metre of the dialogue in Greek drama.

Sophocles

ΚΡΕΩΝ: συ δ᾽ εἰπε μοι μη μηκος, ἀλλα συντομως,
ᾐδησθα κηρυχθεντα μη πρασσειν ταδε;
ΑΝΤΙΓΟΝΗ: ᾐδη. τί δ᾽ οὐκ ἐμελλον; ἐμφανη γαρ ἡν.
ΚΡΕΩΝ: και δητ᾽ ἐτολμας τουσδ᾽ ὑπερβαινειν νομους;
ΑΝΤΙΓΟΝΗ: οὐ γαρ τι μοι Ζευς ἡν ὁ κηρυξας ταδε,
οὐδ᾽ ἡ ξυνοικος των κατω θεων Δικη
τοι-ουσδ᾽ ἐν ἀνθρωποισιν ὡρισεν νομους,
οὐδε σθενειν τοσουτον ᾠμην τα σα
κηρυγμαθ᾽ ὡστ᾽ ἀγραπτα κάσφαλη θεων

191

νομιμα δυνασθαι θνητα γ᾽ ὀνθ᾽ ὑπερδραμειν.
οὐ γαρ τι νυν γε κἀχθες, ἀλλ᾽ ἀει ποτε
ζῃ ταυτα, κοὐδεις οἰδεν ἐξ ὁτου ᾽φανῃ.

Sophocles, Antigone 446-57.

The Greek world

The Greek revival

In the 4th century AD the Roman empire split in two: a western half, ruled only nominally from Rome because the real centres of power had moved north to places like e.g. Ravenna; and an eastern half, centred on Constantinople (ancient Byzantium, Istanbul), the city earlier created by Constantine to keep Greek élites in the east happy with a Rome of their own.

It is important to point out that it was only the western empire which 'fell' in the 5th century AD. The Greek eastern 'Byzantine' empire, based on Constantinople, continued to flourish till the Ottoman Turks took it on 29 May 1453, and this was where Greek literature and learning survived. In the west, with the demise of Rome, they completely disappeared from cultural and educational life. The Bible, read in Rome up till the 3rd century AD in Greek, was otherwise read only in various Latin versions and this accounts for the supremacy of Latin in Christianised western Europe after the fall of the western Roman empire. Incidentally, St Jerome's Latin 'Vulgate', produced in the late 4th century AD, did not become standard and unify the traditions till the 8th century AD.

For the return of Greek to the west we must therefore wind forward to the turmoil of the Byzantine empire under Turkish attack. Turks ('Turchu') had been coming westwards from the far east from the 9th century AD. They converted to Islam (whose founder was Mohammed *c.* 620 AD) and set about establishing themselves in the eastern Mediterranean. The threat to the Byzantine empire and Constantinople in particular was obvious, and as the threat increased, so Byzantine scholars starting seeking refuge in the west, bringing their precious manuscripts of Greek literature with them. It is from these manuscripts that our texts of Greek literature derive. Italy was especially receptive to these Byzantine scholars, and it was here from the 14th century AD that classical scholarship as we think of it began. The invention of printing secured the survival of Greek and Latin literature in the 15th century. Greek began to be taught again in Italy in 1387, and in 1492 the first Greek teaching post in England was established at Oxford. Translations of Greek literature into Latin and then vernaculars started to appear. The renaissance had begun.

Answers
Lucian
We reached the place where it was necessary for him, sitting down, to listen to the prayers ... So Zeus, sitting down at the first [opening] and removing the lid, offered himself to those praying. They prayed from all over the world for different and varied [things]. The prayers were like this: 'O Zeus, may it come about for me to be king'; 'O Zeus, may it come about for me that my onions and garlic grow'; 'O gods, may it come about for me that my father dies quickly'; 'May it come about for me to win my court-case'; 'May it come about for me to be crowned at the Olympics'. Of those sailing, one prayed for the north wind to blow, the other for the south, the farmer asked for rain, the potter for sun. Zeus, listening, and precisely examining each prayer, did not promise all, 'but one the father granted, the other he refused'.

The Bread of Life
Use your Bible.

Antigone
K: And tell me not at length, but briefly: did you know the edict not to do these things?

A: I knew. Why was I not likely to? For it was clear.

K: And still you dared to transgress these laws?

A: [Yes] for Zeus was not the one announcing these-things to me at all. Nor did Justice, who lives with the gods below, lay down such laws among men. Nor did I consider your edicts, being at-any-rate mortal, to have the power so much as to be able to override the unwritten and unfailing laws of the gods. For these laws live not now merely at-any-rate and yesterday, but always ever, and no one knows from where they [these laws] appeared.

GRAMMATICAL SUMMARY

VERBS

PRESENT ACTIVE

1. Present indicative active παυ-ω 'I stop'

1s	παυ-ω	'I stop' 'I do stop' 'I am stopping'
2s	παυ-εις	'you (s) stop', 'you do stop', 'you are stopping'
3s	παυ-ει	'he, she, it stops', 'he, she, it does stop/is stopping'
1pl	παυ-ομεν	'we stop', 'we do stop', 'we are stopping'
2pl	παυ-ετε	'you (pl) stop', 'you do stop', 'you are stopping'
3pl	παυ-ουσι(ν)	'they stop', 'they do stop', 'they are stopping'

<u>Imperative</u>

2s	παυ-ε	'stop!' (addressed to one person)
2pl	παυ-ετε	'stop!' (addressed to more than one person)

<u>Infinitive</u>

	παυ-ειν	'to stop'

<u>Participle</u>

m. παυων (παυοντ-), f. παυουσ-α, n. παυ-ον (παυοντ-) 'stopping'

<u>Subjunctive</u>

1s	παυ-ω	'I (may) stop'
2s	παυ-ης	'you (s) (may) stop'
3s	παυ-η	'he, she, it may stop/stops'
1pl	παυ-ωμεν	'we (may) stop'
2pl	παυ-ητε	'you (pl) (may) stop'
3pl	παυ-ωσι	'they (may) stop'

2. Present indicative active of νικαω 'I conquer'

1s	νικ-ω	'I conquer'
2s	νικ-ας	'you conquer'
3s	νικ-α	'he, she, it conquers'
1pl	νικ-ωμεν	'we conquer'
2pl	νικ-ατε	'you conquer'
3pl	νικ-ωσι	'they conquer'

<u>Imperative</u>

2s	νικ-α	'conquer!'
2pl	νικ-ατε	'conquer!'

<u>Infinitive</u>

	νικαν	'to conquer'

194

Participle
　　m. νικων (νικωντ-), f. νικωσ-α, n. νικων (νικωντ-) 'conquering'

3. Present indicative active of φιλε-ω 'I love'

1s	φιλ-ω	'I love'
2s	φιλ-εις	'you love'
3s	φιλ-ει	'he, she, it loves'
1pl	φιλ-ουμεν	'we love'
2pl	φιλ-ειτε	'you love'
3pl	φιλ-ουσι	'they love'

Imperative
2s	φίλ-ει	'love!'
2pl	φιλ-ειτε	'love!'

Infinitive
　　φιλειν　　　　'to love'
Participle
　　m. φιλων (φιλουντ-), f. φιλουσ-α, n. φιλουν (φιλουντ-) 'loving'

PRESENT PASSIVE

4. Present indicative passive of παυ-ω 'I am being stopped'

1s	παυ-ομαι	'I am being stopped'
2s	παυ-η	'you (s) are being stopped'
3s	παυ-εται	'he, she, it is being stopped'
1pl	παυ-ομεθα	'we are being stopped'
2pl	παυ-εσθε	'you (pl) are being stopped'
3pl	παυ-ονται	'they are being stopped'

Infinitive
　　παυ-εσθαι　　'to be stopped'
Participle
　　παυ-ομεν-ος η ον　'being stopped'

PRESENT MIDDLE

5. Present indicative middle of ἐρχ-ομαι 'I come, go'

1s	ἐρχ-ομαι	'I go',
2s	ἐρχ-η	'you (s) go'
3s	ἐρχ-εται	'he, she, it goes'
1pl	ἐρχ-ομεθα	'we go'
2pl	ἐρχ-εσθε	'you (pl) go'
3pl	ἐρχ-ονται	'they go'

Imperative
2s	ἐρχ-ου	'go!'
2pl	ἐρχ-εσθε	'go!'

Infinitive

ἐρχ-εσθαι   'to go'

Participle

ἐρχ-ομεν-ος η ον 'going'

Subjunctive

1s	ἐρχ-ωμαι	'I (may) go'
2s	ἐρχ-ῃ	'you (s) (may) go'
3s	ἐρχ-ηται	'he, she, it may go/goes'
1pl	ἐρχ-ωμεθα	'we (may) go'
2pl	ἐρχ-ησθε	'you (pl) (may) go'
3pl	ἐρχ-ωνται	'they (may) go'

IMPERFECT ACTIVE

6. Imperfect indicative active of παυ-ω 'I stop'

1s	ἐ-παυ-ον	'I was stopping'
2s	ἐ-παυ-ες	'you were stopping'
3s	ἐ-παυ-ε(ν)	'he, she, it was stopping'
1pl	ἐ-παυ-ομεν	'we were stopping'
2pl	ἐ-παυ-ετε	'you were stopping'
3pl	ἐ-παυ-ον	'they were stopping'

7. Imperfect indicative active of νικα-ω 'I conquer'

1s	ἐνικ-ων	'I was conquering'
2s	ἐνικ-ας	'you were conquering'
3s	ἐνικ-α	'he, she, it was conquering'
1pl	ἐνικ-ωμεν	'we were conquering'
2pl	ἐνικ-ατε	'you were conquering'
3pl	ἐνικ-ων	'they were conquering'

8. Imperfect indicative active of φιλε-ω 'I love'

1s	ἐφιλ-ουν	'I was loving'
2s	ἐφιλ-εις	'you were loving'
3s	ἐφιλ-ει	'he, she, it was loving'
1pl	ἐφιλ-ουμεν	'we were loving'
2pl	ἐφιλ-ειτε	'you were loving'
3pl	ἐφιλ-ουν	'they were loving'

IMPERFECT PASSIVE

9. Imperfect indicative passive of παυ-ω 'I stop'

1s	ἐ-παυ-ομην	'I was being stopped'
2s	ἐ-παυ-ου	'you were being stopped'
3s	ἐ-παυ-ετο	'he, she, it was being stopped'

1*pl*	ἐ-παυ-ομεθα	'we were being stopped'
2*pl*	ἐ-παυ-εσθε	'you were being stopped'
3*pl*	ἐ-παυ-οντο	'they were being stopped'

IMPERFECT MIDDLE

10. Imperfect indicative middle of πορευ-ομαι **'I travel'**

1*s*	ἐ-πορευ-ομην	'I was travelling'
2*s*	ἐ-πορευ-ου	'you were travelling'
3*s*	ἐ-πορευ-ετο	'he, she, it was travelling'
1*pl*	ἐ-πορευ-ομεθα	'we were travelling'
2*pl*	ἐ-πορευ-εσθε	'you were travelling'
3*pl*	ἐ-πορευ-οντο	'they were travelling'

AORIST ACTIVE

11. Aorist indicative active of παυ-ω **'I stop'**

1*s*	ἐ-παυσ-α	'I stopped'
2*s*	ἐ-παυσ-ας	'you stopped'
3*s*	ἐ-παυσ-ε(ν)	'he, she, it stopped'
1*pl*	ἐ-παυσ-αμεν	'we stopped'
2*pl*	ἐ-παυσ-ατε	'you stopped'
3*pl*	ἐ-παυσ-αν	'they stopped'

<u>Infinitive</u>

    παυσ-αι   'to stop'

<u>Participle</u>

    m. παυσ-ας (παυσαντ-), f. παυσασ-α, n. παυσαν (παυσαντ-)
    'stopping'

AORIST MIDDLE

12. Aorist indicative middle of πορευ-ομαι **'I travel'**

1*s*	ἐ-πορευσ-αμην	'I travelled'
2*s*	ἐ-πορευσ-ω	'you travelled'
3*s*	ἐ-πορευσ-ατο	'he, she, it travelled'
1*pl*	ἐ-πορευσ-αμεθα	'we travelled'
2*pl*	ἐ-πορευσ-ασθε	'you travelled'
3*pl*	ἐ-πορευσ-αντο	'they travelled'

<u>Infinitive</u>

    πορευσ-ασθαι   'to travel'

<u>Participle</u>

    πορευσ-αμεν-ος η ον 'travelling'

13. Stem changes in the aorist

The sign of the regular aorist is -σα-.

1. Where the present ends in a consonant, that consonant usually changes by contact with the σ. Thus:

φ + σ = ψ	e.g. γραφ-ω	ἐγραφσ-	= ἐγραψ-α	'I wrote'
π + σ = ψ	e.g. πεμπ-ω	ἐπεμπσ-	= ἐπεμψ-α	'I sent'
σκ + σ = ξ	e.g. διδασκ-ω	ἐδιδασκσ-	= ἐδιδαξ-α	'I taught'
κ + σ = ξ	e.g. διωκ-ω	ἐδιωκσ-	= ἐδιωξ-α	'I chased'
γ + σ = ξ	e.g. λεγ-ω	ἐλεγσ-	= ἐλεξ-α	'I said'
ττ + σ = ξ	e.g. κηρυττ-ω	ἐκηρυττσ-	= ἐκηρυξ-α	'I announced',
	πραττ-ω	ἐπραττσ-	= ἐπραξ-α	'I did, acted, fared'

2. Where the stem ends in α or ε (i.e. is a contract verb), those vowels lengthen before the σ, e.g.

ζαω   aor. ἐζησα
μισεω   aor. ἐμισησα

ALTERNATIVE AORIST ACTIVE

14. Aorist indicative active ἠλθ-ον 'I came/went'

1s	ἠλθ-ον	'I went'
2s	ἠλθ-ες	'you went'
3s	ἠλθ-ε(ν)	'he, she, it went'
1pl	ἠλθ-ομεν	'we went'
2pl	ἠλθ-ετε	'you went'
3pl	ἠλθ-ον	'they went'

ALTERNATIVE AORIST MIDDLE

15. Aorist indicative middle ἀφικ-ομην 'I came, arrived'

1s	ἀφικ-ομην	'I arrived'
2s	ἀφικ-ου	'you arrived'
3s	ἀφικ-ετο	'he, she, it arrived'
1pl	ἀφικ-ομεθα	'we arrived'
2pl	ἀφικ-εσθε	'you arrived'
3pl	ἀφικ-οντο	'they arrived'

IRREGULAR VERBS

16. Present indicative of εἰμι 'I am'

1s	εἰμι	'I am'
2s	εἰ	'you (*singular*) are'
3s	ἐστι(ν)	'he, she, it, there is'

198

1*pl*	ἐσμεν	'we are'
2*pl*	ἐστε	'you (*plural*) are'
3*pl*	εἰσι(ν)	'they are'

<u>Infinitive</u>

εἶναι   'to be'

<u>Participle</u>

m. ὤν (ὀντ-), f. οὖσ-α, n. ὀν (ὀντ-) 'being'

<u>Subjunctive</u>

1*s*	ὦ	'I may be, I am'
2*s*	ἦς	'you (*s*) may be, are'
3*s*	ἦ	'he, she, it may be, is'
1*pl*	ὦμεν	'we may be, are'
2*pl*	ἦτε	'you (*pl*) may be, are'
3*pl*	ὦσι(ν)	'they may be, are'

17. Imperfect indicative of εἰμι, ἦ(ν) 'I was'

1*s*	ἦ(ν)	'I was'
2*s*	ἦσθα	'you were'
3*s*	ἦν	'he, she, it was, there was'
1*pl*	ἦμεν	'we were'
2*pl*	ἦτε	'you were'
3*pl*	ἦσαν	'they were, there were'

18. Present indicative of οἶδα 'I know'

1*s*	οἶδα	'I know'
2*s*	οἶσθα or οἶδας	'you know'
3*s*	οἶδε(ν)	'he, she, it knows'
1*pl*	ἴσμεν or οἴδαμεν	'we know'
2*pl*	ἴστε or οἴδατε	'you know'
3*pl*	ἴσασι(ν) or οἴδασι(ν)	'they know'

<u>Infinitive</u>

εἰδεναι   'to know'

<u>Participle</u>

m. εἰδώς (εἰδοτ-), f. εἰδυι-α 'knowing'

RULES OF CONTRACT

19. α-contract verbs

α + ε = α
α + ει = α
α + any ο-ω = ω

20. ε- contract verbs

ε + ω = ω

ε + ε or ει = ει
ε + ο or ου = ου

PARTICIPLES

Participles ('-ing') have m., f. and n. forms.

21. -μενος

Participles ending in -μεν-ος follow the m., f., n. pattern of καλ-ος η ον. See **25** below.

22. -ων -ουσα

Participles ending in -ων (e.g. m. παυ-ων f. παυ-ουσα) follow the pattern given here (omitting neuter):

	M	F
	M	F
Nom. *s*	-ων	-ουσ-α
Nom. *pl*	-οντ-ες	-ουσ-αι
Acc. *s*	-οντ-α	-ουσ-αν
Acc. *pl*	-οντ-ας	-ουσ-ας
Gen. *s*	-οντ-ος	-ουσ-ης
Gen. *pl*	-οντ-ων	-ουσ-ων
Dat. *s*	-οντ-ι	-ουσ-η
Dat. *pl*	-ου-σι(ν)	-ουσ-αις

23. -σας -σασα

Participles ending in -σας (e.g. m. παυ-σας f. παυ-σασα) follow the pattern given here (omitting neuter):

	M	F
	M	F
Nom. *s*	-σας	-σασα
Nom. *pl*	-σαντες	-σασαι
Acc. *s*	-σαντα	-σασαν
Acc. *pl*	-σαντας	-σασας
Gen. *s*	-σαντος	-σασης
Gen. *pl*	-σαντων	-σασων
Dat. *s*	-σαντι	-σαση
Dat. *pl*	-σασι(ν)	-σασαις

THE DEFINITE ARTICLE

'The' is the most important word in ancient Greek.

First, it gives the clue to the case and number of the noun it goes with.

Second, since its forms are used by a huge range of nouns and adjectives (as you can see under ADJECTIVES below), if you know Def Art, you save yourself a great deal of work.

24. The definite article

	M	F	N
Announcing subject, singular (nom.):	ὁ	ἡ	το
Announcing subject, plural:	οἱ	αἱ	τα
Announcing object, singular (acc.):	τον	την	το
Announcing object, plural:	τους	τας	τα
Announcing 'of ', singular (gen.):	του	της	του
Announcing 'of ', plural:	των	των	των
Announcing 'to, for' singular (dat.):	τῳ	τη	τῳ
Announcing 'to, for' plural:	τοις	ταις	τοις

ADJECTIVES

Adjectives (which include participles) have m., f. and n. forms since their job is to describe m., f. and n. nouns. Observe how all the adjectives below follow the pattern of Def Art very closely.

25. Adjectives like καλ-ος

Adjectives ending in -ος are very common indeed. Here is an example in full, καλος 'beautiful, fine, good':

	καλ-ος M	καλ-η F	καλ-ον N
Singular			
Nom.	καλ-ος	καλ-η	καλ-ον
Acc.	καλ-ον	καλ-ην	καλ-ον
Gen.	καλ-ου	καλ-ης	καλ-ου
Dat.	καλ-ῳ	καλ-η	καλ-ῳ
Plural			
Nom.	καλ-οι	καλ-αι	καλ-α
Acc.	καλ-ους	καλ-ας	καλ-α
Gen.	καλ-ων	καλ-ων	καλ-ων
Dat.	καλ-οις	καλ-αις	καλ-οις

Note

Adjectives whose stem ends in -ι, ρ, or ε replace η with α in the f. singular, e.g. δικαι-ος, f. δικαι-α, δικαι-αν etc.

PRONOUNS

A pronoun takes the place (Latin *pro*) of a noun: not 'Jimmy' but 'he', not 'table' but 'it', not 'the boys' but 'we', and so on. Here are the three most common words for 'he, she it' in Greek, in m., f. and n. forms:

201

26. αὐ-τος 'he'

	αὐ-τος, 'he' M	αὐ-τη, 'she' F	αὐ-το, 'it' N
Singular			
Nom.	αὐ-τος	αὐ-τη	αὐ-το
Acc.	αὐ-τον	αὐ-την	αὐ-το
Gen.	αὐ-του	αὐ-του	αὐ-της
Dat.	αὐ-τῳ	αὐ-τῃ	αὐ-τῳ
Plural			
Nom.	αὐ-τοι	αὐ-ται	αὐ-τα
Acc.	αὐ-τους	αὐ-τας	αὐ-τα
Gen.	αὐ-των	αὐ-των	αὐ-των
Dat.	αὐ-τοις	αὐ-ταις	αὐ-τοις

27. οὑ-τος 'he, this person'

	οὑ-τος, 'he, this man' M	αὐ-τη, 'she, this woman' F	του-το, 'it, this thing' N
Singular			
Nom.	οὑ-τος	αὐ-τη	του-το
Acc.	του-τον	ταυ-την	του-το
Gen.	του-του	ταυ-της	του-του
Dat.	του-τῳ	ταυ-τῃ	του-τῳ
Plural			
Nom.	οὑ-τοι	αὐ-ται	ταυ-τα
Acc.	του-τους	ταυ-τας	ταυ-τα
Gen.	του-των	του-των	του-των
Dat.	του-τοις	ταυ-ταις	του-τοις

28. ἐκειν-ος 'he, that person'

	ἐκειν-ος, 'he, that man' M	ἐκειν-η, 'she, that woman' F	ἐκειν-ο, 'it, that thing' N
Singular			
Nom.	ἐκειν-ος	ἐκειν-η	ἐκειν-ο
Acc.	ἐκειν-ον	ἐκειν-ην	ἐκειν-ο
Gen.	ἐκειν-ου	ἐκειν-ης	ἐκειν-ου
Dat.	ἐκειν-ῳ	ἐκειν-ῃ	ἐκειν-ῳ
Plural			
Nom.	ἐκειν-οι	ἐκειν-αι	ἐκειν-α
Acc.	ἐκειν-ους	ἐκειν-ας	ἐκειν-α
Gen.	ἐκειν-ων	ἐκειν-ων	ἐκειν-ων
Dat.	ἐκειν-οις	ἐκειν-αις	ἐκειν-οις

Note

When any form of οὑ-τος and ἐκειν-ος is followed by a form of Def Art, οὑ-τος means 'this' and ἐκειν-ος means 'that', e.g.

ἐκεινος ὁ οἰκος ἐστιν ἀγαθος 'that [the] house is good'
γραφω ταυτην την ἐπιστολην 'I am writing this [the] letter'

29. ἐγω 'I/we' and συ 'you'

	'I/me'	'we/us'	'You' *s*	'You' *pl*
Announcing subject, singular (nom.):	ἐγω		συ	
Announcing subject, plural:		ἡμεις		ὑμεις
Announcing object, singular (acc.):	(ἐ)με		σε	
Announcing object, plural:		ἡμας		ὑμας
Announcing 'of ', singular (gen.):	(ἐ)μου		σου	
Announcing 'of ', plural:		ἡμων		ὑμων
Announcing 'to, for' singular (dat.):	(ἐ)μοι		σοι	
Announcing 'to, for' plural:		ἡμιν		ὑμιν

NOUNS

As you know, we have not examined in detail the endings of any nouns. We have learnt the noun-stem to give us the meaning, and have relied on Def Art to give us the rest of the information (case, *s*/*pl*, m., f., n.).

Like Latin, nouns are divided into different types, called declensions. The most important patterns are:

First and second declension nouns, following the pattern of Def Art.

Third declension nouns, following the pattern of the endings (not the stem) of the m. participle (see **22** above).

Here then, purely for reference, are examples of the nouns from these three major declensions:

30. First declension, feminine, like ἡ ἀγαπ-η

Singular
Nom.   ἀγαπ-η
Acc.   ἀγαπ-ην
Gen.   ἀγαπ-ης
Dat.   ἀγαπ-ῃ
Plural
Nom.   ἀγαπ-αι
Acc.   ἀγαπ-ας
Gen.   ἀγαπ-ων
Dat.   ἀγαπ-αις

Note
Feminine nouns ending in -α like e.g. ἡ ἀδικι-α follow this pattern too, with -α generally replacing -η throughout the singular.

31. Second declension, masculine, like ὁ θε-ος

Singular
Nom.   θε-ος
Acc.   θε-ον
Gen.   θε-ου
Dat.   θε-ῳ
Plural
Nom.   θε-οι
Acc.   θε-ους
Gen.   θε-ων
Dat.   θε-οις

32. Second declension, neuter, like το τεκν-ον

Singular
Nom.   τεκν-ον
Acc.   τεκν-ον
Gen.   τεκν-ου
Dat.   τεκν-ῳ
Plural
Nom.   τεκν-α
Acc.   τεκν-α
Gen.   τεκν-ων
Dat.   τεκν-οις

33. Third declension, masculine or feminine, like Ἕλλην, Ἑλλην-

Singular
Nom.   Ἕλλην
Acc.   Ἕλλην-α
Gen.   Ἕλλην-ος
Dat.   Ἕλλην-ι
Plural
Nom.   Ἕλλην-ες
Acc.   Ἕλλην-ας
Gen.   Ἕλλην-ων
Dat.   Ἑλλη-σι(ν)

Note
You can be sure of first and second declension nouns. If they are of the

GRAMMATICAL SUMMARY

right gender and have the right ending in the nom. *s* (-η, or -ος, or -ον), their declension is secure.

But there are many different types of third declension. The pattern I have given is followed by e.g. ἀνηρ ἀνδρ-, γυνη γυναικ-, παις παιδ- but e.g. ἡ πολις follows a quite different pattern, as does το πληθος (note: το, not ὁ, so not second declension).

PREPOSITIONS

34. + accusative

προς	'to', 'towards'
εἰς	'into'
δια	'through, because of'

35. + genitive

ἀπο, ἀπ, ἀφ'	'(away) from'
ἐκ, ἐξ	'out of'
δια	'through, because of'
ὑπερ	'on behalf of'
ὑπο, ὑπ', ὑφ'	'by'
περι	'around, concerning'

36. + dative

ἐν	'in'

LEARNING VOCABULARY

ἀγαθ-οι (nom. *pl*, i.e. referring to many people) 'good', 'brave'

ἀγαθ-ος (nom. *s*, i.e. referring to one person) 'good', 'brave'

ἀγαθ-ος η ον 'good', 'brave'

ἀγαπα-ω 'I love'

ἡ ἀγαπ-η '[the] love'

ὁ ἀγγελ-ος 'the angel', 'messenger'

ἀδικε-ω 'I harm, (do) wrong, hurt'

ἡ ἀδικι-α 'the injustice, crime, wrong'

ἀδικ-ος 'unjust'

αἱ 'the' nom. *pl* f.

το αἱμα 'blood'

αἰσχυν-ομαι 'I feel ashamed'

ὁ αἰων (αἰων-) 'eternity'

αἰωνι-ος 'eternal'

ἀκου-ω 'I hear, listen to' + gen. if hearing a person

ἡ ἀληθει-α '[the] truth'

ἀληθ-ης 'true'

ἀλλα 'but' (ἀλλ' when next word starts with a vowel, e.g. ἀλλ' ἐστι)

ἀλληλ-οι 'each other'

ἀλλ-ος η ο 'other'

ὁ ἀνηρ (ἀνδρ-) 'man, husband'

ὁ ἀνθρωπ-ος 'human, man, fellow'

ἀπαγ-ω 'I arrest'

ἀπεθανον 'they died'

ἀπεκρινα-μην aor. of ἀποκρινομαι

ἀπο, ἀπ, ἀφ' '(away) from'

ἀπεκριθη 'he replied'

ἀποκριν-ομαι 'I reply'

ἀπολογε-ομαι 'I defend myself'

ὁ ἀποστολ-ος 'the apostle'

ἀρα *indicates question*

ἡ ἀρχ-η 'the beginning; rule; principle'

ἀρχ-ομαι 'I begin'

αὐτ-η 'she' ('her')

αὐτ-η 'this woman, she'

αὐτο 'it'

αὐτ-ος 'he' ('him')

ἀφικ-ομην 'I came, arrived'

βαλλ-ω 'I throw (missiles)'

βαρβαρ-οι (nom. *pl*) 'non-Greek speakers'

βαρβαρ-ος (nom. *s*) 'non-Greek speaker'

το βιβλι-ον 'the book, bible'

ὁ βι-ος '[the] life'

βοα-ω 'I shout'

βουλευ-ομαι 'I advise'

βουλ-ομαι 'I wish, want'

γαρ 'because, for' (second or third word in Greek, first in English)

γε 'at any rate'

γενοιτο μοι 'may it come about for me'

ὁ γεωργ-ος 'farmer'

ἡ γ-η 'the land'

γιγν-ομαι 'I become, am made/born, am'

γι(γ)νωσκ-ω 'I recognise, get to know, learn'

γογγυζ-ω 'I murmur, grumble'

γραφ-ω 'I write'

ἡ γυνη (γυναικ-) 'woman'

το δαιμονι-ον 'the divine sign; (biblical) devil, demon'

δε (on its own) 'and, but';

206

following μεν, 'on the other hand'

δει 'it is necessary for X (acc.) to Y (infinitive)'

δηλ-ος η ον 'clear, evident'

ἡ δημοκρατι-α 'the people (δημος)-power (κρατος), the democracy'

ὁ δημ-ος 'the people'

δια, δι, + acc., gen. 'through, because of'

διακωλυ-ω 'I prevent'

διανοε-ομαι 'I plan, intend, realise'

διδασκ-ω 'I teach'

δικαια 'justly'

δικαι-ος 'just, lawful, right'

οἱ δικαστ-αι 'the jurors'

ἡ δικ-η 'judgement, trial, court-case'

διωκ-ω 'I pursue, chase'

δοκε-ω 'I seem'

δυνα-μαι 'I can, am able to' + infin.

ἐαν 'if (ever)' + subjunc.

ἐγεν-ομην 'I was born, made, I became, happened'

ἐγραψ- aor. γραφω

ἐγω 'I' (nom. s)

ἐδιωξ- aor. διωκω

ἐθελ-ω 'I wish, want'

εἰ 'you are'

εἰδεναι 'to know'

εἰδ-ον 'I saw'

εἰδως (εἰδοτ-) 'knowing'

εἰμι 'I am'

εἰναι 'to be'

εἰπειν 'to speak'

εἰπ-ον 'I said, spoke'

εἰπέ μοι 'tell me'

εἰς 'into'

εἰσι 'they are'

εἰχ-ον 'I was having' (imperf. of ἐχω)

ἐκ, ἐξ 'out of' + gen.

ἐκαστ-ος 'each'

ἐκειν-η 'she, that woman'

ἐκειν-ος 'he, that man'

ἐκηρυξ- aor. of κηρυττω

ἐλεξ- aor. of λεγω

Ἑλλην (nom. s) 'Greek'

Ἑλλην-ες (nom. pl) 'Greeks'

ἐμαχεσ- aor. of μαχομαι

ἐμε 'me' (acc. s)

ἐμειν- aor. of μενω

ἐμοι 'to, for me' (dat. s)

ἐμου 'of me' (gen s)

ἐν 'in' + dat.

ἡ ἐντολ-η 'the command, order'

ἐξεστι 'it is permitted to Y (dat.) to X (infin.)'

ἐπειδη 'when'

ἐπεμψ- aor. of πεμπω

ἐπραξ- aor. of πραττω

ἐπυθ-ομην 'I heard, enquired'

ἡ ἐπιστολ-η 'the letter'

το ἐργ-ον 'the work, deed'

ἡ ἐρημ-ος 'the desert'

ἐρχ-ομαι 'I come, go'

ἐσμεν 'we are'

ἐστε 'you (pl) are'

ἐστι 'he, she, it, there is'; + dat. 'there is to X', i.e. 'X has'

ἐσχατ-ος η ον 'last'

εὑρισκ-ω 'I find'

ἡ εὐχ-η 'prayer'

εὐχ-ομαι 'I pray'

ἐφαγον 'they ate'

ὁ ἐχ-ις 'snake'

ἐχ-ω 'I have'

ἐψηφισ- aor. of ψηφιζομαι

ζα-ω 'I live'

ζης 'you live'

ζη 'he, she, it lives'

ζην 'to live'

ζησει 'he will live'

ζητε 'you live'

ζητε-ω 'I seek'

ἡ ζω-η '[the] life'

ζωμεν 'we live'

ζωσι 'they live'

ἠ 'I was'

ἡ 'the' (nom. s fem.)

207

ἡ 'he, she, it may be' (subjunc. of
  εἰμι)
ἠγαπησ- aor. of ἀγαπαω
ἠθελησ- aor. of ἐθελω
ἠκουσ- aor. of ἀκουω
ἠλθ-ον 'I went/came'
ἡμας 'us' (acc. *pl*)
ἡμεις 'we' (nom. *pl*)
ἡμεν 'we were'
ἡ ἡμερ-α 'the day'
ἡμιν 'to, for us' (dat. *pl*)
ἡμων 'of us' (gen. *pl*)
ἠν 'he, she, it, there was'
ἠρ-ομην 'I asked'
ἡς 'you may be' (subjunc. of εἰμι)
ἠσαν 'they, there were'
ἠσθα 'you were'
ἠτε 'you may be' (subjunc. of εἰμι)
ἠτε 'you were'
ηὐξ- aor. of εὐχομαι
ηὑρ-ον 'I found'
ἡ θαλαττ-α 'the sea'
ὁ θανατ-ος 'death'
θελ-ω 'I wish, want'
οἱ θε-οι '[the] gods' (nom. *pl*)
ὁ θε-ος '[the] god' (nom. *s*)
του Θεου 'of God'
ὁ Ἰησους '[the] Jesus'
ἱνα 'in order that' + subjunc.
ἰσασι 'they know'
ἰσμεν 'we know'
ἰστε 'you know'
κἀγω = και ἐγω
καθευδ-ω 'I sleep'
καθεζ-ομαι 'I sit'
καθως 'as'
και 'and', 'too', 'as well', 'also'
καιτοι 'and yet'
κακα 'evilly'
κακοι 'bad', 'evil' (nom. *pl* m.)
κακος 'bad', 'evil' (nom. *s* m.)
κακ-ος η ον 'bad', 'evil'
καταβαιν-ω 'I come down,
  descend'
καταψηφιζ-ομαι 'I condemn' +
  gen.
ὁ κατηγορ-ος 'accuser'

καλε-ω 'I call'
καταβας 'descending, coming
  down' (nom. *s* m.)
κελευ-ω 'I order'
ἡ κεφαλ-η 'head'
κηρυττ-ω 'I announce'
ὁ κινδυν-ος 'danger'
ὁ κοσμ-ος 'the world'
ὁ κυρι-ος 'the Lord'
λαλε-ω 'I talk, speak'
λεγ-ω 'I say, speak'
ὁ λογ-ος 'the word, reason,
  argument'
ὁ μαθητ-ης 'the student, disciple'
μαλακως ἐχω 'I feel poorly'
μαρτυρε-ω 'I bear witness'
ἡ μαρτυρι-α '[the] witness,
  evidence'
μαχ-ομαι 'I fight'
με 'me' (acc. *s*)
μεγαλ- 'great, large, weighty'
μεν ... δε 'on the one hand ... on
  the other hand'
μεν-ω 'I remain, wait, stay'
μετα, μετ', μεθ' 'with' + gen.
μη 'not'; 'don't' + imperative
μισε-ω 'I hate'
μοι 'to, for me' (dat. *s*)
μον-ος η ον 'alone, sole'
μου 'of me' (gen. *s*)
νικα-ω 'I conquer, win, am
  victorious'
ὁ νομ-ος 'law, custom'
νυν 'now'
ὁ 'the' (nom. *s* m.)
ὁ-δε ἡ-δε το-δε 'this'
οἱ 'the' (nom. *pl* m.)
οἰδα 'I know'
ὁ οἰκ-ος 'house, home'
οἰσθα 'you know'
ὀλιγ-οι 'few' (nom. *pl* m.)
ὁ μεν...ὁ δε...ὁ δε...'the one...the
  other...the other'; (*pl*)
  'some...others'
ὁμολογε-ω 'I confess, admit'
ὀντ- 'being' (m., n. stem of
  participle of εἰμι)

ὁρα-ω 'I see'
ὅς ἀν 'whoever' + subjunc.
ὅτι 'that'
οὐ, οὐκ (when a vowel comes
   next, e.g. οὐκ ἐστι), and οὐχ
   (when 'h' comes next, e.g. οὐχ
   Ἑλλην) 'no, not'; οὐχι 'no'
οὐδε 'nor, and...not'
οὐδεν 'nothing'
οὐδεποτε 'never'
οὐδεπω 'not yet'
οὐν 'therefore' (second or third
   word in Greek, first in
   English)
οὐ μη 'never'
ὁ οὐραν-ος 'the heaven'
οὐσ- 'being' (f. stem of participle
   of εἰμι)
οὔτε...οὔτε 'neither...nor'
οὗτ-οι 'they, these men'
οὗτ-ος 'he, this man'
οὕτως 'in this way'
το παιδι-ον 'the small child,
   small slave'
ὁ, ἡ παις (παιδ-) 'child'
παν ποιων 'doing everything'
πανταχοθεν 'from all sides'
παρ-ειμι 'I am present'
παρεχ-ω 'I provide, offer'
ὁ Πατηρ (Πατ(ε)ρ-) 'the Father'
παυ-ω 'I stop'
πειθ-ομαι 'I obey, trust' + dat.
πεμπ-ω 'I send'
περι + gen., 'around, concerning'
πιν-ω 'I drink'
πιστευ-ω 'I trust, have faith in,
   believe' + dat., or προς + acc.
το πληθ-ος 'the mob, crowd'
ποιε-ω 'I make, do'
ὁ πολεμ-ος 'war'
ἡ πολ-ις 'the city, city-state'
πολλακις 'often'
πολλ-οι 'many' (nom. pl m.)
πορευ-ομαι 'I walk, journey'
ὁ ποταμ-ος 'river'
που; where?

το πραγμα (πραγματ-) 'the
   affair, business, matter'
πραττ-ω 'I make, do, fare, act'
προς 'to', 'towards'
ῥᾳδι-ος 'easy'
ἡ σαρξ, σαρκ- 'flesh'
σε 'you' (acc. s)
ἡ σκοτι-α 'the darkness'
το σκοτ-ος 'the darkness'
σοι 'to, for you' (dat. s)
σου 'of you' (gen. s)
συ 'you' (nom. s)
τα 'the' (nom., acc. pl n.)
ταις 'the' (dat. pl f.)
τας 'the' (acc. pl f.)
ταυτ- stem of αὑτη 'this woman,
   her' (see οὑτος)
ταυτα 'these things' (nom., acc.
   pl n. of οὑτος)
το τεκμηρι-ον 'evidence'
το τεκν-ον 'the child, son, young
   man'
το τελ-ος 'the end, aim, purpose'
τηρε-ω 'I guard, keep'
τί 'what?', 'why?'
τίνες; 'who?' (nom. pl)
τίς; 'who?' (nom. s)
τις 'someone, anyone' (nom. s)
τη 'to/for the' (dat. s f.)
την 'the' (acc. s f.)
της 'of the' (gen. s f.)
το 'the' (nom., acc. s n.)
τοις 'to/for the' (dat. pl m., n.)
τολμα-ω 'I dare'
τον 'the' (acc. s m.)
του 'of the' (gen. s m., n.)
τους 'the' (acc. pl m.)
τουτ- 'this' (m., n. stem of οὑτος)
τρωγ-ω 'I eat'
τῳ 'the' (dat. s m., n.)
των 'of the' (gen. pl m., f., n.)
ὁ Υἱ-ος '[the] Son'
ὑμας 'you' (acc. pl)
ὑμεις 'you' (nom. pl)
ὑμιν 'to, for you' (dat. pl)
ὑμων 'of you' (gen. pl)
ὑπερ 'for, on behalf of' + gen.

ὑπο, ὑπ', ὑφ' 'by'
φαγειν 'to eat'
φαγη 'he may eat'
φαιν-ομαι 'I seem, appear'
φερ-ω 'I carry, bear, endure'
φευγ-ω 'I flee, run away from, escape'
φιλε-ω 'I love'
φιλ-ος η ον 'dear, friendly, beloved, one's own'
φοβε-ομαι 'I fear'
το φως (φωτ-) 'the light'
χαιρ-ε 'hello' (addressing one person), χαιρ-ετε 'hello' (addressing more than one)

χαλεπ-ος η ον 'difficult'
χρη 'it is necessary for X (acc.) to Y (infinitive)'
ὁ Χριστ-ος '[the] Christ'
ψηφιζ-ομαι 'I vote'
ὠ 'O' (addressing someone)
ὠ 'I may be' (subjunc. of εἰμι)
ὠμεν 'we may be' (subjunc. of εἰμι)
ὠν 'being' (nom s m.)
ὡς 'as'
ὠσι 'they may be' (subjunc of εἰμι)
ὡσπερ 'as if, like'

ENGLISH-GREEK VOCABULARY

agree ὁμολογε-ω
announce κηρυττ-ω
appear φαιν-ομαι
asked ἠρ-ομην
bear φερ-ω
become γιγν-ομαι
begin ἀρχ-ομαι
born, be γιγν-ομαι
came ἠλθ-ον, ἀφικ-ομην
chase διωκ-ω
come ἐρχ-ομαι
conquer νικα-ω
endure φερ-ω
enquired ἐπυθ-ομην
fare πραττ-ω
fight μαχ-ομαι
find εὑρισκ-ω
flee φευγ-ω
get to know γιγνωσκ-ω
go ἐρχ-ομαι
Greek nom. s Ἑλλην
Greeks nom. pl Ἑλληνες
happen γιγν-ομαι
happened ἐγεν-ομην
harm ἀδικε-ω
hate μισε-ω
have ἐχ-ω
have faith πιστευ-ω
he is ἐστι
hear ἀκου-ω
heard ἐπυθ-ομην
hullo χαιρ-ε(τε)
I ἐγω
I am εἰμι (see 16)
journey πορευ-ομαι
keep τηρε-ω
know οἰδα (see 18)
lead ἀγω

learn γιγνωσκ-ω
love ἀγαπα-ω, φιλε-ω
made, be γιγν-ομαι
make ποιε-ω, πραττ-ω
me acc. με
order κελευ-ω
Paul Παυλ-ος
Peter Πετρ-ος
pray εὐχ-ομαι
pursue διωκ-ω
*Question, to ask: use question
   word or* ἀρα
recognise γιγνωσκ-ω
reply ἀποκριν-ομαι
said εἰπ-ον
saw εἰδ-ον
say λεγ-ω
see ὁρα-ω
seek ζητε-ω
seem δοκε-ω
send πεμπ-ω
she is ἐστι
shout βοα-ω
stay μεν-ω
stop παυ-ω
talk λαλε-ω
teach διδασκ-ω
tell me εἰπέ μοι
they are εἰσι
travel πορευ-ομαι
us acc. ἡμας
'used to': *use imperfect*
walk πορευ-ομαι
was *see* 17; 'was –ing' *use
   imperfect*
we ἡμεις
we are ἐσμεν
who? *pl* τίνες

211

who? *s* τίς

wish βουλ-ομαι

write γραφ-ω

wrong, do wrong ἀδικε-ω

you nom. *s* συ

you nom. *pl* ὑμεις

you acc. *s* σε

you acc. *pl* ὑμας

you are *s* εἰ

you are *pl* ἐστε

INDEX

References in bold type are to the Grammatical Summary.

INDEX

214

END-PIECE

In this magical passage from Homer's *Odyssey*, Odysseus falls asleep
on the boat that is transporting him from the heroic world of Troy and
his fantastic adventures by sea to his homeland of Ithaca, where
further trials await him – to win back his wife and home from the
depredations of others. Listen to the sound of it – the peace of Odysseus'
sleep, the grave dignity of his past trials, the buck of the horses, the lift
of the boat, and the hiss and surge of the sea.

The sign / indicates word order to be reversed.

Metre: hexameters (the metre of epic). I have marked the long
syllables. See scansion notes throughout **15b**.

καὶ τῷ νῆδυμος ὕπνος ἐπὶ βλεφάροισιν ἔπιπτε,
And on-him sweet sleep on (his) eyes began-to-fall,
νήγρετος ἥδιστος, θανάτῳ ἄγχιστα ἐοικώς.
unwaking sweetest, to-death most-closely similar.
ἡ δ', ὥς τ᾽ ἐν πεδίῳ τετράοροι ἄρσενες ἵπποι
It [the ship], as on (a) plain four-linked male horses
πάντες ἅμ᾽ ὁρμηθέντες ὑπὸ πληγῇσιν ἱμάσθλης,
all together setting-off under blows of (the) lash
ὑψόσ᾽ ἀειρόμενοι ῥίμφα πρήσσουσι κέλευθον,
up-high rising easily make (the) journey,
ὣς ἄρα τῆς πρύμνη μὲν ἀείρετο, κῦμα δ᾽ ὄπισθε
so then its stern rose, (a) wave/while behind
while, behind, a wave
πορφύρεον μέγα θῦε πολυφλοίσβοιο θαλάσσης.
dark huge seethed [a wave] of (the) loud-resounding sea.
ἡ δὲ μάλ᾽ ἀσφαλέως θέεν ἔμπεδον· οὐδέ κεν ἴρηξ
It/and very safely ran secure: nor would (a) falcon
κίρκος ὁμαρτήσειεν, ἐλαφρότατος πετεηνῶν.
bird keep-pace, swiftest of-birds.
ὣς ἡ ῥίμφα θέουσα θαλάσσης κύματ᾽ ἔταμνεν,
So it, lightly running, (the) sea's waves (it) cut,
ἄνδρα φέρουσα θεοῖς ἐναλίγκια μήδε᾽ ἔχοντα,
(a) man carrying to-(the)-gods similar mind having
carrying a man having a mind similar to the gods
ὃς πρὶν μὲν μάλα πολλὰ πάθ᾽ ἄλγεα ὃν κατὰ θυμόν
who previously very many (he) suffered pains his- in - heart
suffered very many pains in his heart

215

ἀνδρῶν τε πτολεμους ἀλεγεινα τε κυματα πειρῶν,
men's/both wars   painful-/and – waves enduring,
    enduring both wars of men and painful waves,
δη   τοτε   γ'   ἀτρεμας εὐδε, λελασμενος ὁσσ' ἐπεπονθει.
indeed then at-any-rate unafraid he-slept, forgetting all he-had-suffered.

Homer, Odyssey 13.79-92

"More trouble. Something called the Romans."